Alexander Balmain Bruce

The Kingdom of God

Or, Christ's teaching according to the synoptical gospels

Alexander Balmain Bruce

The Kingdom of God
Or, Christ's teaching according to the synoptical gospels

ISBN/EAN: 9783337244859

Printed in Europe, USA, Canada, Australia, Japan

Cover: Foto ©Lupo / pixelio.de

More available books at **www.hansebooks.com**

THE KINGDOM OF GOD;

OR,

CHRIST'S TEACHING ACCORDING TO THE SYNOPTICAL GOSPELS.

BY

ALEXANDER BALMAIN BRUCE, D.D.,

PROFESSOR OF
NEW TESTAMENT EXEGESIS IN THE FREE CHURCH COLLEGE, GLASGOW;
AUTHOR OF
"THE TRAINING OF THE TWELVE," "THE HUMILIATION OF CHRIST,"
ETC. ETC.

SCRIBNER & WELFORD,
743 AND 745 BROADWAY,
NEW YORK.
1889.

TO

OLD STUDENTS

OF

GLASGOW FREE CHURCH COLLEGE

AS

A MEMORIAL OF HOURS SPENT

IN

THE STUDY OF THE WORDS OF CHRIST

THIS BOOK

IS RESPECTFULLY DEDICATED

BY

THE AUTHOR.

PREFACE.

THE first ten of the fifteen chapters contained in this volume appeared a few years ago in the pages of the *Monthly Interpreter*. They have been carefully revised and brought down to date. The remaining five chapters, with the *Introduction*, appear here for the first time.

This book is a first instalment of a projected work on the leading types of doctrine in the New Testament concerning the Good that came to the world through Jesus Christ, whereof the plan is briefly outlined in the last section of the *Introduction*.

A. B. BRUCE.

GLASGOW, *September* 1889.

CONTENTS.

CRITICAL INTRODUCTION.

SECTION	PAGE
I. The sources,	1
II. Luke's variations,	14
III. The motives of Luke's variations,	28
IV. The synoptical type of doctrine,	38

CHAPTER I.

CHRIST'S IDEA OF THE KINGDOM.

Two opposed tendencies,	43
Senses of the expression: *The Kingdom of God*,	46
Idea suggested by prophecy,	47
The mysteries of the kingdom,	49
Words of grace,	50
Effect of Christ's preaching,	51
To whom Christ preached,	53
Significance of Christ's attitude towards social abjects,	54
Sayings involving universalism,	55
Sayings of apparently contrary import,	56
Spirituality of the kingdom: the kingdom of *Heaven*,	58
The kingdom in outline,	59

CHAPTER II.

CHRIST'S ATTITUDE TOWARDS THE MOSAIC LAW.

Reticence of Christ,	63
Think not I came to destroy,	64
Destroying by fulfilling,	65
Scale of moral worth,	66
Straws showing the stream of tendency,	68

CONTENTS.

	PAGE
Silence concerning circumcision,	68
The things that defile,	69
The statute of divorce,	71
The Sabbath,	72
Made for man,	74
Summary,	79
The least in the kingdom greater than John,	80
John's doubt of Christ,	82
Christ's method of working,	83

CHAPTER III.

THE CONDITIONS OF ENTRANCE.

Repent and believe,	85
Repentance as conceived by Christ and the Baptist,	86
Repentance no arbitrary requirement,	89
Disciples called on to repent,	90
The cities of the plain,	93
Faith the chief condition of admission,	94
Signifies a new departure,	95
Christian universalism,	96
Typical narratives showing Christ's estimate of faith,	97
The woman who was a sinner,	97
The psychology of faith,	100
The Roman centurion,	101
The Syro-Phœnician Woman,	103
"Faith Alone,"	107

CHAPTER IV.

CHRIST'S DOCTRINE OF GOD.

The divine Father,	109
The new element in Christ's idea,	110
God's Fatherhood in relation to men in general,	111
The providential aspect,	111
The gracious aspect: parables in Luke xv.,	112
Universalism involved,	114
God's Fatherhood in relation to disciples,	114
The providential aspect,	115
Value of Christ's doctrine on,	119
Parables of *The Selfish Neighbour* and *The Unjust Judge*,	120
The gracious aspect,	122
Parable of *The Blade, the Ear, and the Full Corn*,	124
The Fatherhood of God still imperfectly comprehended,	127

CHAPTER V.

CHRIST'S DOCTRINE OF MAN.

The doctrines of God and of man ever kindred,	128
Significance of Christ's attitude towards the poor and the depraved,	129
Immortality,	131
Social salvation,	132
Ideal and reality,	133
Human depravity in Christ's teaching and in scholastic theology,	134
The "Lost,"	136
Zacchæus,	137
The lost sheep of the house of Israel,	138
True and false holiness,	140
Why Christ addressed Himself to the humbler classes,	142
The *Two Debtors*,	143
The *Lost Sheep* and the "Lapsed Masses,"	143
The people of the land,	145

CHAPTER VI.

THE RELATION OF JESUS TO MESSIANIC HOPES AND FUNCTIONS.

Had Jesus a Messianic idea?	148
His idea a transformed one,	149
Its nature,	150
He claimed to be this Messiah,	153
The proof,	153
Genesis of Christ's Messianic consciousness,	158
Did Jesus ever doubt His Messiahship?	161
Aids to faith in His Messianic vocation,	162
His Messianic consciousness free from ambition,	164

CHAPTER VII.

THE SON OF MAN AND THE SON OF GOD.

Was the *Son of Man* a current Messianic title?	166
Its use in the Book of Enoch,	167
Old Testament source of the title,	169
Its use in the Gospels,	171
The texts classified,	172
The unprivileged man,	172

	PAGE
The sympathetic man,	173
The apocalyptic aspect,	174
Future glory and present humiliation,	175
An incognito,	177
The title *Son of God*,	178
The official sense,	178
The ethical sense,	179
The filial consciousness of Jesus analysed,	180
The metaphysical sense,	184
The two titles in relation to the doctrine of the kingdom,	186

CHAPTER VIII.

THE RIGHTEOUSNESS OF THE KINGDOM—NEGATIVE ASPECT.

Criticism an inevitable task for the Christ,	187
The task faithfully performed,	188
Yet temperately,	189
And with discrimination,	190
Origin of Rabbinism,	191
The process of degeneracy,	192
Examples of fencing the law,	193
Multiplication of rules,	194
Arts of evasion,	196
The Sabbath laws: *Erubin*,	197
Neglect of the great commandments,	198
Externalism,	199
Spiritual vices of Rabbinism,	200
Pharisaic righteousness outside the kingdom,	203
The strait gate and the narrow way,	205

CHAPTER IX.

THE RIGHTEOUSNESS OF THE KINGDOM—POSITIVE ASPECT.

The righteousness of God: its contents,	207
Right thoughts of God,	208
The rabbinical God,	209
Perfect as the Father in heaven,	211
Filial righteousness: characteristics,	213
Righteousness of discipleship,	217
Imitation of Christ,	219
Righteousness of citizenship,	221
Parables of *The Treasure* and *The Pearl*,	222
The three aspirants,	222

CONTENTS. xiii

	PAGE
Perfection,	223
Parable of *Extra Service*,	225
Parable of *The Labourers in the Vineyard*,	226
General reflections,	226

CHAPTER X.

THE DEATH OF JESUS AND ITS SIGNIFICANCE.

The doctrine of the cross,	231
First lesson : for righteousness' sake,	231
Second lesson : for the unrighteous,	235
A ransom for the many,	236
The temple-tax,	239
Third lesson : dies in love to men,	243
Mary of Bethany,	244
The wastefulness of love,	245
Fourth lesson : for the remission of sins,	246
The new covenant,	247
The new era,	249
Characteristics,	250
The Holy Supper,	251

CHAPTER XI.

THE KINGDOM AND THE CHURCH.

The kingdom of God an ideal craving embodiment,	252
The choice of the twelve,	253
"*My Church*,"	254
Election, how to be understood,	256
The sacraments : Baptism,	257
The Trinitarian formula,	258
The Holy Spirit in Christ's teaching,	259
The nature of the Church,	260
On this rock : Peter,	261
The Church Christian,	262
The Church and the kingdom,	264
The righteousness of the kingdom realized therein,	266
Training of the apostles,	268
Christ's promise and prophecy conditional,	271
Is the Church a failure ?	271

CHAPTER XII.

THE PAROUSIA AND THE CHRISTIAN ERA.

	PAGE
Conflicting texts,	273
A lengthened history anticipated by Christ,	274
Parables of *Growth*,	275
A delayed *Parousia*,	276
Exhortations to *Watch*,	278
Parable of *The Upper Servant*,	278
A Gentile day of grace,	280
The times of the Gentiles,	283
The other class of texts,	284
The coming of the Son of Man,	285
Three kinds of coming,	287
The eschatological discourse,	288
Of that day knoweth no one,	289
Variations in synoptical reports,	291

CHAPTER XIII.

THE HISTORY OF THE KINGDOM IN OUTLINE.

Chequered character of the history,	293
Optimistic parables: *Mustard Seed* and *Leaven*,	294
The reverse side: parable of *The Sower*,	294
Parable of *The Tares* and *The Drag Net*,	296
Parable of *The Children in the Market-place*,	299
Parable of *The Great Supper*,	300
Rejection of the Jews: relative parables,	302
Christ's predictions of His resurrection,	304
Their meaning,	305
"Destroy this temple,"	306
Import of the saying,	307

CHAPTER XIV.

THE END.

The ideal will be realized,	311
Purity by separation,	312
Three judgment programmes,	312
Judgment of Christendom,	312
Judgment of antichristendom,	313
Blasphemy against the Holy Ghost,	314

Judgment of heathendom, ... 315
This judgment purely ethical, ... 317
"Eternal" punishment, ... 318
Eternal sin, ... 319
The everlasting fire not prepared for man, . . . 321
Christ's doctrine of election, ... 322
Rewards and punishments, ... 323
Judgment according to natural law, ... 325
Pictorial representations of eternal states, . . . 326
The true object of dread, ... 327

CHAPTER XV.

THE CHRISTIANITY OF CHRIST.

"Back to Christ," 328
The Christian revival, ... 331
Gospellers, ... 331
The Shorter Catechism, ... 333
A Christian primer, ... 334
Church creeds: what to do with them, ... 335
Reunion, ... 337
New apologetic, ... 339
Can we know Christ? 340

INDEX, ... 342

CRITICAL INTRODUCTION.

SECTION I.—THE SOURCES.

THE first three Gospels, from their homogeneous character called synoptical, differ widely from the fourth; as in other respects, so also and very specially, in the account which they give of our Lord's teaching. And there can be little doubt that, as compared with the fourth Gospel, the synoptical Gospels present that teaching in its original form. To the question, What did Christ really teach? What were the very words He spoke? the answer must be sought in the first place from them. Their reports are more indisputably apostolic in their ultimate source, and to all appearance much less influenced by reflection on the part of the writers.

But the question may be raised, even in reference to the Synoptists, whether they can be regarded as giving a perfectly trustworthy report of the sayings of Jesus. Even if they did not, their report of these sayings would still form an interesting subject of study. But it is obviously important to know how far the best sources extant are reliable; for the supreme desire of all Christians is to know exactly the mind of the Master.

It would inspire great confidence in the synoptical records to be assured that they were compiled by certain of the men who "had been with Jesus." These men were eye and ear witnesses of Christ's ministry; they knew much if not all that He said and did, and they could be trusted to tell honestly and with substantial accuracy what they knew.

But there is no sufficient evidence that any one of the first three Gospels, in the form in which we have them, proceeded from the hand of an apostle. The most that can be said is, that their reports are based on apostolic traditions, preserved either orally or in written form. That these traditions, originating ultimately, without doubt, in apostolic preaching, had, before our Gospels were written, assumed a comparatively stereotyped form, is apparent from the extensive resemblance in the synoptical accounts both in substance and in style.

The literary relations subsisting between these Gospels are such as to make it probable, if not certain, that written accounts of Christ's words and deeds were previously in existence, and were accessible to the evangelists. From the preface to the third Gospel, it may be inferred that there had been considerable activity in the production of such accounts, and that at the time Luke wrote, evangelic collections had been multiplied to such an extent, as to create embarrassment to one who aimed at giving in moderate compass a full narrative of the more important facts in the life of Jesus.

How many documents Luke used in the compilation

of his Gospel cannot be known; but two sources, at least, of outstanding importance, seem to have been at his command, and to have supplied the main body of his narrative—one a collection of sayings, the other a collection of narrations similar in contents to the second Gospel. By a comparison of his Gospel with the other two, the inference is suggested that these two sources form the basis of all three synoptical Gospels. Whether we should identify the collection of narrations with the Gospel of Mark, or distinguish it therefrom as an original Mark, is a question on which critics are divided; but there is general agreement of opinion as to a book similar in contents to Mark forming the basis of the common matter of the first three Gospels relating to the deeds of Jesus. Whether, again, the collection of sayings used by Luke was identical in contents and form with that used by the first evangelist, is a matter of dispute; but the extensive similarity between the first and third Gospels in their respective reports of Christ's sayings, leaves little room for doubt that they either drew from one source, or from sources so kindred in character as to suggest the conjecture that they were different editions of the same original writing, formed under different influences.

Recent criticism recognises in these two sources of the synoptical tradition the "Mark" and "Matthew" of Papias,—the former either to be identified with the canonical Mark, or to be regarded as its original, and resting on the preaching of Peter as its ultimate authority; the latter written by the Apostle Matthew, and forming the basis of the canonical Matthew. Critics differ in their interpretations of the statement of Papias as to the character and contents of the two sources, some contending, *e.g.*, that the book of *Logia*, said to have been compiled by Matthew, contained nothing but sayings, while others argue that it must at least have contained such brief narratives as were necessary to make the sayings intelligible. In like manner it is disputed whether Mark consisted only of narrations, or did not in its original form contain more of Christ's words than are found in canonical Mark, *e.g.* the Sermon on the Mount.[1] But we shall not err greatly if we say that the two sources differed in their characteristics at least: the one being predominantly a collection of sayings, the other chiefly a collection of narrations.

What mainly interests us is the collection of *Logia*. What would one not give to have that book which the Apostle Matthew wrote, just as he wrote it! But the wish is idle; the only course open to us is to make ourselves acquainted with its contents at second-hand through the writings of the two evangelists, who have drawn so freely from it, comparing their reports one with another so as to arrive at a probable conclusion as to the original form of the sayings recorded. Attempts have been made to reconstruct the *Logia* from the synoptical Gospels;[2] but such attempts can be little more than ingenious conjectures. We cannot at this date resurrec-

---

[1] For information as to the present state of opinion on these questions, readers may consult the *Introductions to the New Testament* by Weiss and Holtzmann. Weiss thinks the main source of apostolic tradition was the *Logia*, which he thinks contained many narrations as well as sayings; Holtzmann contends for an Urmarkus as the main source.

[2] *Vide* Wendt's *Die Lehre Jesu*, Erster Theil.

tionize a lost apostolic document; all that is possible for us is to make ourselves acquainted with extant reports of our Lord's words, and when these vary, to do our best to determine which version is primary and which secondary.

It does not take long study of the first and third Gospels to be satisfied that if their authors did really use a common source in reporting the words of Jesus, they have made respectively a very different use of it. It is, indeed, not easy to understand how such diversity could exist in reports based on the same document. Compare, *e.g.*, the two reports of the Sermon on the Mount. How strangely divergent on the whole, and yet too similar in detail to admit of any doubt that they are different versions of the same discourse. One of two inferences is inevitable. Either one of the reporters (or possibly both) has taken considerable liberties with the source, or the source existed in different recensions, arising in different circles, and under different influences. Either supposition is possible; in either case the causes producing the diversity might be to a large extent the same, only operating in different ways. In case the variations were due to the evangelists, we should have to acknowledge the action to a considerable extent of editorial intention, guided by possibly ascertainable motives. If, on the other hand, the variations arose gradually in copies of the *Logia* in the possession of different persons, before they came under the eye of the evangelists, then we may conceive them creeping in insensibly under the action of motives of which the agents in producing variation were hardly conscious.

The latter view is adopted by Weizsäcker in his recently published work on *The Apostolic Age*. His idea of the matter is to this effect. Collections of Christ's sayings began to be formed, not in a historical spirit, but simply to meet the practical needs of disciples desirous of guidance in life. It was recorded that on this point and on that the Master spoke thus and thus. Thus groups of sayings arose, ever increasing as time went on. But the purpose aimed at not being the preparation of an exact historical record, but the instruction of the faithful, comments, glosses, explanations grew up simultaneously, and gradually became mixed with the words of the Lord. "The tradition was from the first not mere repetition, but was bound up with creative activity. And, as was natural, this activity increased in course of time. Explanations became text. The single word became multiplied with the multitude of its applications, or the words were connected with a definite occasion and shaped to suit it."[1] In this way, according to this writer, many, if not all, the variations in the reports of Christ's words are to be accounted for. The conscious editorial activity of the evangelists he seems inclined to reduce to a minimum. For the wide divergence of Luke's report of the Sermon on the Mount from that of Matthew, he is not disposed to make the evangelist responsible. He is of opinion that Luke found the Sermon in that form in his source. Even the Pauline, universalistic, element in Luke's Gospel he seems willing to impute not to Luke personally, but to the spirit of a school within Palestine

[1] *Das Apostolische Zeitalter*, S. 406.

and the Jewish Church, originating in the influence of such men as Stephen and Barnabas. It is the product and witness of a universalism independent of Paul within the bosom of Hebrew Christianity.

This new view is certainly a great improvement on the tendency-criticism of the Tübingen school, headed by Baur, and it probably contains a large amount of truth. In the way indicated arose, in all likelihood, variations in the reports of Christ's sayings which were a *datum* for the evangelists. But it is not at all unlikely that a certain number of the existing variations are due to the evangelists themselves. It is a nowise inadmissible supposition, that they so far exercised their discretion in the use of their sources as to make the material serviceable to the edification of those for whose special benefit they wrote—acting not in a spirit of licence, but with the freedom of men who believed that it was more important that their readers should get a true impression of Christ than that they should know the *ipsissima verba* of His sayings. Thus may be accounted for alterations of words and phrases occurring in the documents, and omissions of material found there not deemed suitable for his purpose by the compiler. To take one or two examples. In Luke's version of the Sermon on the Mount there are two verbal variations from Matthew's text: the substitution of χάρις (thanks, grace) for μισθός in the saying: "If ye love them which love you, what reward have ye?"[1] and of οἰκτίρμονες (merciful) for τέλειοι in the saying: "Be ye therefore perfect even as your Father which is in heaven

[1] Matt. v. 46; Luke vi. 32.

is perfect."[1] Assuming that the sayings stood in Luke's source the same as in Matthew's, we can easily conceive him making these changes to remove an element of apparent legalism from our Lord's utterances, and to bring them into more complete harmony with evangelic, or Pauline, habits of thought and expression. It is noticeable that Luke introduces the word χάρις no less than three times in the passage referred to, as if he took pleasure in repeating this watchword of Pauline theology. Of course these changes might have been made before Luke wrote, and his function at this point may have been merely to transcribe; but the other alternative, that he made the alterations for the reason assigned, is at least equally probable.

The very significant and characteristic word of Jesus, "I came not to call the righteous but sinners," appears in Luke's Gospel with the addition "unto repentance."[2] This may have been an explanatory gloss that had crept into the text used by the evangelist, but it may quite as well have been a change made by him to render the meaning clear, and possibly to guard against the misconstruction that Christ invited sinners to the Kingdom of heaven without repentance.

Not only alterations but omissions might be made out of regard to edification. The story of the Syro-Phenician woman does not occur in Luke's Gospel. It by no means follows from this that he was ignorant of it, or that it was missing in his sources. He may have left it out to avoid the risk of scandalizing Gentile readers by the appearance therein of a grudging attitude on the

---

[1] Matt. v. 48; Luke vi. 36.   [2] Matt. ix. 13; Luke v. 32.

part of Jesus towards the Pagan world. Other omissions might be due not to any fear of wrong impressions being made, but simply to the consideration that the matters omitted were not of special interest or concern to the first readers. Thus may be accounted for the absence from Luke's narrative of many sections relating to Christ's conflict with Pharisaism. In a roundabout way, a regard to edification might explain yet another class of omissions from the third Gospel: viz. duplicate incidents, such as the second feeding of the multitude, and the second storm on the lake. By such omissions we may conceive Luke making room for important matter peculiar to his Gospel, his desire being to introduce this new matter without unduly extending his narrative; for all inspired writers seem to have sensitively shrunk from being tedious, knowing that the feeling of weariness is fatal to edification.

These instances may suffice to show how an evangelist might with perfect loyalty and a good conscience exercise an editorial discretion in the use of sources. But the point of importance for us is not in what way variations arose, but the fact that they exist, and the question which of the varying reports comes nearer to the original. This resolves itself largely into a question as to the relative merits of Matthew's and Luke's reports of our Lord's sayings in point of exactness. The question is not altogether a simple one. In some cases the evidence seems to be in favour of one evangelist, in other cases the balance inclines towards the other. Thus one can have little hesitation in pronouncing in favour of Matthew's form of the saying, "I came not to call the righteous;" whereas on the other hand in the case of the saying, "Seek ye first the kingdom of God" (Matt. vi. 33; Luke xii. 31), the critical decision gives the preference to the simple brief form of Luke, "But rather seek ye the kingdom of God," regarding the clause "and His righteousness" in Matthew as an added gloss, designed to bring the counsel into correspondence with the drift of the whole discourse, which is to contrast the righteousness of God with the righteousness of the scribes.[1] There are cases even in which in the same narrative the probabilities are on opposite sides. Thus comparing Luke's report of the introduction to the Sermon on the Mount with Matthew's, one is inclined to give his form of the "macarisms:" "Blessed be ye poor, Blessed are ye that hunger, Blessed are ye that weep,"—the preference on account of their brevity; but, on the other hand, the "woes" which he appends to them seem out of keeping with the spirit of the discourse, and rather inferences from the words spoken by Jesus, than sayings actually uttered by Him.

On the whole, the evidence, by the general confession of critics, is in favour of the comparative originality of Matthew's reports.[2] Thus reverting to the Sermon on the

---

[1] So Weiss (*Das Matthäus-Evangelium*) and Wendt, *Die Lehre Jesu*, S. 117. The ultimate decision of the question depends on the view we take as to the original form of the Sermon. If Christ discoursed on righteousness as Matthew reports, it would be quite natural that He should give the above counsel as it appears in the first Gospel. I hesitate to give my assent to the opinion of Weiss and Wendt.

[2] From this view Pfleiderer, in his recent work *Das Urchristenthum* (1887), decidedly dissents. In his whole views of the Gospels, and their relation to each other, as set forth in this work, he departs widely from the general current of critical opinion. "Mark" he

Mount, the two substitutions above referred to ($\chi\acute{a}\rho\iota\varsigma$ for $\mu\iota\sigma\theta\acute{o}\varsigma$, and $oi\kappa\tau\acute{\iota}\rho\mu\omega\nu$ for $\tau\acute{\epsilon}\lambda\epsilon\iota o\varsigma$) wear the aspect of an attempt to replace difficult expressions by words of simpler meaning, just because their sense is less obvious. Matthew's phrases are to be regarded as the more original. Another point may be noted here: the less frequent use of the title "Father" for God in Luke's Gospel, as compared with Matthew's. Thus for the expression "the children of your Father which is in heaven" (Matt. v. 45), Luke gives "the children of the Highest" (vi. 35); and for Matthew's "your heavenly Father feedeth them" (the birds, vi. 26), Luke has the colder "God feedeth them" (xii. 24). The change seems due to a desire to restrict the Fatherhood of God within the spiritual sphere, ignoring the general aspect of Divine Paternity revealed in ordinary Providence. There can be little doubt that the broader presentation of the first evangelist is truer to the style of the Master, and that Jesus saw in the sunshine and in the rain a revelation of

regards as the earliest Gospel—the first attempt to present the gospel of Jesus, as the Christ which Paul had preached as a theological doctrine, in the form of a history, written under the influence of the great apostle whose scholar the author probably was (S. 360). "Luke" comes second; it is based on "Mark," and contains additions due not so much to other historical sources as to the literary genius of the writer, who also was much under Paul's influence (S. 417). "Matthew" was the latest, originating some time after the beginning of the second century. It is throughout dependent on "Mark" and "Luke," and is a harmonizing combination of the two in a Churchly interest, written by a man who was imbued with the spirit of the old Catholic Church: universalistic yet not Pauline, rather neonomian (S. 479, 493). In comparison with "Luke," the words ascribed to our Lord in "Matthew" are held to be for the most part secondary.

God's paternal love to all, not less than in the communication of His Holy Spirit a revelation of the same love to the citizens of His kingdom. The restriction is made in the interest of edification, that the faithful might value more God's special love to them; nevertheless it is a narrowing of the great doctrine of God's Fatherhood, as taught by Christ.

The epilogue of the Sermon on the Mount as given by Luke is manifestly secondary. One can trace throughout the hand of an editor modifying, expounding, abbreviating, all with a view to general edification. For Matthew's "Whosoever heareth *these* sayings of mine," suited to the original hearers, Luke has "Whosoever *cometh to me*, and heareth *my sayings*," adapted to the case of all disciples, and to the whole of Christ's teaching. In Luke's version the diverse action of the two builders to whom hearers of different characters are compared, in reference to the foundation of the house, is very carefully described. The one builder is represented as digging deep till he came to the rock, while the other is represented as beginning to build on the surface, without a foundation. This is a useful commentary on the Speaker's words as reported in the first Gospel, but it is a commentary, not an exact report. The description of the oncome of the storm that was to try the two houses is very graphic in Matthew. "Descended the rain, came the floods, blew the winds:" this is in the impassioned style natural to one winding up an impressive, solemn discourse. The eloquence disappears in Luke's narrative, and for it we have simply the prosaic statement: "When a flood arose, the stream dashed against the house."

The discourses of Jesus, as reported by Matthew, both in substance and in style, correspond to the actual circumstances in which the Speaker was placed: they recall the world of Judea as it existed in the days of our Lord. On the other hand, as reported by Luke, these discourses seem to be adapted to the circumstances and needs of a somewhat later time, that of the Apostolic Church. Critics may have carried this distinction too far, and discovered traces of it where they are not to be found; but, as a general observation, the statement just made is beyond doubt. The badge of the apostolic age, and the proof that its needs and modes of thought influenced the compiler of the third Gospel, may be found in the frequent use of the two phrases "the Lord" and "the apostles" in narratives where "Jesus" and "the disciples" are the expressions used by the other Synoptists.[1] The Great Teacher is the Lord of the Church, and the writer reports His sayings in forms deemed best fitted for the instruction of its members. The "disciples" of a bygone time are now the apostles, and the lessons they received from the Master are conceived of as the training which fitted them for their high position, and are reported from that point of view. Thus, for example, in narrating the institution of the Holy Supper, Luke states that "when the hour was come He sat down, and the twelve *apostles* with Him." He thinks of them as getting their lesson how to celebrate the sacred rite commemorative of the Lord's redeeming death.

[1] The remark applies specially to the latter of the two phrases. For examples of its use *vide* Luke vi. 13; ix. 10; xvii. 5; xxii. 14. The title "Lord" occurs chiefly in sections peculiar to Luke; *vide* x. 1; xi. 39; xii. 42; xiii. 15; xvii. 5; xviii. 6.

Assuming the comparative originality of Matthew's report as established, it may be worth while to form an approximate idea of the character and extent of Luke's variations, as also to consider more fully the influences or motives to which they probably owe their origin. These will be the subjects of inquiry in the two following sections.

SECTION II.—LUKE'S VARIATIONS.

The phenomena of variation in Luke's report of our Lord's words, as compared with Matthew's, may be classed under three heads: *modifications, omissions, and additions.* Besides these, there are well-known and broadly marked differences between the two evangelists in the grouping and setting of sayings; the general fact here being that Matthew's habit is to collect into large masses sayings of kindred import, while Luke's is to disperse the material of these collections over his pages, assigning to the dissociated utterances distinct occasions. This diversity of treatment in some instances has a by no means unimportant influence on the sense; nevertheless, it is not proposed to take any further notice of it here, beyond making the remark that it is obviously incumbent on the interpreter to be on his guard against laying too much stress on supposed historical connection. In certain cases the occasions on which sayings were uttered can be definitely ascertained, and in all such cases the most should be made of the setting to illustrate the meaning of the word. But there are instances not a few, especially in the long section of Luke's Gospel, ix. 51–

xviii. 14, in which to lay emphasis on the occasion would be to follow a misleading guidance. The evangelist found valuable materials in his sources, whose exact place in the history was not known, and he introduced them into his narrative where it seemed expedient, and with such preface as the contents suggested.

I. We have to notice, then, in the first place, Luke's *modifications*. These occur wherever a saying of Christ found in both Gospels (we leave Mark out of account), in terms so similar on the whole as to put the identity beyond doubt, is given in the third Gospel with more or less variation in the expression. Such modifications are too numerous to be exhaustively indicated here; all that can be done is to give a selection of samples with tentative notes suggesting possible motives for variation. The instances which have been already alluded to in the previous section are omitted.

1. Luke viii. 12 compared with Matthew xiii. 19. Of the wayside hearer Jesus, according to Matthew, said: *When any one heareth the word of the kingdom, and understandeth it not, then cometh the wicked one* (ὁ πονηρός), *and snatcheth away that which hath been sown in the heart.* Luke reports the saying with minor variations, and appends this significant addition: *lest they should believe and be saved.* This looks like a gloss, stating in current Pauline or Apostolic Church phraseology the end contemplated in the preaching of the word.

2. Luke viii. 21 compared with Matthew xiii. 50 (Mark iii. 35). To those who informed Him of the desires of His relatives to see Him, Jesus, according to Matthew, replied: *Whosoever shall do the will of my Father which*

is in heaven, he is my brother and sister and mother. Mark has *the will of God*, a minor variation. But in Luke occurs the major modification: "my mother and my brethren are those *which hear the word of God and do it.*" "Word" takes the place of "will," and the spiritual brotherhood of Christ are described by a phrase which sounds secondary and stereotyped: "Those who hear the word." It recurs again and again in Luke's Gospel. Mary sat at the feet of Jesus and *heard His word* (x. 39). To the woman in the crowd who exclaimed: "Blessed is the womb that bare Thee, and the breasts which Thou didst suck!" Jesus replies: "Yea, rather blessed are they that hear the word of God and keep it" (xi. 28). The substitution of "word" for "will" makes Christ's saying concerning His brethren more evangelical, and brings it more into line with the phraseology current among believers in the apostolic age.

3. Luke ix. 18–27 compared with Matthew xvi. 13–28 (Mark viii. 27–ix. 1). There are several points at which Luke's narrative appears secondary as compared with Matthew's. For Matthew's form of Peter's confession: *Thou art the Christ, the Son of the living God,* Luke has the tame expression: *the Christ of God;* what was for the disciple a great originality, uttered with passionate vehemence, having become in the circle for which Luke writes, or from which his version emanated, a commonplace. In the saying concerning cross-bearing: *If any man will come after me, let him deny himself and take up his cross and follow me,* Luke inserts "daily" ($\kappa\alpha\theta$' $\dot{\eta}\mu\acute{\epsilon}\rho\alpha\nu$) after the cross, which seems a gloss intended to adapt the counsel to the facts of spiritual experience. In the final

prediction that some of those present with the speaker would live to see the Son of Man coming in His kingdom, this vivid concrete form of expression is replaced in Luke's text by the vague general phrase: *till they see the kingdom of God.* There can be little doubt as to which is the more original version; there may be some doubt as to the motive of the change.

4. Luke xi. 13 compared with Matt. vii. 11. The saying is: *If ye then, being evil, know how to give good gifts unto your children; how much more shall your Father which is in heaven give good things* (ἀγαθὰ) *to them that ask Him?* Luke retains the "good gifts" (δόματα ἀγαθὰ) of the first clause, but in place of the "good things" of the second he puts the "Holy Spirit" (πνεῦμα ἅγιον), God's best gift, the gift the children of the kingdom most desire, the gift of which so frequent mention is made in the Pauline Epistles, though it is referred to but seldom in the synoptical record of Christ's teaching. There is nothing to be said against the substitution, except that it is in all probability a comment on what Christ said, rather than an exact report of His precise words.

5. Luke xi. 20 compared with Matt. xii. 28. In the discourse in which He defended Himself against the blasphemous suggestion of the Pharisees that He cast out devils by the aid of Beelzebub, Jesus, as reported by Matthew, says: *If I by the Spirit of God* (ἐν πνεύματι θεοῦ) *cast out the devils, then the kingdom of God is come unto you.* For "by the *Spirit* of God" Luke reads "by the *finger* of God" (ἐν δακτύλῳ θεοῦ). Matthew's version is obviously more in keeping with the connection of thought, as it offers a defence of Christ's *moral* character,

assailed by the charge of being in league with Satan. Luke's form of the saying gives prominence to Christ's claim to be in possession of *miraculous* power, which, however well founded, was not the point requiring to be insisted on. It seems, however, to have been one of the points which the evangelist desired to make conspicuous in his narrative. It is observable in his reports of miraculous incidents that he is ever careful to bring out two features—the *power* and the *benevolence* of Jesus. The power he magnifies by specifying particulars tending to show the aggravated character of the disease healed. Peter's mother-in-law is taken with a *great* fever (iv. 38), the leper is *full* of leprosy (v. 12), the blind man at Jericho needs to be conducted to Jesus (xviii. 40, "Jesus stood and commanded him to be brought unto Him"). These heightening phrases are not necessarily exaggerations of the fact, but they reveal a desire to make the most of the fact as a foil to the power of Christ. The benevolence of the Saviour, Luke signalizes by specifying particulars tending to show the greatness of the calamity from which He delivers, as when he mentions that the subject of a miracle is an only child (widow's son, vii. 12; Jairus' daughter, viii. 30; epileptic boy, ix. 47), or that the withered hand cured on the Sabbath day was the *right* one, the hand by which the man earned his bread (vi. 6).

6. Certain modifications seem to have sprung out of a desire to tone down the severity of Christ's sayings. The following are instances: Luke ix. 60: "Let the dead bury their dead, *but go thou and preach the kingdom of God*," compared with Matthew's: "Follow Me, and let the

dead bury their dead." A special vocation and the urgent claims of the kingdom justify neglect of ordinary duties. Luke xvii. 2: "It were better for him (through whom offences come) that a millstone were hanged about his neck, and he cast into the sea, than that he should offend one of these little ones." How tame compared with Matthew's: "It were better for him that a millstone *turned by an ass* (μύλος ὀνικός, larger than one worked by the hand, — Luke's phrase is λίθος μυλικὸς) were hanged about his neck, and that he were drowned in the *depth* of the sea" (ἐν τῷ πελάγει τῆς θαλάσσης; Luke: εἰς τὴν θάλασσαν). There is a passion in these words which is allowed to evaporate in the milder version of the third Gospel. Luke xviii. 17: "Verily I say unto you, Whosoever shall not receive the kingdom of God as a little child, shall in nowise enter therein." This is Luke's equivalent for Matthew's stern word of rebuke addressed to ambitious disciples: "Except ye be converted, and become as little children, ye shall not enter into the kingdom." Think of future apostles being spoken to in that manner! Luke xii. 51: "Suppose ye that I am come to give peace on earth? I tell you, Nay; but rather *division*" (διαμερισμόν, in place of Matthew's *sword*—μάχαιραν, x. 34).

As an offset to these examples of subdued expression may be cited a case in which Luke's report intensifies the severity of one of Christ's hard sayings. For the word: "He that loveth father or mother more than Me, is not worthy of Me; and he that loveth son or daughter more than Me, is not worthy of Me" (Matt. x. 37). Luke has: "If any man come to Me and *hate* not his father and mother, and wife and children, and brethren and sisters, yea, and his own life also, he cannot be My disciple" (xiv. 26). Which of the two forms is the original; and if Matthew's be, whence this solitary example of intensified expression in a Gospel whose general tendency seems to be to make prominent the mildness and amiability of Jesus? I incline to the view that Matthew's form is the more original, and that in Luke's report we have an exception to his rule requiring to be accounted for. And the most probable account seems to be that the word " hate " reflects the actual experience of the Church. Matthew's form gives the theory of Christian discipleship as quietly spoken by the Master into the ears of his companions, before the great conflict his mission was destined to originate had properly begun. Luke's gives the experience of Christian disciples when faith in Jesus was found to create profound alienations within families, unbelieving members cherishing bitter hatred against members that had become believers; and believers, if not hating unbelieving relatives, being compelled by their faith to assume such an attitude towards them as bore to the world's eye, and possibly to their own feeling at times, an aspect of hatred. Nothing divides and alienates so completely as earnest divergence in religious belief and practice. The word "hate" in Luke's report of the Lord's *logion* bears testimony to this truth. Probably he found it in his sources.

II. Luke's *omissions*. By an omission is meant not merely a certain saying or discourse of Christ given by Matthew and not found in Luke's Gospel, but a saying or discourse with which the compiler of his source, or

Luke himself, was acquainted, but which for some reason was omitted by either the one or the other. The distinction between a non-appearance and an omission is important. The former presupposes ignorance, and tends to throw doubt on the authenticity of an unreported saying. The latter is intentional; and when the intention is discovered, the absence of a particular saying from the record given in one Gospel does not weaken the testimony to its genuineness borne by another Gospel in which it is found, but rather tends to confirm it. The position of matters then is: one evangelist knew and reported, another evangelist knew, but for an assignable reason did not report.

That Luke was not ignorant of all he does not report, may in some instances be demonstrated. A notable and instructive example may be found in the omission from his Gospel of the materials contained in the long section of Matthew's Gospel, chap. xiv. 22–xvi. 12, to which in the main corresponds Mark vi. 45–viii. 27. These materials belonged to the common synoptical tradition, with which there is every reason to believe Luke was acquainted. And by inspection of his narrative at the place where the gap occurs we can detect traces of intentional omission. At the beginning of the omitted section we find Jesus, after the feeding of the five thousand, alone praying (Matt. xiv. 23; Mark vi. 46); at the close of it comes in the narrative of the conversation at Cæsarea Philippi (Matt. xvi. 13; Mark viii. 27). Luke connects the praying with the conversation thus: "And it came to pass as He was alone praying, His disciples were with Him; and He asked them, saying,

Whom say the people that I am?" (ix. 18), so, as it were, bringing together the two edges of the gap, and giving apparent continuity to a fragmentary narrative. The materials contained in this demonstrably intentional omission will be found very instructive as to the motives of omissions, and of variations in general.

Luke's omissions of teaching material are extensive, and of serious import in connection with an attempt to give a connected account of the doctrine of Christ.

1. The anti-Pharisaic utterances of Christ are very much curtailed. The sections relating to alms-giving, praying, and fasting in Matthew's version of the Sermon on the Mount are not found in the third Gospel. We miss also the encounters between Jesus and the Pharisees regarding washing of hands and divorce. The great anti-Pharisaic discourse in Matt. xxiii. likewise disappears, or dwindles to a couple of verses, in which the speaker warns His hearers against the ostentation of the scribes, who walked in long robes, loved salutations in the market-places, and chief seats in the synagogues, and against their detestable hypocrisy in cloaking robbery of the defenceless with long prayers (Luke xx. 46, 47). Some of the material of this discourse, indeed, is to be found elsewhere (Luke xi. 37–52); but important portions, such as the section referring to the immoral casuistry of the Rabbis in connection with oaths (Matt. xxiii. 16, 22), are entirely lacking. The effect of these omissions is, that from Luke's Gospel alone it would be impossible to present a complete view of Christ's moral criticism of the prevalent religion; in other words, of His doctrine of righteousness on its negative side.

2. The sayings of Jesus bearing on the meaning of His own death are very imperfectly recorded in the third Gospel. Jesus taught His disciples four lessons on that subject, contained in as many texts, which are either not found at all in Luke, or very partially reported. The first lesson was given at Cæsarea Philippi, where Jesus taught His disciples that His death would be the result of His moral fidelity, and so far from being a peculiar event, was only one instance of a law according to which all who live faithfully must bear a cross. Luke's report of the words which form the basis of this doctrine is very defective (ix. 22-24, cf. Matt. xvi. 22-25).[1] The second lesson was conveyed in the words: "The Son of man came not to be ministered unto, but to minister, and to give His life a ransom for the many" (Matt. xx. 28; Mark x. 45). This saying does not occur in Luke, nor the story of the ambitious request of James and John in connection with which it was uttered. The third lesson was given on the occasion of the anointing in Bethany, when Jesus declared that wherever the gospel was preached in the whole world, Mary's deed would be spoken of to her honour,—implying an affinity between her act and His own in laying down His life. The whole of this beautiful story, lovingly narrated by Matthew and Mark, has, to our surprise, been omitted by Luke. The last lesson was taught in the words spoken at the institution of the supper: "This is My blood, shed *for the*

[1] To be noted is the omission of the rebuke administered to Peter for opposing his Master's purpose to meet death at Jerusalem. On this Pfleiderer remarks: "He (Luke) is everywhere the man of peace, who will remove every dark shadow from the sacred personalities of the primitive Church." *Urchristenthum*, S. 585.

remission of sins." The vital phrase: "for the remission of sins," is wanting in Luke's version. These omissions, assuming acquaintance with the material omitted, are perplexing. How are they to be explained? Shall we say that Luke was not a theologian, but a moralist, and that therefore we must not be surprised if we find not in his pages a special doctrine of atonement, but only a general doctrine of grace or mercy?

3. Luke's Gospel contains no words of Christ referring to the *Church*. According to Matthew, Christ made a very important declaration on that subject at Cæsarea Philippi, pointing to the founding of a religious society to be identified with His name, and indicating its relation to the kingdom of God which had been the main theme of His preaching. As the passage in question is not found in Mark, it may legitimately be inquired whether this is to be regarded as an intentional omission on Luke's part. In any case, the fact remains that the section concerning the Church is lacking in his Gospel, and that he supplies no materials for a doctrine on that subject expressly taught by the Master.

4. It is not necessary to do more than simply state that we miss in Luke's Gospel nearly the whole of the utterances in which, according to Matthew's report of the Sermon on the Mount, Jesus defined His attitude to the Mosaic law.

5. Among the surprises of Luke's Gospel is the absence from its pages of the gracious invitation: "Come unto Me, all ye that labour." Can it be that the evangelist, who seems to take delight in presenting Jesus in word and deed as the Gracious One, passed over that

beautiful word, having it before his eye in his sources? I have stumbled on a hypothetical solution of this problem which I shall explain in the following section. If there be anything in it, it will show in at least one instance a very close connection between Luke's omissions and his *additions.*

III. Luke's *additions.* These are sufficiently extensive to have made it necessary to make room for them in the narrative by reducing the matter taken from the common tradition, and to have raised the question, for a compiler who desired to keep his narrative within moderate limits, what could best be spared. They have for the most part a common character, being nearly all fitted and presumably intended to bring into view the benevolence or loving-kindness of Christ. The earliest within the period of the public ministry, the account of the discourse in the synagogue of Nazareth (iv. 16–30), may be said to furnish the keynote of the whole. The words Jesus spake on that occasion the evangelist characterizes as "words of grace." All, or nearly all, his additions to the stock of evangelic traditions may be said to be reports either of "words of grace" or of acts of grace. To the latter head may be referred the raising of the son of the widow of Nain (vii. 11), and the healing of the woman who had a spirit of infirmity (xiii. 10). The gracious reception given to the woman who was a sinner (vii. 36–50), and to Zacchæus the chief publican (xix. 1), exhibit in a signal manner Christ's humane bearing towards persons belonging to proscribed classes. The Samaritan incidents, the rebuke of the proposal to call down fire from heaven (ix. 51), and the healing of ten lepers, one being a Samaritan, and he the only grateful one (xvii. 11), exhibit the same benignant spirit towards a people treated by the Jews as pagans. The words of grace, preserved alone by Luke, are many and beautiful, comprising the parables of the *two debtors*, the *good Samaritan*, the *great supper;* the three parables concerning the *finding of the lost*, and that of the *Pharisee and the publican*.

For the sake of these words and works of grace, Luke might well deem himself justified in leaving out of his narrative materials of a different character already well known, or of less value at least for those whose benefit he had specially in view; such as severe words against the patrons of counterfeit righteousness, duplicate miracles teaching the same lesson, and incidents or sayings liable to be misunderstood, or that might tend to obscure the very grace which he made it his business to magnify, like that of the Syro-Phœnician woman.

It may be taken for granted that for all these additions Luke found vouchers among his sources. It seems not improbable that he modified sayings by added glosses or substituted expressions, but there is not the slightest reason to believe that he invented *logia*. How far his editorial liberties might go, we may learn from one of his additions not yet referred to—the mission of the seventy. Even such a critic as Weiss is inclined to think that this mission did not take place, but that Luke simply attached it as a heading to the second of two versions of the instructions to the twelve which he found in his sources. I do not deem a second mission of some kind so improbable as some imagine. Our

Lord's word, " the harvest is plenteous, but the labourers are few," shows His anxiety for an increase in the number of sympathetic evangelists. It is therefore likely that He would send out more if they were forthcoming; and that they were, appears from the account of the three aspirants in Luke ix. 57–62. He might send them forth as they presented themselves, not waiting till a large number had been accumulated, but despatching them piecemeal two and two. Tradition may have made the number thus sent out amount to the symbolical seventy, and transformed a mission in detail into a solemn mission of the whole at one time, accompanied by such instructions as Luke records. This is conceivable; that it is what actually occurred, I do not say. But suppose the fact were that there was no mission but that of the twelve, and that the mission of the seventy is an invention of Luke, or of those to whom he owed his information, the point to be noted is that for this "invented" mission there are no invented *instructions*. The instructions are simply a repetition in substance of those given to the twelve. If Luke furnished unhistorical settings for some sayings of Jesus, this was the limit of his editorial licence: he reported no sayings which he did not believe to be in substance genuine *logia* of the Master. This we observe to be the case where, as in the instance before us, we have the means of controlling him, and we may confidently assume that it is his way where he reports words not elsewhere found.[1]

[1] Luke's care in preserving valuable sayings left orphans through his omissions, by affiliating them with favourite utterances to which

SECTION III.—THE MOTIVES OF LUKE'S VARIATIONS.

As the long section, Matt. xiv. 22–xvi. 12, supplies us with the most probable instance of intentional omission on Luke's part, an analysis of its contents may form a suitable introduction to a study of the causes or motives of the variations specified in the foregoing section. It contains (1) a storm on the lake of Gennesaret, a second of the kind (xiv. 25–33); (2) an encounter between Jesus and the scribes in regard to neglect of ceremonial ablutions (xv. 1–20); (3) the story of the Syro-Phœnician woman (xv. 21–28); (4) the feeding of 4000, a second incident of the kind (xv. 32–38); (5) the demand of the Pharisees with the Sadducees for a sign from heaven (xvi. 1–12). The five sections reduce themselves to three classes: two *duplicates*, two *encounters with the representatives of current religion*, and one example of *apparent limitation of sympathy within the bounds of the chosen people*. The categories under which they are thus

---

they become as adopted children, can be illustrated from his version of the Sermon on the Mount. By the omission of the section, Matt. v. 38–42, concerning the law of retaliation ("an eye for an eye"), the ethical maxim "resist not evil" and its concrete examples: if one smite thee on the right cheek, turn to him the left; if one take thy coat, let him have thy cloak also—become orphaned. They are too good to lose. What does Luke do? He brings these sayings under the head of the great law of love: "Love your enemies," etc., which appears in his version of the Sermon as the sum of all ethical precepts. By this device all that is valuable is preserved. That it is an editorial device appears from the repetition of the precept: "Love your enemies" (vi. 27, 35). In this instance we see Luke showing himself careful of words, careless of original historical connections.

grouped suggest the probable motives of omission. Omissions of the first class are very intelligible, and we can easily conceive the evangelist making them without a moment's hesitation. He may, however, have had two thoughts before finally deciding on the other omissions. For some of the words spoken by Jesus on the occasions to which the omitted sections refer are very remarkable, *e.g.* these: *Ye have made the commandments of God of none effect by your tradition;* and *not that which goeth into the mouth defileth a man, but that which cometh out of the mouth, this defileth a man.* These utterances, so pregnant with moral significance and revolutionary in tendency, must have possessed deep interest for a man of Pauline sympathies like Luke, and one would imagine also for the readers he had chiefly in view. Why, then, does he pass over the narrative in which they occur? No more likely answer suggests itself than that the encounter it records belonged to a local and temporary controversy between Jesus and the representatives of traditional religion in Judæa, which, however fierce in spirit and tragic in result, appeared to the evangelist of secondary importance to the permanent interests of the Christian faith. These conflicts were to him but the morning mists through which the Sun of righteousness had to clear His way to meridian splendour. If this motive was at work, it would account not only for the two omissions in the passage now under consideration, but for the disappearance from Luke's Gospel of large masses of material relating to the same general subject. The plain-spoken working out of the principle, that not that which goeth into the mouth defileth, might bring into play a feeling of delicacy as a subsidiary motive for omission in connection with the earlier of the two incidents.

The appearance of a grudging, unsympathetic attitude towards the pagan world, presented by the behaviour of Jesus towards the Syro-Phœnician woman, in all probability supplied at least one motive for the omission of that pathetic story. The evangelist shrank from recording anything that might create in the minds of his readers the false and injurious impression that the Author of the Christian faith was animated by anti-Gentile prejudices. This motive may have been assisted by another—the feeling that the incident in question might be omitted without loss of anything valuable, as virtually a duplicate. For the story of the centurion, as related in Luke's Gospel, is so constructed as to present the good features of the kindred story of the woman of Canaan without its drawbacks. An excessive humility is ascribed to the centurion, which in effect echoes the sentiment: "We Gentiles are *dogs*." Then the intercession of the elders of the Jews takes the place of the entreaties of the disciples for the distracted Syrian mother. Finally, the compliance of Jesus, and His unfeigned admiration for the faith displayed, appear with their value undiminished by any preliminary hesitations.[1]

From this group of omissions, as above explained, combined with the prevailing character of Luke's additions, we may draw this general inference: that the third evangelist, having supreme regard to the religious edification of his readers, omitted matter which appeared comparatively useless, unprofitable, or liable to be misunder-

[1] Luke vii. 1-10.

stood, to make room for matter tending to exhibit Christ in the fulness of His grace as the friend of sinners, publicans, Samaritans, and even Gentiles. Now, if this motive influenced him in any part of his work as the compiler of a Gospel, it is not unreasonable to assume that it would influence him throughout. In other words, we may trace the influence of a regard to edification, not only in omissions and additions, but also in modifications of sayings by alterations in expression. In the notes appended to the samples of such alteration given in the foregoing section, suggestions as to possible motives of change are tentatively offered. These may be reduced to two main heads: the style of Christ's sayings adapted (1) to existing habits of thought and expression on religious topics; and (2) to the sentiments of reverence and love towards the person of Christ cherished by writer or readers, or both. How far changes of this sort originated with Luke, and how far they were a datum for him in his sources, cannot be determined. The question of importance for us is, To what influence are existing variations due? When we have ascertained these, we are furnished with the means of determining with a measure of exactness the primitive form of the words of Christ.

That both the forms of influence just specified, that of the religious life of the Church in general, and that of the idea of Christ cherished by believers in particular, can be traced in Luke's report of our Lord's sayings, must, I think, be conceded. Of exceptional interest for the student are the indications belonging to the latter category. Reading Luke's Gospel with a critical eye, one obtains a very vivid idea of Christ as he conceived Him, and loved to contemplate Him, and to present Him to the view of others. He is full of *grace*, ever revealing itself in word and deed. He is the *sympathetic friend* of the sinful, such as she who came into Simon's house, of publicans like Zacchæus, of Samaritans, of Gentiles like the centurion of Capernaum. He is the *Lord*. He is possessed of unlimited divine power, and works miraculous, astonishing cures by the very *finger* of God. He is Himself divine; the inversion of the order of the temptations in the desert seems due to a desire to make this prominent. Christ's last word in Luke's narrative is: "Thou shalt not tempt the Lord thy God." When that word had been spoken, it was meet that temptation should cease. His fellowship with His Father is uninterrupted and unclouded even in the hour of death. The bitter cry on the cross: "My God, my God, why hast Thou forsaken me?" is replaced by: "Father, into Thy hands I commend my spirit." That the character and public conduct of Jesus had a stern side Luke knows, and does not altogether conceal, but he keeps it well in the background. He reduces the withering exposure of Pharisaism to a minimum, and seeks to soften the seeming asperity of the little he retains by representing Christ, when uttering the words reported, as in friendly relations with the criticized class. The free-spoken words are the table-talk of Jesus sitting at table as the guest of members of the Pharisaic fraternity. Luke thus makes Jesus appear as a genial, wide-hearted man who shuns nobody; eating to-day with publicans and "sinners," to-morrow with "holy" people, but speaking His mind frankly in all companies with royal freedom.[1] He tones down words that seem to be spoken with passionate vehemence, such as that concerning the millstone, and the other in the same discourse to ambitious disciples concerning the necessity of a radical change of spirit in order to admission into the divine kingdom. He does not allow his beloved Lord to appear either as a bitter controversialist or as a pitilessly severe Master. Nor does his Gospel supply even a plausible pretext for the allegation that the founder of the Christian faith was a man of narrow Jewish prejudices. The story of the woman of Canaan is left out, and the hard word, "Let him be unto thee as an heathen man and a publican," given by Matthew in connection with his second reference to the *Church*,[2] is not found in his pages.

For the immediate needs of the section of the Church for which Luke wrote this picture of Christ may have been wisely drawn, and he is not to be blamed for the bias he manifests. Nevertheless, it remains true that the Christ thus presented is a partial, one-sided one, and that the permanent needs of the Church and of the Christian faith demand that the sterner side of passionate, relentless abhorrence of counterfeit sanctity, as exhibited in the Pharisees, and of selfish ambition intruding into the kingdom of God, as exhibited in His own disciples, should be fully shown. Therefore we have reason to be thankful that the partiality of one evangelist is supplemented by the healthy realism of another, who seems to have thought that the

---

[1] *Vide* Luke vii. 36, xi. 37, xiv. 1.
[2] Matt. xviii. 17. The presence of this word in this passage may have been the reason why this second allusion to the Church is also omitted by Luke.

character of Christ could look after itself, and that his business was to state facts, however apparently ungenial. That Matthew had his bias may be true; that he had a less clear insight into the grace of Christ than Luke is probable; it certainly does not receive from him the same broad, effective delineation. But it must be conceded that the face of Jesus, as he shows it, is very real and life-like. And that face inspires us with trust and admiration; trust in His humanity, admiration for His heroic moral fidelity. There He stands, the sympathetic people's Friend, the wise Master, the fearless Prophet— the genuine Jesus of Nazareth.

Luke is *par excellence* the evangelist of grace. But why, then, does he omit matter peculiarly evangelic, *e.g.* the gracious invitation, "Come unto Me, all ye that labour and are heavy laden"? I should be sorry to think it was from ignorance, for that might tend to throw doubt on the authenticity of one of the most charming of all the evangelic *logia*. But if Luke knew the saying, is his omission of it not quite unaccountable? The problem has exercised the critics, and various explanations have been suggested. Weiss thinks that Luke passed the passage over because he found the transition from the previous context too abrupt.[1] Holtzmann is of opinion that Luke stumbled at some of the expressions, such as the epithet ταπεινὸς, humble, applied to Jesus, and ζυγός and φορτίον, as savouring of legalism, and suggesting ideas of bondage and burdensomeness incongruous with the Gospel.[2] But supposing these words were dis-

---

[1] *Das Matthäus-Evangelium, in loc.*
[2] *Die Synoptischen Evangelien,* S. 147.

tasteful to him, one does not see why he could not substitute for them others more evangelic, as he did in his report of the Sermon on the Mount. Accordingly Wendt, who in his reconstruction of the book of *Logia*, assumed to be a source for Luke, includes the gracious invitation, confesses himself unable to offer any explanation of its omission. "This section," he remarks, "Luke has passed over without any perceptible good reason. The words form a very suitable, one may even say necessary, continuation of the foregoing discourse."[1]

When such scholars fail, it may seem presumptuous in any one else to hope to succeed. Nevertheless I will venture to throw out the thought which has occurred to me. It seems to me, then, that Luke found in his source, at the place where the gracious invitation occurs, probably written on the margin, as illustrative examples, the three incidents recorded in Luke x. 25–42, xi. 1–13: the *Good Samaritan* (x. 25–37), *Martha and Mary* (x. 38–42), and the *lesson on Prayer*, in answer to the request of the disciples (xi. 1–13). These incidents occupy much the same place in Luke's Gospel that the gracious invitation occupies in Matthew's. In both, the passage beginning with "I thank Thee, O Father," forms the preceding context, only that Luke appends to that passage, as given by Matthew, the saying: "Blessed are the eyes which see the things that ye see," placed in the first Gospel in a different connection.[2] After the gracious invi-

---

[1] *Die Lehre Jesu*, Erster Theil, S. 92.
[2] Matt. xiii. 16, 17, in connection with the parables. Luke gives it in connection with the results of the evangelistic mission of the Seventy (x. 23, 24).

tation in Matthew's Gospel come the sabbatic incidents: "disciples plucking ears of corn," and "man with withered hand" (xii. 1–14). These Luke, following the order of Mark, disturbed in Matthew's record, records at an earlier stage in his Gospel, so that he passes on directly from the lesson on Prayer to the discourse on Blasphemy, which in Matthew follows immediately after the above-named sabbatic incidents. The three incidents reported by Luke in the place occupied by the gracious invitation in Matthew's Gospel have, moreover, all this in common, that they exhibit Christ as a *Teacher*, and there is no other perceptible link of connection accounting for their being placed side by side. But Christ appears as a teacher in many other passages in the Gospel; why should these three be selected and formed into a group by themselves, as woodcuts, so to speak, illustrating the "Come unto Me"? If there is anything in my hypothesis, it must be because these incidents illustrate the salient points of Matthew's *Logion*. And I think on examination this will be found to be the case. The salient points in the *Logion* are the *Scholar's Burden* — the persons invited to Christ's school are the "labouring and heavy laden;" the *Teacher's Meekness*: "I am meek and lowly in heart;" and the *Rest-bringing Lesson*: "Ye shall find rest unto your souls." The characters brought before us in the three incidents of Luke are all in diverse ways burdened ones. The burden of the lawyer was an artificial Rabbinical system; the burden of Martha, happily escaped by Mary, is the cares of life; the burden of the disciples is unfulfilled spiritual desire, struggling for utterance, despairing of satisfaction. The meekness of the Master is conspicuous in all three instances: in the first He meekly instructs one who comes rather asking captious questions than in the humble guise of a true disciple; in the second He soothes the irritable housewife with a gentle "Martha, Martha;" in the third He enters with deep human sympathy, as well as with superhuman wisdom, into the spiritual perplexities of disciples. And in each case a rest-giving word is spoken. To the lawyer is taught the infinitude of duty, neighbourhood wide as the world, whereby the spirit is allowed to escape like a bird from the cage of artificial restriction into the boundless atmosphere of Humanity. To Martha is hinted the supreme worth of the kingdom, the theme of all the Teacher's discourse; whereby earthly cares are put into their proper place of subordination. To the disciples is given a form of prayer which they can use till they have outgrown the need of it, and a parabolic instruction in the art of waiting for good earnestly desired but long withheld.

What Luke does, therefore, is to give us a substitute for Matthew's gracious invitation. Instead of making Christ say, "Come, ye burdened ones, to My school, and I will give you rest," he conducts us into Christ's school, and shows Him in the act of giving, with the meekness of wisdom, rest-bringing instruction to burdened spirits. It may be asked, indeed, What hindered him from giving both the invitation to school and the samples of work going on in the school; pointing to the one as the inscription over the door, offering the other as inducements to enter? If the gracious invitation was in the text of his source, and the illustrations on the margin, how natural to retain the text and add to it by introducing the marginal comments! Or did comments overlay text, hiding it from view, rendering it illegible? Conjectures are idle. One thing only seems probable, that the saying, "Come unto Me," was a nucleus around which gathered gradually these beautiful stories illustrative of Christ's method as a teacher. The alternative hypothesis, that the stories came first, and that the invitation was abstracted from them, is possible, but unlikely.[1]

SECTION IV.—THE SYNOPTICAL TYPE OF DOCTRINE.

The scope of the study which goes by the name of New Testament Theology may be variously defined. It may be vaguely and comprehensively regarded as an attempt to ascertain and set forth in order the views to be found in the various groups of New Testament books on all manner of religious and theological topics. With so

---

[1] Pfleiderer regards Matt. xi. 28–30 as a free citation out of Sirach li. 23, where the Divine Wisdom invites the ignorant to come to her and dwell in the house of instruction. There is a certain resemblance in some of the expressions which led me, in reading this apocryphal book some years ago, to make a marginal reference to Matt. xi. 28–30. Pfleiderer expresses the opinion that in future we will have to familiarize ourselves with the thought that the light rays of the Gospels have not come so directly from the one point of the historical person of Jesus as to the unaided eye of the Church, in virtue of a natural optical illusion, seemed to be the case, but have emanated also from the creative geniality or inspiration of the evangelists, and are often to be traced only indirectly to the common light-fountain in the Spirit of Jesus. It will be a while before we reconcile ourselves to the view that we have to thank Matthew, rather than Christ, for the Gracious Invitation.

wide a range it is apt to become a rather pointless and wearisome exercise. There is one mode of looking at this department of theological inquiry which, if not exhaustive, has at least the merit of definiteness and unflagging interest, that, viz., which makes it have supreme reference to the main drift and *raison d'être* of the literature to be studied. Why is there a *New Testament*? Because Jesus Christ came into the world an epoch-making personage in the history of religion and revelation. The question of sovereign importance therefore is, What is the significance of the new epoch? what is the good Christ brought to men? The Highest Good it must be, if Jesus be indeed the Christ, the fulfiller of the promises and hopes of foregoing ages. What, then, is the *summum bonum*? The New Testament contains the answer to the question, and New Testament theology has for its chief, if not sole problem, to ascertain what the answer is. It may therefore be defined as the study of the leading types of doctrine concerning the things freely given to us of God in Jesus Christ.

Leading types I say, for the New Testament writings do not all present the gift of divine grace under precisely the same point of view. Four types may be distinguished, not of course antagonistic or mutually exclusive, rather closely related; yet distinct, and capable of being associated with certain books. These types have objective and not merely subjective value; they are more than modes under which particular writers apprehended the truth, deriving their colour from personal idiosyncrasy and peculiar experience, though these elements have their place. They are different aspects of the same thing, having a relative independence, and exhibiting Christianity under distinct relations of resemblance or contrast to other forms of religion. The four types may be described by these titles: *The Kingdom of God, The Righteousness of God, Free Access to God, Eternal Life.* The first is the designation under which the benefit accruing from the advent of Christ appears in the synoptical presentation of our Lord's teaching; the second is the name for the same thing found in the Pauline Epistles; the third indicates the chosen point of view of the author of the Epistle to the Hebrews; the last is the watchword of the Fourth Gospel. We are concerned in the present work with the first of these four types, our task being to give a succinct account of the teaching of Christ as recorded in the first three Gospels.

The doctrine of Christ in these Gospels is the doctrine of the kingdom of God. Under this category all may be ranged; there is no other entitled to be placed above it, or that does not easily find a place under it. The ethical teaching of Christ is very important, and some have given it the first place, and made the doctrine of the kingdom subordinate and secondary.[1] But the ethics of Jesus are the ethics of the kingdom, setting forth the laws by which its subjects are to guide their lives. The function of Christ as Redeemer is a still more important category, and it might seem as if the most appropriate general description of His teaching would be one giving prominence, as He did Himself, to the fact that He came to "save the lost"—the doctrine of *salvation*. But even

[1] So Baur, in *Vorlesungen über neutestamentliche Theologie*.

this heading falls naturally under the doctrine of the kingdom. The doctrine of salvation shows the way by which men enter into the kingdom. Christianity has been described as being, not a circle with one centre, but an ellipse with two foci; the doctrine of the kingdom being one of the foci, the doctrine of redemption the other. But no indignity is done to Christ's redeeming work by including it as a particular under the general head of the kingdom; rather is its fundamental importance thereby signalized. No higher idea can be formed of salvation than to make it consist in citizenship in the divine commonwealth; nor can Christ's importance as Saviour be more conspicuously magnified than by representing Him as one to whom citizens owe their admission to the privilege. I have no hesitation, therefore, in regarding the kingdom of God as an exhaustive category.

THE KINGDOM OF GOD;

OR CHRIST'S TEACHING ACCORDING TO THE SYNOPTICAL GOSPELS.

CHAPTER I.

CHRIST'S IDEA OF THE KINGDOM.

THE KINGDOM OF GOD: what did Jesus mean by that expression? In all that relates to the significance of Christianity, two tendencies of thought have ever revealed themselves in the Church — one to magnify the new element in it, the other to reduce the new element to a minimum; on the one hand, to emphasize the affinity of the Christian religion to that which went before in the history of revelation; on the other, to emphasize the distinctness. The minimizing tendency has ever had on its side the majority. It has its representatives among living theologians in reference to the question now before us. The most recent writer, *e.g.*, on the life of Jesus says: " What this kingdom is Jesus has nowhere expressly stated; He treats the notion as one current among the people. It is therefore quite perverse to regard it as an idea invented by Jesus, and to attempt to construct it out of His sayings. Historically viewed, Jesus can have meant nothing by it save what arose naturally out of the peculiarity of His people and its ways of thinking."[1] I should be very much surprised as well as disappointed if this were true. All the leading writers of the New Testament—Paul and the authors of the Epistle to the Hebrews and the Fourth Gospel—betray in their writings an intense consciousness that some great and *new* thing had come into the world through the mission of Christ. Paul makes Christ the bringer in of a new creation. The author of the Epistle to the Hebrews represents the Christian era as the era of the Better Hope through which we draw nigh to God, in contrast to the Levitical religion which kept men standing at an awful distance. In the Fourth Gospel the distinction between the new and the old dispensations is broadly indicated by the declaration: "The law was given by Moses; grace and truth came by Jesus Christ." We should certainly expect to find the great Initiator not behind His apostolic interpreters in insight into the nature and ultimate outcome of His mission. Without claiming for Him omniscience, we

---

[1] Weiss, *Leben Jesu*, i. 444, 445 (vol. ii. pp. 65, 66, Clark's translation). Students of the works of this distinguished theologian must be on their guard against his bias as an interpreter. His great merits as a critic may lead to indiscriminate discipleship in a sphere in which he is weak and unsatisfactory. His great fault, or at least one of his glaring faults, is an extreme anti-Tübingen bias, a tendency to deny the very fact-basis of the Tübingen theory, reducing all to a colourless neutrality, in place of the extreme antagonisms of Baur. The universalism of Jesus is grudgingly admitted. Even that of Paul is toned down; and on the whole, one wonders how a worldwide Christianity ever grew up out of such beginnings, the initiators having so little of the spirit of the new era.

should at least credit Him with the deep, far-reaching spiritual vision of a unique religious genius. This is also demanded by words of His own, of indubitable authenticity; such as those which represent John the Baptist as less than the least in the kingdom of heaven, and compare the movement with which He Himself was identified to a *new* garment and a *new* vintage. It would require some great epoch-making novelty in religious thought and life to justify such utterances.

It is true, indeed, the name employed by Jesus for the new thing is old. It indicates an attitude less antagonistic to the earlier rudimentary forms of religion than that of Paul, who is consciously and intensely opposed to legalism, and of the author of the Epistle to the Hebrews, who is earnestly bent on asserting and evincing under every aspect the incomparable superiority of Christianity to the Levitical religion. It expresses affinity rather than antagonism, introducing a new world with the least possible shock to old associations. But the choice of it was due to wisdom, not to limitation of knowledge. It was natural and suitable at the initial period of the new age, yet fit for permanent use. It was not a transient name, expressive of a hope that was destined to prove a dream — a restored theocratic kingdom of Israel, cherished by one who was under the influence of the old world that was about to pass away. It was a felicitous suggestive name for the blessing of the New Testament, used with full consciousness of its significance, expressive of eternal truth, and to be reverted to throughout the Christian ages for instruction and inspiration.

Nothing can be at once more necessary and more

legitimate than the endeavour to ascertain by a close study of Christ's words and actions in what sense He used this title. It is necessary, for the title in itself is a form capable of much meaning, but expressly conveying little. It signifies some form of divine dominion. Abstractly viewed, it might denote the reign of the Almighty over all creation through the operation of natural law; or of the moral Governor of the world rendering to every man and nation according to their works; or of the God of Israel ruling over a chosen people, and bestowing on them power, peace, and felicity as the reward of obedience to His divine will. Or it might mean something higher than any of these things, the highest form of dominion conceivable, the advent of which is emphatically fit to be the burden of a gospel, viz. the reign of divine love exercised by God in His grace over human hearts believing in His love, and constrained thereby to yield Him grateful affection and devoted service. Which of all these was present to Christ's mind can be ascertained only by a study of His words and deeds. The first two are excluded by the simple consideration that the kingdom Christ proclaimed was represented by Him as *coming*. They do not come; they are always here and everywhere in all possible fulness. The choice lies between the other two, which are subject to the law of growth. The theocratic kingdom comes as Israel becomes a righteous nation, and grows proportionally prosperous. The kingdom of grace comes as men open their hearts to the benignant love of God, and experience in increasing measure its peace-giving, renewing influence. Which of these, then, was it whose approach Jesus proclaimed?

We must search the Gospels to determine. As either alternative is possible, the question is not to be settled by offhand assumptions. It may be that Jesus had in view, at least in the early period of His ministry, simply the theocratic kingdom of Hebrew prophecy and popular expectation,—a politico-ethical commonwealth, differing from the multitude only in placing the ethical element before the political as its indispensable condition; but the mere use of the expression "the kingdom of God" is no proof of this. The only legitimate and satisfactory course is to try to ascertain which hypothesis fits best into the particular statements and general drift of the evangelic history.

Our Lord is represented as opening His ministry with the announcement, "The time is fulfilled, and the kingdom of God is at hand."[1] The fact seems to favour what we may call the Judaizing hypothesis. The "time" referred to, it is natural to suppose, is Israel's time of merciful visitation, and the "kingdom" the realization of Israel's hope as depicted by the prophets. But even on this view the question at issue is not settled. For, on any hypothesis, Israel had a vital and prior interest in the kingdom now declared to be at hand; and as for the prophetic ideal of the kingdom, it is not quite so simple a matter to determine as one may at first be inclined to think. The general strain of Hebrew prophecy seems indeed to point to such a state of things as Zacharias longed for: Israel delivered out of the hands of her enemies, and serving God without fear, and amid prevalent prosperity.[2] Yet there are stray

[1] Mark i. 15.   [2] Luke i. 74.

utterances here and there which suggest the doubt whether this idyllic picture was ever to find a place in the realm of reality. There is, *e.g.*, the ominous word, uttered towards the close of the prophetic period, which not obscurely hints that God's kingdom might come not merely so as not to be the monopoly of Israel, but even so as to involve for her a doom of reprobation. The prophet Malachi represents Jehovah, in disgust at the Pharisaical, heartless service of an ungodly race, exclaiming: "Oh that some one would shut the temple doors, that ye may no more kindle in vain a fire upon Mine altar;" and declaring, "for from the rising of the sun, even unto the going down of the same, My name shall be great among the Gentiles; and in every place incense shall be offered unto My name, and a pure offering: for My name shall be great among the heathen, saith the Lord of hosts."[1] Here it is no more all the nations coming to Jerusalem with gold and incense in their hands, as in Isaiah's bright vision,[2] but the temple shut up and forsaken, and an acceptable worship offered to God in every place where human souls are found worshipping the true God in spirit and in truth. Those who, like the father of the Baptist, waited for the consolation of Israel in Christ's time, might overlook such passages, but we are not to suppose that Christ Himself was blind to them. He had an eye for overlooked texts, a mind that could appreciate forgotten or neglected truths, a spiritual insight that could discern the undercurrents of

---

[1] Mal. i. 10. The rendering in the Authorized Version makes the text contain a charge of mercenariness against the priests.
[2] Isa. lx.

prophetic thought. Withal He was a most original interpreter; this we must ever remember if we would understand His teaching. He was, to an inestimable extent, original in every way. He was original as a thinker and actor, not the mere creature of historical development. He was likewise original as an exegete and as a fulfiller of Scripture. He was not the slave of Old Testament texts, which it was His official duty as Messiah to fulfil. He brought out of His treasure things new as well as old; He spiritualized, idealized the utterances of the prophets, and He fulfilled them by filling them full to *overflowing*, bringing to the world in Himself and His teaching more than it is possible to find in all Old Testament prophecies put together, apart from the light shed on them by the gospel history.

Many things in that history point to the deeper mystic sense of the phrase now under consideration as the true one. Some of these can conveniently be mentioned here.

First, there is the very term "mystery" applied by Jesus to the kingdom in explaining to His disciples the parable of the Sower. "A mystery," it has been well remarked, "is a truth revealed for the first time by Jesus only, and by the Spirit of God who continues His work, and unknown to previous generations: we see, then, by that very term, that the idea which presents itself to our study will contain characters absolutely new, and which it will require special instruction to enable us to seize and comprehend."[1] The comparison of the scribe instructed in the things of the kingdom to a house-

[1] Reuss, *Theologie Chrétienne*, i. 174.

holder who bringeth out of his treasure things new and old, points in the same direction. The parable, a familiar story of natural life, is the old; the new is a truth relating to the kingdom which the parable embodies.

The expression "the kingdom of grace," so familiar to us, nowhere occurs in the Gospels, and even the word "grace" ($\chi άρις$) in the Pauline sense is of rare occurrence. The latter is, however, found once in Luke, in his account of Christ's preaching in the synagogue of Nazareth, where it is said: "All bare Him witness, and wondered at *the words of grace*[1] which proceeded out of His mouth."[2] The reference is to the substance of the discourse, not to its manner. We can well believe that there was a peculiar charm in the speaker's manner, but it sprang from His heart being filled with enthusiasm for the mission on which He had been sent. The grace of manner had its source in the grace that lay in the message. He had come to preach the gospel to the poor, to heal the broken-hearted, to proclaim the acceptable year of the Lord. The words of the prophet quoted and descanted on take us involuntarily into a higher region than a restored theocratic kingdom of Israel. There can be no doubt how the evangelist regarded them, and in what sense he called them "words of grace." He has taken the scene in the synagogue of Nazareth out of its true historical place, and set it in the forefront of his Gospel, to signify that the mission of Jesus concerned men's souls, and that it concerned all men. That scene, as it stands there, stamps Christ's whole ministry with the attributes of spirituality and universality, proclaims

---

[1] $ἐπὶ τοῖς λόγοις τῆς χάριτος$.   [2] Luke iv. 22.

it to be throughout a ministry of love to all the sinful, sorrowful sons of men. True, the evangelist's thought is not necessarily the thought of Jesus; and in transferring that scene from its true place, late in the evangelic history, he may be conveying a false impression as to the views and hopes with which the Herald of the kingdom *began* His ministry. But the presumption, to say the least, is the other way. The frontispiece of Luke's Gospel makes for the hypothesis that the doctrine of the kingdom from the first moved on a higher plane than that of vulgar expectation.[1]

The nature of Christ's preaching may be inferred from the effect of it on the minds of those who welcomed it. The disciples of Jesus conducted themselves as men who had received good news. They fasted not, they resembled rather a bridal party going to a wedding feast, according to the testimony of their own Master. Did their joy spring from the hope that the theocratic kingdom was about to be restored to Israel, and unrighteousness, misery, and the Romans expelled from the Holy Land? In that case we should have expected the disciples of the Baptist to share the joy, for their thoughts admittedly ran in that direction. But they did not: it was the marked difference in habit and temper between the two discipleships that gave Jesus occasion to make the striking comparison of His own disciples to a bridal party. Whence this difference? Why were the followers of Jesus like people going to a wedding, and

[1] The scene in the synagogue of Nazareth has the same typical significance in Luke's Gospel that the Sermon on the Mount has in Matthew's. On this point, see my *Galilean Gospel*.

the followers of John like a band of pilgrims faring towards a holy place, doing penance for their sins? It must have sprung from totally diverse conceptions of the kingdom whose approach both Masters proclaimed, imbibed from the teaching of those Masters. Jesus and John used much the same form of words, but they cannot have meant the same thing. We know what John meant when he spoke of the kingdom. He meant the people of Israel converted to righteousness, and in consequence blessed with national prosperity. And that being his ideal and aim, he was a gloomy man, and those who were about him became infected with his gloom. For he saw too soon and too well that the conversion of Israel to righteousness was a very improbable event. And so, despairing of the nation, and hoping only for the salvation of a small remnant, he began to talk of a winnowing-fan to separate wheat from chaff, and of an axe of judgment to hew down the worthless tree. In the mouth of one in this grim, desponding mood, the announcement of the approaching kingdom was a message of doom rather than of hope; it was awful tidings rather than good tidings, for the greater number at least, and indeed for all; for who could tell who should be able to stand the King's keen scrutiny, "who may abide the day of His coming?" All one could do was to labour painfully at self-reformation, fasting, praying, scrupulously cleansing body and soul, humbly trusting he might have a chance of standing at Jehovah's dread appearing. From the joy of Christ's disciples, we infer that He meant something different. He did not expect national repentance, though He desired it, and faithfully worked for it; therefore He never despaired. He did not come merely making a legal demand, and commanding men to be righteous under penalties. He came as one conscious that he had a message to proclaim that would help men to be good and happy. Therefore He was glad and hopeful, and all who came near Him felt His presence as a warm summer sun.

Another significant indication of the nature of the kingdom Jesus preached may be found in the kind of people to whom He principally and by preference addressed His invitations to enter. He preached the gospel of the kingdom to the poor;[1] He defined His mission by such sayings as these: "I am not come to call the righteous, but sinners;"[2] "the Son of Man is come to seek and to save the lost."[3] He threw the gates of the kingdom open to all comers irrespective of antecedent character, even if they had been really as bad as the Pharisees deemed those whom they branded as "publicans and sinners." Many morally disreputable persons responded to His call. This fact was in His view when He uttered the remarkable saying: "From the days of John the Baptist until now the kingdom of heaven suffereth violence, and the violent take it by force."[4] Publicans, sinners, harlots, the moral refuse of society,—such were the persons who in greatest numbers and with greatest earnestness pressed into the kingdom,—

---

[1] Matt. xi. 5.   [2] Matt. ix. 13.   [3] Luke xix. 10.
[4] Matt. xi. 12. Some take the statement in a bad sense, as implying that the people were seeking the kingdom in a worldly spirit, bent on setting up a political kingdom, irrrespective of ethical conditions. This view is unsuitable to the connection of thought.

a phenomenon astonishing to reputable, "righteous," religious people. The kingdom of God was being made a cave of Adullam, whither every one that was in distress or deep in moral debt resorted. The city of God was being taken possession of by "dogs," whose proper place was without; it was, as it were, being stormed by rude, lawless bands, and taken from those who thought they had an exclusive right to it. What a violence! what a profanation! Perhaps so; but one thing is clear: those persons who by their passionate earnestness were storming the kingdom would not suppose that *they* had any right to it. They listened to Christ's call, because they gathered from His preaching that the kingdom was a gift of grace, meant, in fact, God's sovereign, unmerited love to unworthy men, blessing them with pardon, and so gaining power over their hearts. And they felt that it did gain power, and that the dominion was real. Forgiven much, they loved much. Christ also was aware of the fact, and that was one of His reasons for seeking citizens of the kingdom in such a quarter; and that He did seek them there, for such a reason, shows very plainly what His idea of the kingdom was: *a kingdom of grace in order to be a kingdom of holiness.*

The attitude of Jesus towards the social abjects is in many ways significant. It implies, as we shall see, a new idea of man; but what I wish now to point out is the tendency it indicates towards *universalism*. This part of Christ's public action, as the records show, created much surprise, and provoked frequent censure. This is not to be wondered at. It really meant an incipient religious revolution. It manifested a disregard for conventional social distinctions, involving a principle which might one day be applied on a much wider scale, in the form, viz., of a disregard of distinctions not merely between classes within the bounds of the chosen people, but between races and nations; Jew and Gentile being treated as one, both needing salvation, neither having any claim to it, and the Gentile being not less capable of it than the Jew. In maintaining sympathetic relations with the "publicans and sinners," Jesus said in effect: "The kingdom is for them too; it is for all who need it and make it welcome. It opens its gates, like ancient Rome, to all comers, on condition that they conduct themselves as good citizens, once they are within its walls. From east, west, north, south, let them come; they shall not be refused admittance." The jealous guardians of Jewish prerogative did well, therefore, to take alarm at this novel interest in the lost sheep of Israel, whom they themselves had abandoned to their fate.

The universalistic drift revealed in Christ's love for the low and lowly found expression in many of His *words*. I refer to such as these: "Ye are the salt of the earth;" "ye are the light of the world;" "the field is the world."[1] The human race is regarded as the subject of the salting and enlightening influence of the children of the kingdom, and the field to be sown with the word of the kingdom; so that we are not surprised to find one

[1] Of course it is open to criticism to raise doubts as to the genuineness of such sayings. Weiss thinks the interpretation of the parable of the Tares, in which the last of the above sayings occurs (Matt. xiii. 38), does not proceed from Christ; and one of his arguments is, that He *could* not have said so absolutely "the field is the world." *Vide* his *Matthäus-Evangelium, in loc.*

Gospel closing with the injunction from the Master to His disciples: "Go ye therefore, and teach all nations;" and another with a similar command: "Go ye into all the world, and preach the gospel to the whole creation." There is a width of horizon in such utterances that is totally irreconcilable with the hypothesis that Jesus was merely a patriotic Jew, whose sympathies as well as His work were confined to His countrymen, and whose aim was to make Israel first a righteous nation, and then a free, prosperous kingdom.

But we may be reminded that there are things in the Gospels pointing in a contrary direction, which imply either that Christ's teaching and action were not self-consistent, or that the evangelists do not give us a reliable record of His ministry. They are such as these: the refusal of Jesus to grant the prayer of the woman of Canaan, on the ground that His mission was to Israel; the exclusion of Samaria from the sphere of the mission on which the twelve were sent; and such apparently contemptuous expressions towards pagans as those in the Sermon on the Mount: "When ye pray, use not vain repetitions as the heathen do," "after all these things do the Gentiles seek;" the still more offensive term "dogs" employed with the same reference in the interview with the Syro-Phœnician; and the direction given to the future ministers of the kingdom to treat an obstinately impenitent offender "as an heathen man and a publican." It is not a very formidable array of counter-evidence. When Jesus said: "I am not sent save to the lost sheep of the house of Israel," He did certainly speak seriously. He did regard Himself, in His individual capacity, as a messenger of God to the Jewish nation exclusively, unless when good cause could be shown for making an exception. But that is a very different thing from regarding the kingdom of God, in its essential nature and ultimate destination, as a matter in which Jews alone had any interest. Assuming that the kingdom was destined to universality, it might still be the wisest method for founding a universal, spiritual monarchy to begin by securing a footing within the boundaries of the elect people; and that could be done only by one who devoted his whole mind to it, determined not to be turned aside by outside opportunities, however tempting, or by random sympathies, however keen, with sin and misery, beyond the Jewish pale. The utterance in question only shows the thoroughly disciplined spirit of Jesus in abiding at His own appointed post. As He was willing to be the corn of wheat cast into the ground to die, that through death there might be great increase, so He was willing to be God's minister to the Jews, as the best preparation for a future ministry among the Gentiles. The other particulars above referred to hardly need explanation. The direction given to the disciples not to go to the Samaritans is sufficiently explained by their spiritual immaturity. The two allusions to pagan practice in prayer have no animus in them: they are simple statements of fact brought in to illustrate the speaker's meaning. There is certainly an animus in the term "dogs," but it is not an animus of hatred. It was used to experiment on the spirit of the person addressed. One who really hated the Gentiles would neither have taken the trouble to make the experiment, nor been so gratified with the result. As for the saying last quoted, the possibility of misapprehension is precluded by the familiar facts of Christ's personal history. We know what the publicans were to Him; and if He felt towards the heathen in like manner, they were to Him objects not of aversion or contempt, but of humane, yearning compassion.

One fact more I mention, as surely indicating the *spiritual* character of the kingdom Jesus preached. It is the alternative name for the kingdom of frequent occurrence in the first Gospel. Mark and Luke call it the kingdom of God. Matthew almost uniformly calls it the kingdom of *heaven*. The expression suggests the thought that the kingdom is an ideal hovering over all actual societies, civil or sacred, like Plato's Republic, to be found realized in perfection nowhere on this earth, the true home of which is in the supersensible world.[1] In all probability, the title was used alternatively by Jesus for the express purpose of lifting the minds of the Jewish people into a higher region of thought than that in which their present hopes as members of the theocratic nation moved; just as, in addressing censors of His conduct in associating with publicans and sinners, He spoke of the joy in *heaven* over a sinner repenting to gain an entrance into their minds for the conception of a love in His own heart whereof as yet they had not so much as dreamed. There is no reason to doubt that the phrase belonged to the vocabulary of Jesus, though a writer already quoted confidently affirms that it cannot have belonged to the apostolic tradition, in other words, was

[1] So Baur.

not employed by Christ.[1] The opinion carries no weight, for it is a mere assertion, but it is very interesting as an indirect testimony on the part of its author that the designation in question does not fit well into his theory as to the nature of the kingdom Jesus proposed to found. The argument is: "The kingdom was to be the fulfilment of theocratic hopes, therefore it cannot have been called by Jesus the kingdom of heaven. That name must have come in when the hope of a restored kingdom of Israel was seen to be a dream." Strange that this unhistorical name should occur in the first Gospel, the most theocratic of all the four!

It would be a mistake to suppose that, in using this name, Jesus meant to banish the kingdom from earth to the skies, from this present life to the future world. As He presented it, it was very lofty in nature, yet near men, yea in their very hearts; there if anywhere. It concerned men here and now; all men eventually, Israelites in the first place, as they were the people of the old election, and the Herald of the kingdom was their countryman. It was to become a society on earth,

---

[1] Weiss, *Lehrbuch der Biblischen Theologie des Neuen Testaments*, S. 47. Jost, *Geschichte des Judenthums*, i. 397, says that what the wise in Israel in the time of our Lord aimed at was simply the highest piety of life, the union in modes of feeling and action which was called the kingdom of heaven, though they did not express their meaning clearly; and that Rabbinical expressions concerning the so-called King Messiah were all of later date. If this view be correct, the phrase "the kingdom of heaven" was current then, and had a purely ethical or spiritual meaning. Jost represents the "kingdom of heaven" of Jewish theology as a refuge to the devout from the degradation of the temple-worship by unworthy high priests, and from the bondage under which the people sighed, and as such as a pioneer to Christianity.

ever widening in extent, for a kingdom is a social thing; it could not fail to become such if it met with any reception from those to whom it was proclaimed, for the spirit of the kingdom is love, and impels to fellowship. It was the highest good of life, the hidden treasure which men should willingly buy with all their possessions, the precious pearl for which all else should be gladly exchanged. It was accessible to all: to the poor, the hungry, the weeping, the social outcasts, and the depraved; not to them exclusively, but to them very specially, as most needing its blessings and most likely to welcome them. It was spiritual. The conditions of admission, the sole conditions so far as appears, and as I shall hereafter try to prove, were repentance and faith, or in one word *receptivity*—readiness to make the kingdom welcome. It was associated with, may almost be said to have consisted in, a certain doctrine of God, and a kindred doctrine of man. "Briefly stated, the religious heaven of Jesus meant the Fatherliness of God for men, the sonship of men for God, and the infinite spiritual good of the kingdom of heaven is Fatherhood and Sonship."[1] It was all this from the beginning of Christ's ministry. Jesus did not begin to cherish and utter these gracious, spiritual, universal thoughts in the later sorrowful days of His public ministry, after painful experience had taught Him that the aim with which He started was a generous patriotic delusion. The career He ran was not this: The Nazarene prophet goes forth from His home full of youthful enthusiasm, bent on realizing the hope which prophecy had nursed, with

[1] Keim, *Geschichte Jesu von Nazara*, 54.

this as His watchword and programme—*first*, the kingdom of God and His righteousness; next, food and raiment, or in one word, prosperity. First a righteous nation, then a people free and happy. He goes about preaching the approach of the kingdom in this sense, and dispensing benefits especially to the poor and the sick with Messianic bountifulness. The people, especially in the northern province, receive Him and His doctrine and His benefits with enthusiasm. They welcome the kingdom, and they hail Him King. But their programme is not His; it is His inverted. They desire political independence and temporal well-being first and unconditionally, and as much righteousness as can be made forthcoming after that. This once made manifest, at the Capernaum crisis, Jesus enters emphatic dissent, and the charm is gone. The multitude melts away; and the eyes of Jesus are opened. It is all over with the dream of a theocratic kingdom of Israel with Himself for its King. What awaits Him, He now sees, is not a throne but a *cross*. If He is to have a kingdom, it must be one of a different sort. He seeks it meantime with sad heart in the formation of a separate society gathered out of Israel; and gradually His mind opens up to the great inspiring thought of spiritual dominion, gained through death over human hearts, not in Judea only, but in all lands.[1] Far other was the actual course of Christ's history. His greatest thoughts were present to His mind, in germ at least, from the first, though they underwent development in correspondence with outward

---

[1] This is substantially the scheme worked out by Weiss in his *Leben Jesu*. It involves new interpretations of many texts.

events. He had a spiritual, universal kingdom in view the day He preached the Sermon on the Mount, as the opening sentences clearly show. He expected a tragic end at the time when He defended His disciples for the neglect of fasting. If it seem unnatural that one capable of entertaining such wide-ranging ideas, and visited with such gloomy forebodings, should devote Himself with singleness of heart to the limited and also thankless task of the regeneration of Israel, it will be well to remember that Hebrew prophets had done much the same thing. Isaiah and Jeremiah went forth in God's name to preach to their countrymen righteousness, with small hope of bringing them to repentance; nevertheless they did their duty faithfully and nobly, at all hazards to themselves, as their recorded prophecies amply attest.

CHAPTER II.

CHRIST'S ATTITUDE TOWARDS THE MOSAIC LAW.

THE first impression produced by a perusal of the Evangelic records with reference to this topic, is one of surprise at the reticence of Christ regarding a subject of such importance. We might have expected Him to say distinctly whether Jewish law and custom were to prevail in the kingdom that was coming; whether, *e.g.*, the rite of circumcision was or was not to be observed in the new era. Yet throughout the whole range of His utterances, as recorded in the Synoptical Gospels, Jesus does not once mention circumcision.

While maintaining silence regarding that particular rite of fundamental importance in the old covenant, Jesus on one or two occasions expressed Himself in general terms concerning His relation to the Mosaic Law, and that in a manner which does not seem to harmonize with the idea of the kingdom sketched in the last chapter. The chief of these utterances is the well-known passage in the Sermon on the Mount, in which the Preacher declares that He is come, not to do away with the Law and the Prophets, but rather to fulfil them. He speaks as if He were conscious that an opposite *rôle* would be expected of Him, and desired as early as possible to correct the misapprehension. "*Think* not I came to destroy." With solemn emphasis He goes on to affirm that while heaven and earth last, the minutest particle of the law shall remain valid, till all things be accomplished. Then, as if to ensure for the declaration a permanent lodgment in the minds of His hearers, He asserts the inferiority of the destroyer of any existing laws, however unimportant, to the man who inculcates and keeps the laws great and small; and the little esteem in which the one is held in the kingdom of heaven in comparison with the other.[1] The whole passage seems to teach that the laws of Moses, without exception or distinction, are to be observed while the world endures. Hence Baur, despairing of interpreting the words in accordance with what he believed to be the real attitude of Jesus, comes to the conclusion that they do not give a correct account of what the Speaker said, and sums up his discussion of them in these terms: "As Jesus did not in fact confirm the ritual law, and as, on the other hand, if He did not intend to confirm it, He could not have expressed Himself in such a way as to its enduring validity, the only course left us is to assume that His words received from the evangelist a Judaistic bias which they had not as they came from His mouth."[2]

There are, however, some features of this same utterance, even as it stands, which provoke reflection, and suggest the doubt whether our first impression of its meaning be correct. Does not the repudiation of an intention to destroy imply a consciousness that the effect of His work is to be such as may appear a destroying in

[1] Matt. v. 17–20. [2] *Neutestamentliche Theologie*, S. 55.

CHRIST'S ATTITUDE TOWARDS THE MOSAIC LAW. 65

the eyes of many? Then why say of one who by word or deed sets aside any of the commandments that he is the *least* in the kingdom of heaven; instead of saying of him, as of the Pharisee, that he cannot enter the kingdom: the position taken up by the conservative party in the Apostolic Church when they said to the Gentile Christians, "Except ye be circumcised after the manner of Moses, ye cannot be saved."[1] It seems as if it were not a question of mere destroying, but rather of the right way of doing it, and as if the attitude of the Preacher were something like this: He was aware that His appearance on the stage of history might bring about a crisis in reference to the law, and inaugurate a new era in which much would be changed. But He was conscious at the same time that He came not in the spirit of a destroyer, full of headlong zeal against rude imperfect statutes and antiquated customs, but rather in the spirit of profoundest reverence for ancient institutions, believing that everything in the law, down to its minutest rules, had a meaning and value in the system of religion and morals to which it belonged, and not doubting that the least important of the commandments could not, any more than the most weighty, pass away till their purpose had been fulfilled. Coming in this spirit, He felt entitled to repudiate abrogation as an aim, whatever of that nature might come in the way of necessary effect. He had no taste for the work of a mere destroyer, no inclination towards the vocation of a legal reformer demanding the abolition of this or the other particular statute or custom as no longer useful, no sympathy with

[1] Acts xv. 1.

the iconoclastic zeal which rushes passionately at abuses, bent on demolishing, and heedless what may come in the idol's place. For those who pursued such an occupation He had not unqualified esteem, though they might be very conscientious; nor did He think they would take a high place in the kingdom of God. Were the question put, "Who is the greatest in the kingdom?" He would certainly not say, the mere reformer or destroyer. He should esteem him the least, whoever might be the greatest: greater than him He should account the man who honestly did all things enjoined, and taught others to do them. Him He called great in the kingdom.

Great, but be it observed not even he is called the *greatest*. That place is reserved for one who not merely does the commandments and teaches respect for them, but *fulfils* them, realizes in Himself all their meaning, and only so, if at all, brings about the annulment of any. Thus we get an ascending scale of moral worth. The Pharisee, the man of form, who cares more for the little than for the great commandments, has no moral worth, and is not in the kingdom at all.[1] The reformer who has a keen eye for abuses, who is impatient of laws whose utility is doubtful, and urgently calls for change where he thinks it is greatly needed, is of some worth; he is in the kingdom, though not occupying a high place there. The man who spends not his energies in attacking abuses, but puts his heart into all duties, and so redeems from formality the minutest details of conduct, and teaches others so to live, is of greater worth; is not only in the kingdom, but a person of consideration there.

[1] Matt. v. 20.

Finally, he who not only does, but fulfils,—*that is,* by his life-work inaugurates a new time that shall be the ripe fruit towards which the old time with its institutions was tending; and so satisfies the hearts of the children of the new time, that without formal abrogation much that belonged to the old shall be allowed eventually to fall quietly into desuetude: this one is the greatest in the kingdom, the man of absolute moral worth.

This interpretation of the remarkable saying in question is at least legitimate, if not the only one conceivable. It is an interpretation, doubtless, which but for the light of subsequent events, we might not have thought of. The idea of a distinction between doing and fulfilling, or of a fulfilling which may at the same time be more or less an undoing, is one we take not out of the mere words, but out of history. We know that there is a fulfilling which is at the same time an undoing at all critical periods, and we bring our knowledge as a help to the interpretation of words spoken by one who has proved to be the greatest of all Initiators, and conclude that the very claim to fulfil involves a virtual intimation of eventual antiquation to a greater or less extent. More than this we cannot make of the solemn declaration on the Mount. We cannot learn from it what in Law or Prophets should, in being fulfilled, be at the same time annulled. By the nature of the case, such information was excluded, because to give such information, and say, *e.g.,* " Circumcision must ere long pass away," would have been to belie the position taken up, and to exchange the high vocation of a fulfiller for the comparatively low vocation of a reformer. For the same reason we ought not to expect explicit information of that kind—a list of laws marked like trees in a forest to be cut down—anywhere in Christ's teaching. The utmost we can look for are hints, incidental indications showing like straws in what direction the stream of tendency was flowing. Such indications are not wanting; indications which confirm the interpretation given of the text in the Sermon on the Mount, and help us also to determine for ourselves in what respects Christ in fulfilling was at the same time to annul.

The very silence of Christ concerning the fundamental rite of the old Covenant is, as Reuss has remarked, very significant. Its import is, indeed, ambiguous; it might be held to mean that Christ never thought of calling in question the perpetual obligation of circumcision. But it is hard to credit this while reading the golden sentences wherewith the Sermon on the Mount opens, and in which are set forth the requirements for citizenship in the kingdom of heaven. The qualifications specified are exclusively spiritual. The Beatitudes take us away into an entirely different world from that of ritualism. We can hardly imagine Jesus uttering these words: Blessed are the poor, the meek, the pure, the peacemakers, the persecuted, with the mental reservation, "provided always that they be Israelites and circumcised." We cannot help feeling that the kingdom must be wider than Israel, and its blessings independent of merely external and ritual conditions. The rite by which men became members of the theocratic commonwealth is quietly ignored.

Another significant hint that in the new kingdom the

ceremonial law at least was destined to fall into desuetude, may be found in the words spoken by Jesus when His disciples were blamed for neglecting customary ritual ablutions before eating: "Hear me, all of you, and understand: there is nothing from without a man that going into him can defile him, but the things which proceed out of a man are those that defile a man."[1] By this emphatic utterance Jesus in effect, as Baur remarks, declared the observance of the Mosaic laws of purification to be something morally indifferent. It is true, indeed, that the fault imputed to the disciples had not been disregard of the Mosaic ritual law, but neglect of the traditions of the elders relating to ablutions which were designed to form a hedge about the law, and ensure its strict observance. But it is manifest that the word addressed to the people enunciates a principle whose range of application is much wider than these traditions, and which, when it has got a firm hold of the popular mind, must in the end lead to the non-observance of the Mosaic laws of purification, as well as of the rules superadded by the Rabbis. That it was taken in this wide scope in the Apostolic Church, and specially in the circle of which Peter formed the centre, may be inferred from the reflection appended by the second evangelist to the explanation of His own saying given by Christ to the disciples: "*This He said*, making all meats clean."[2] It has, however, been maintained of late that the saying of

---

[1] Mark vii. 14, 15. Matthew's version (xv. 10, 11) is less emphatic.

[2] Mark vii. 19, last clause, according to the approved reading, which substitutes $\kappa\alpha\theta\alpha\rho\iota\zeta\omega\nu$ for $\kappa\alpha\theta\alpha\rho\iota\zeta\sigma\nu$.

Jesus to the multitude is parabolic, and that it must be understood as referring throughout to things belonging to the physical sphere. The things that proceed out of a man are not, as in the subsequently given interpretation, moral offences, but matters discharged from the body whether in health, in diseases like leprosy, or in death. These, not the eating of forbidden meats, defiled in the Levitical sense, and it was against the defiling influence of these that the Mosaic rules of purification were directed. The effect, therefore, of Christ's saying was to condemn the Pharisaic additions as plants which God had not planted, but to confirm the obligation of the Mosaic laws of purification as of divine authority.[1] This is ingenious but not convincing. If Christ meant to tell the multitude that ceremonial defilement proceeded from matters discharged from the body, not from the kind of food taken, it is difficult to see why in the subsequent conversation with His disciples He gave a spiritual turn to the thought, and made the things which proceed out of a man, evil thoughts, fornications, thefts, and the like. Why not rather explain to them, the future apostles, His exact position on the topic raised by Pharisaic criticism, viz. that what He condemned was simply Rabbinical additions to Mosaic rules, and that He believed in the perpetual obligation of the latter? The reference to the moral evils proceeding from the heart lifts the whole subject above the level of ceremonialism, and irresistibly conveys the impression that, in the view of the Speaker, the only cleanness and uncleanness that are real and worth minding are

[1] Weiss, *Leben Jesu*, ii. S. 116.

those which arise from morally right and wrong feelings and actions.

A third straw showing the direction of the stream of tendency may be found in the word spoken by Jesus in Peræa towards the close of His ministry concerning the Mosaic statute of divorce: "Moses out of regard to the hardness of your heart suffered you to put away your wives, but from the beginning it was not so."[1] It was a distinct declaration that this particalar law was a concession on the part of the Jewish legislator to a rude moral condition, and a departure from the primitive ideal. In Mark's narrative, the conversation between Christ and His captious interrogators is so arranged that there is less of the appearance of calling in question the authority of Moses than in Matthew's version of the incident. The first evangelist makes Christ, in answer to His interrogants, at once announce the original law of marriage as ordained by God at the creation, whereby Moses seems to be set in antagonism to the Creator, as ordaining an inferior law, though not without excuse in the moral condition of his people. In the account given by the second evangelist, on the other hand,[2] Jesus meets the question put by the Pharisees with another, What did Moses command you? It is possible that He meant thereby to hint that Moses had given more than one law on the subject, regarding the primitive law in Genesis as his, not less than the law in Deuteronomy. In that case He merely appealed from Moses to Moses; from what Moses allowed under pressure of circumstances, to what Moses must have known, if, as all Jews believed, he was

[1] Matt. xix. 8.   [2] Mark x. 2-9.

the author of the five books, and doubtless approved as the ideally perfect law concerning the relation of the sexes. Nevertheless, assuming Mark's version to be the more accurate, and the drift of Christ's argument to be as indicated, the fact remains that the Deuteronomic statute regulating, and by implication sanctioning, divorce for other reasons besides adultery, was explicitly declared to be a statute "not good," adapted to the *sklerokardia* of Israel. And as that statute did not stand alone, but was only a sample of many of the same kind, the general position was virtually laid down that the whole Mosaic civil code was far from perfect, and consequently could not be permanently valid, but must pass away in that kingdom where the *sklerokardia* is removed, and is replaced by the "new heart."[1]

From these indications of Christ's attitude towards the ceremonial and civil laws of Moses, we pass to inquire what position He assumed in reference to what we are wont to call the "moral" law, that is, the Decalogue. The interest here concentrates on the institution of the weekly rest, which, some think, ought to be included in the same category as circumcision, maintaining also that it was actually so regarded by Jesus. I shall here go into the question so far only as is necessary to ascertain how far the latter allegation is correct. And I begin with the observation that it is antecedently unlikely that Jesus would treat circumcision and the Sabbath as in all

---

[1] See on the above topic, Weiss in his *Leben Jesu*, and also in his two works on the Gospels of Matthew and Mark. He contends for the accuracy of Mark's version, and does his utmost to minimize the significance of Christ's words as a criticism on Mosaic legislation.

respects of the same nature. They were certainly not so treated under the law. For though circumcision was of fundamental importance in the covenant between Jehovah and Israel, yet it was not thought necessary to put it among the Ten Words; whereas the law of the Sabbath does find a place there along with precepts generally admitted to be ethical in their nature, and therefore of perpetual obligation in their substance. Why is this? Apparently because circumcision concerned Israel alone, whereas in the Ten Words it was intended that that only should find a place which was believed to concern all mankind. The Decalogue wears the aspect of an attempt to sum up the heads of moral duty, put in a form, and enforced with reasons, it may be, adapted to the history and circumstances of the chosen race, but in their substance concerning not Jews only, but men in general. Speaking of the Decalogue as the work of Moses, we may say that from it we learn what in his judgment all men ought to do in order to please God, and live wisely and happily. And we can see for ourselves that circumcision and the Sabbath are in important respects entirely different institutions. Circumcision was purely ritual, a mere arbitrary sign or symbol, a mark set on Israel to distinguish and separate her from the heathen peoples around. But the Sabbath was essentially a good thing. Rest from toil is good for the body, and rest in worshipful acknowledgment of God as the Maker and Preserver of all is equally good for the spirit. Rest in both senses is a permanent need of man in this world, and a law prescribing a resting day as a holiday and holy day is a beneficent law, which no one having a regard to human wellbeing can have any wish to abrogate.

Turning now to the Gospel records: do we find Jesus speaking of the Sabbath as, say, of ritual washings—*i.e.* as a thing morally indifferent, whose abolition would be no real loss to men? We do not. On the contrary, we find Him invariably treating the institution with respect, as intrinsically a good thing; and His quarrel with the Pharisees on this head was not as to observance, but as to the right manner of observing the law. The Pharisees made the day not a boon, but a burden; not a day given by God to man in mercy, but a day taken from man by God in an exacting spirit. Having this idea of the weekly rest in their minds, they naturally made it as burdensome and irksome as possible, not a delight, but a horror, giving ridiculously minute definitions of work, and placing the merit of Sabbath-keeping in mere abstinence from work so defined, apart altogether from the nature of the work. With this Pharisaic idea of the Sabbath, and the manner in which it was worked out in practice, Jesus had no sympathy. He conceived of the institution, not as a burden, but as a boon; not as a day taken from man, but as a day given to him by a beneficent Providence. This idea He expressed in a remarkable saying, found, curiously enough, only in Mark, but doubtless a most authentic apostolic tradition: "The Sabbath was made on account of man, not man on account of the Sabbath."[1] He meant to say that God appointed the Sabbath for man's good, and that it must be so observed as to realize the end originally contem-

[1] Mark ii. 27.

plated; men must not be made the slaves of the Sabbath, as they were by the Pharisaic method of interpreting and enforcing the statute. This being His meaning, He consistently said, the Sabbath was made for *man*, not the Sabbath was made for *Jews*, so giving the saying a universal character. One who so thought of the institution could have no interest in its abolition. He would rather desire to extend the benefit, and He would favour only such changes as might be needful to make the benefit as great and as wide-reaching as possible. Accordingly, Jesus did not propose to abolish the beneficent institute. He did, indeed, claim lordship over the Sabbath-day. But He claimed it not with a view to abolition, but in order to give full effect to the principle that the Sabbath was made for man, that is, for his good, and to emphasize the true motive of observance, love, the supreme law of His kingdom. In other words, Christ's claim of lordship was a claim of right to *humanize* the Sabbath, in opposition to the Pharisees who had *Rabbinized* it, and made it a snare to the conscience and a burden to the spirit.

An esteemed writer has given an entirely different interpretation to the saying recorded by Mark, according to which Christ meant to draw a distinction between the laws that are of permanent validity and those that are transient, including the Sabbath in the latter category. The permanent laws are those which are an end for man, the transient are those which have man for their end. The former set forth man's chief end—the moral ideal; the latter are merely means subservient to some temporary human interest.[1] I gravely doubt the soundness

[1] Ritschl, *Die Entstehung des Altkatholischen Kirche*, S. 30.

of the construction thus put on our Lord's words. And as for the distinction taken between two sorts of laws, it depends on the respect in which a law has man for its end, whether it be of a temporary character or otherwise. If a law have man for its end, in the sense of having for its aim his highest wellbeing, then it is not transient, even on the principle enunciated by the author referred to, for in that case it is at the same time an end for man. The moral ideal and man's highest happiness coincide. On this view there is no good reason for the Sabbath passing away. It is made for man, doubtless, but not in the sense in which the statute of divorce was made. The latter was an accommodation to man's moral weakness, the former was instituted to promote man's physical and spiritual wellbeing, and it is fitted to serve that end in perpetuity. The kingdom of God therefore cannot frown on the Sabbath as it must frown on the concession made by Moses to the rude moral condition of Israel in the matter of marriage. It must regard the day of rest with favour, even if it looked on it as an outside institution, and not of strictly ethical contents; wherever the spirit of the kingdom prevails, the general desire will be, not for its abolition, but for its retention. Christianity countenances the Sabbath just as, and on the same general ground that it discountenances slavery. Even as, though not formally condemning slavery, yet being hostile to it, as injurious to the moral dignity of man, the Christian religion surely tended towards its abolition; so, though not formally decreeing the perpetuating of a seventh day rest, yet being favourable to it as promotive of man's wellbeing, the Christian religion surely tended from the first towards the perpetuation and the extension of the blessings it conferred throughout the world.

Quite in accordance with the view I have given of our Lord's attitude towards the Sabbath was the manner of His defence against the Pharisaic charge of Sabbath-breaking. He did not admit that He and His disciples were Sabbath-breakers, but took up the ground that their conduct was in accordance with the Sabbath law rightly interpreted. The correct view of the Sabbath being that it was meant to be a boon, not a burden—that it was made for man's benefit—the right observance was that which best promoted the end aimed at—man's good; the wrong that which frustrated the design, and turned a boon into a burden. In applying this principle to His own works of healing, Jesus said: not, It is permissible to do any sort of work on the Sabbath, for the law is no longer binding; but, It is lawful to do *well* on the Sabbath.[1] In defence of His disciples, who, according to current ideas, had been guilty of working in rubbing the ears of corn (it was a kind of thrashing!), Jesus reminded the fault-finders of God's word: "I will have mercy and not sacrifice," and told them that had they laid to heart the divine oracle, they should not have condemned the guiltless.[2]

It remains to add that Christ's favourable attitude towards the Sabbath becomes all the more significant when it is contrasted with the free position He took up in reference to the civil and ceremonial law. Had He, as some think, been an indiscriminate conservative, treating with equal reverence all parts of the Mosaic system,

[1] Matt. xii. 12. [2] Matt. xii. 7.

His respect for the day of rest would have been no argument in favour of its perpetuity. That institution might have been doomed, notwithstanding, to pass away, like circumcision, with the old Jewish world to which both alike belonged. But when we find one who could freely criticize venerable customs resting on the authority of the Hebrew legislator, in the light of the new era, so careful to clear Himself of all suspicion of irreverence towards the fourth commandment, we cannot help feeling that the rest therein enjoined does not altogether belong to the old world about to pass away, but is worthy to find a place in the new order of things. There may be a sense in which, as Paul taught, the Sabbath belonged to the era of shadows; but there must be a sense also in which it belongs to the era of spiritual realities.

Of the other precepts of the Decalogue Christ ever spoke respectfully as enjoining duties incumbent on all; as when He said to the young ruler, "If thou wilt enter into life, keep the commandments,"[1] enumerating the first four of the second table to illustrate His meaning. But, while recognising the perpetual obligation of these commandments, He preferred to sum up duty in the one comprehensive word Love: "Love God with all thy heart, and thy neighbour as thyself." On these two commands, said He, hung all that the law required and the prophets taught.[2] The originality of the saying lay not in the mere words, for they occur in the Pentateuch, but in the new emphasis put upon it. Because of that Jesus was, and claimed to be, a fulfiller, in the pregnant sense, of the Decalogue in particular, as of the law and prophets

[1] Matt. xix. 17.   [2] Matt. vii. 12, xxii. 37–40.

in general. In the Sermon on the Mount He illustrated the sense in which He claimed to be a fulfiller by taking up successively several precepts of the Decalogue, and insisting, in connection with each, not on the outward act of obedience only, but on conformity of inward disposition to the principle embodied in the precept. The law said, "Thou shalt not kill," and when men abstained from taking away each other's lives, the law, as a code for the government of a nation, was satisfied. But the Preacher said, "Whosoever is angry with his brother shall be in danger of the judgment;"[1] so interdicting not only murder but hatred, not only violent deeds but wicked passions. Thus He transformed a law of the Decalogue into a law of the divine kingdom.

The result of our inquiry then is this: Christ came to fulfil the law of the Ten Words by going back with new emphasis on its great underlying principle—love to God and to man; He came to fulfil the meaning, and not immediately, but as foreknown eventual result, to annul the obligation of the ceremonial law by putting substance in place of shadow, spiritual reality in place of ritual emblem; He came to antiquate the civil law by removing the *sklerokardia*, and raising up a race who should be able to order their lives according to a higher ideal. All this He did, however, after the manner of a prophet rather than after the manner of a legislator. He came not to be a rival to Moses, but to originate a new life which should be *self-legislative*.

When we consider the manner in which the hints, whereon the foregoing induction is founded, were given,

[1] Matt. v. 22.

we see how truly Christ could say: "I came not to destroy." They were uttered for the most part in self-defence. It seems as if, had He been left alone, He would have been content to introduce the new life, and leave it to create for itself congenial habitudes without giving any indication what these were to be. As it was, He said no more than was barely necessary to defend Himself against accusers. In spite of much provocation, at the very last, He counselled the people to give heed to the teaching of the scribes who sat in Moses' seat, bidding them only beware of their practice. He would not on any account be irritated into becoming a stirrer up of discontent, or an agitator against existing customs, or a hot-headed leader of zealots bent on overturning an ancient social and religious system. All things considered, therefore, the conclusion, well expressed by Baur, must be accepted as just, that while Jesus introduced into some of His expressions what might form the ground of an opposition on principle, not only against the prescriptions of the Pharisees, but even against the continued absolute validity of the law, He did not wish to come to an open breach, but left the development of the opposition already existing in implicit form, to the spirit of His doctrine, which must of itself lead eventually thereto.

In view of this conclusion, we are able to understand that saying of Christ concerning the Baptist, which has been somewhat of a puzzle to interpreters: "Among them that are born of women there hath not risen a greater than John the Baptist; notwithstanding, he that is least in the kingdom of heaven is greater than he."[1] We are

[1] Matt. xi. 11.

not obliged to have recourse to the ingenious construction put by Chrysostom on the last part of the sentence: "I, Jesus, who as yet am less than John in public esteem, am greater than he in the kingdom of heaven, though not in the judgment of the world." Keeping in mind the great word in the Sermon on the Mount, wherein the Preacher defined His relation to the legal economy, and expressed His judgment in reference to diverse types of character, we have no difficulty in seeing the truth and point of this saying, viewed as a declaration that one occupying a comparatively humble place in the kingdom of heaven was greater than John, supremely great though he was in his own line. For John was in tendency and temper a destroyer, not indeed with reference to Mosaic institutions, but with reference to the actual religious life of his time. He lived the life of a hermit in the wild, taking no part apparently in the temple services, through an unconquerable disgust at prevailing hypocrisy. He denounced the Pharisees, whom he saw on the outskirts of the crowd that gathered around him by the Jordan, as a generation of vipers. He declared that the axe was already at the root of the tree, ready to hew down an unproductive vine. He proclaimed the approach of one who with fan in hand should separate wheat from chaff, and burn the chaff in unquenchable fire. And when the coming One had come, and had been long enough at work to show the manner of His working, John, now a prisoner, doubted whether He were after all the Man he had looked for. Why? Because he saw no axe or fan in His hand. He heard reports of deeds of mercy,

F

and of gracious words spoken unto the poor, but he heard no reports of deeds of judgment. This was too genial a Messiah for his taste. The method of Jesus was also too leisurely for the prophet's ardent temperament. Assuming that He had the same general end in view as himself—a kingdom of righteousness—He was far too tolerant in His spirit. John desiderated an immediate crisis or catastrophe. Separate the good from the bad, destroy the bad and make the good, like Noah's family, the nucleus of a new godly nation. Simple, thoroughgoing programme, most satisfactory to a prophet's earnest temper! But no such programme did Jesus seem to have. He went about in Galilee doing all the good He could, and left the religious world of Judæa, of whose hollowness He was well aware, to go its own way. Therefore John stood seriously in doubt of Him. And this doubt of John's is one of the most convincing proofs that his kingdom of God and that of Christ were not the same thing. There can be no greater mistake in the interpretation of the Gospel history than to explain away that doubt, or to minimize its significance. It is an index showing how wide apart in idea and spirit were the two great ones, who nevertheless were fellow-workers for God and righteousness among their people. That Christ did not under-estimate its significance the saying now under consideration proves. He divined what was passing through the prophet's mind when he sent the message of inquiry, and He said in effect: "John is great, none greater of his kind, a true hero of moral law, who has braved the wrath of earth's mighty ones, and told them their duty, regardless of consequences. I deeply honour him, though he now stand in doubt of me. Yet John is a one-sided defective man. Strong in zeal, he is weak in love; strong in denunciation of evil, he is weak in patience towards the sinful; strong in moral austerity, he is weak in the social sympathetic affections. In these respects any one in the kingdom of heaven animated by its characteristic spirit of love and patient hope is greater than he."

In so speaking of John, Christ, it is hardly necessary to remark, did not mean to shut him out of the kingdom, though an impression to the contrary constitutes for many the chief difficulty of the saying. Possibly the use of the comparative—the less in the kingdom—indicates a desire to avoid the appearance of such an intention. But even taking the comparative as having the force of a superlative, the exclusion of John from the kingdom is to be understood simply in the sense that John had not identified himself openly with the movement of which Jesus was the centre. That was a simple matter of fact. John was intensely interested in the kingdom; he had laboured for it as a pioneer; he had announced its near approach; he prayed daily for its coming. But his conception of the kingdom differed so widely from the kingdom as it actually appeared in the person of Jesus and the society that gathered around Him, that he was not able to give the reality a hearty welcome; he stood aloof, a doubting, puzzled spectator, wondering what it might all mean.

So understood, Christ's judgment of the Baptist confirms our interpretation of the text in the Sermon on the Mount, and throws light on the attitude of the

Messianic King towards established law and custom. The Inaugurator of the new era declined the part which His forerunner had assigned to Him—declined to adopt as his *insignia* the axe and the fan, and to come before the world as the embodiment of divine disgust and fury. He preferred to appear as One " full of grace and truth.' He knew well that the axe and the fan were needed, but He did not believe in the Baptist's method of reaching the desired end. His way was not that of reform but of regeneration, not of judgment but of mercy, not of impatience and intolerance and rupture, but of quiet, silent influence, leading slowly but surely to the new creation, bringing it in noiselessly, gradually, like the dawn of day. Ultimately the kingdom was to bring about much more extensive change than John was prepared for; but the means were to be, not the axe and the fan, but the vital force of a new life, the fermentation of the new wine. The bottles of Judaism must burst some day, but what need for passionately tearing them to pieces? The wine will do the work, in good time, of itself.

CHAPTER III.

THE CONDITIONS OF ENTRANCE.

THE second evangelist represents our Lord as commencing His public ministry in Galilee with the announcement, "The kingdom of God is at hand: repent ye, and believe in the good news."[1] Repentance and faith were thus at the outset declared to be the conditions of admission into the kingdom. What did Christ mean by the words, and why are the things denoted indispensable to citizenship?

The doctrine of Jesus on repentance and faith, especially the former, can be fully understood only when we have become acquainted with other parts of His teaching, particularly His doctrine concerning God, man, and the righteousness of the kingdom. The contents of the idea of repentance must depend on the views set forth on these cardinal topics. If God be a Father, then repentance will mean ceasing to regard Him under any lower aspect; if man be a being of infinite importance as a moral subject and son of God, then repentance will mean realizing human dignity and responsibility; if the righteousness of the kingdom be spiritual and inward, having reference not merely to outward acts but to motives, then the summons to repentance will be a call not merely to

[1] Mark i. 15.

a life for moral ends, but to self-criticism, so as to discern between true and false righteousness. For the present, our inquiry must refer more to form than to matter, to principles rather than to details. These, after all, are the chief points; for when we have settled the general nature of repentance, as Christ preached it, the particulars can be filled in afterwards without difficulty.

On this subject, as in reference to the idea of the kingdom, there is a marked difference in tone and drift between Christ's teaching and that of the Baptist. Both use the same form of words, but they do not mean the same thing. The one instance of divergence is the effect of the other. Christ's conception of repentance springs out of His new thoughts concerning the kingdom of heaven. "When heaven and earth move towards each other, as in Christ's preaching of the kingdom, then on the part both of God and man must the Nay give place to the Yea, anger to love, fear to joy, shame to right action; and in festive attire, not in mourning weeds, all that has affinity for the Divine goes to meet the approaching God, proud to be or to become like Him."[1] The contrast between Jesus and John is specially apparent at two points. There is first an *inwardness* in Christ's doctrine that is wholly lacking in John's. To perceive this, we have only to compare the Sermon on the Mount with the directions given by the Baptist to publicans, soldiers, and others, who inquired what he would have them do.[2] The Sermon, which considered

---

[1] Keim, *Jesu von Nazara*, ii. 77.
[2] Luke iii. 10-14. This is one of Luke's additions, but doubtless he had a voucher for it in his sources. The particulars supplied in

positively is an exposition of the righteousness of the kingdom, may be regarded negatively as an aid to self-criticism and exhortation to repentance. With this view it bids men look into their hearts, and examine their affections and the motives from which apparently good actions spring. John, on the other hand, directed attention merely to outward conduct, admonishing penitents to practise neighbourliness, honesty, contentment with their wages. It was enough, if the coming kingdom was merely the restored theocratic kingdom of Israel, a secular kingdom, only more virtuous than usual. In a kingdom of this world the ruler can take cognizance only of external acts. If the people abstain from stealing, violence, lying, adultery, they are in the eye of law a righteous nation; and they are treated as such even by the moral order of the world, for every nation which practises these and kindred virtues is found to prosper. The fact that Christ turned the thoughts of His hearers from acts to dispositions, shows conclusively that He had in view a kingdom of another and higher description,—" not of this world."

The other point of contrast is that repentance as John preached it was an affair of details, while as Christ preached it, it was a matter of principle, a radical change in the chief end of life. John came preaching in the wilderness of Judæa, saying, " Repent, for the kingdom of heaven is at hand." He meant, " Alter your ways wherever they are amiss, for the great, dread King is near."

these verses as to the counsels given by John to inquirers may be accepted at the very least as a true reflection of the impression which John's preaching had made on the popular mind.

His call resembled a summons to the population of a city to which the monarch is about to make a royal visit, to remove all nuisances out of the way, and to put on holiday attire, and turn out into the street to give their sovereign a worthy reception. But Christ called men to more than a reform of this or that bad habit, even to a radical change of mind, consisting in the recognition of the kingdom as the highest Good, and the most important subject that could engage their attention. "Seek ye first," He said, "the kingdom of God, and His righteousness;"[1] meaning, "Hitherto ye have been living as if life were no more than meat, and the supreme question for you has been, What shall we eat, what shall we drink, wherewithal shall we be clothed? Henceforth let a loftier aim guide you, even to be citizens of the Divine kingdom, and to have a character becoming members of that holy commonwealth." The form of the exhortation shows that the kingdom the Speaker had in view was not the theocratic kingdom of popular expectation. In that case He would have said, Seek ye first the righteousness of the kingdom, and only in the second place its temporal advantages; for the people were seeking the kingdom in the national sense already, their only fault being that they put the material and political aspects of it before the moral. That was in effect what the Baptist said. He assumed that his hearers desired the coming of the kingdom, and bade them prepare for it by repentance and the culture of right conduct, lest its coming should prove to them the reverse of a blessing. Christ, on the other hand, was conscious that He had in

[1] Matt. vi. 33.

His eye a kingdom for whose advent the average Jew did not long, which, nevertheless, would be a priceless boon to all who received it. Therefore He said not merely, Seek the righteousness of the kingdom, but, Seek the kingdom itself and its righteousness. And the call, as already said, was a summons to a radical repentance, a true μετάνοια, a change of mind not in reference to this or the other department of conduct, but in reference to the fundamental question, What is man's chief end and chief good?

Thus understood, the call to repentance issued by Jesus is seen to be no arbitrary requirement, but the indication of an indispensable condition of citizenship. If the kingdom be the highest conceivable object of human aims and hopes, it ought to be regarded and treated as such; and if men have not been hitherto doing that, to ask them to do it is, in other words, to summon them to repentance. And this being the meaning of the summons, we further perceive why it should be addressed to all, as it was by Jesus. For it is certainly not the way of men anywhere to make the kingdom of God of Christ's gospel their chief end and chief good. For the many material goods, "food and raiment," are the first objects of desire. "After these things do the Gentiles seek." After these things, it is to be feared, the majority of Israelites sought more than after righteousness, even in the lower sense of right conduct, justice, truth, honesty. There was therefore an urgent need for repentance even from the Baptist's point of view; and if his call had been generally responded to, it would have brought about an immense improvement in the actual state of things.

How much greater was the need of repentance if man's chief end was to seek the righteousness and the kingdom Christ preached, a righteousness of the heart, a kingdom of filial relations with God! How rare the men even in Israel who cared supremely or at all for these high matters!

With such a high ideal of life, we are not surprised to find Christ preaching repentance even to His own disciples at a late stage of His intercourse with them. The admonition to seek first the kingdom had been addressed principally if not exclusively to them, towards the commencement of the Galilean ministry; and towards its close their Master found it necessary to give them this more stern one: "Except ye turn, and become as the children, ye shall in no wise enter into the kingdom of heaven."[1] The term employed to denote the moral change is new,[2] but the thing insisted on is the same, even a radical change of mind with regard to the chief end of life. It may indeed appear that in this case it is rather the correction of a special fault, pride or ambition, that is pointed at, than the great revolution of an initial spiritual crisis; a conversion in detail rather than in principle. Such special conversions or repentances are to be looked for in the course of religious experience, even in those who have already undergone radical renewal; for after the new principle of life has been adopted, it has to be worked out in all departments of conduct; and while this is being done, conflicts with

---

[1] Matt. xviii. 3.

[2] στραφῆτε. The compound ἐπιστρέφω occurs three times in Luke's Gospel; twice in i. 16, 17, and in xxii. 32. In Acts the verb and the corresponding noun are used to denote the conversion of Gentiles from Paganism to Christianity.

old habits of thought and feeling and action are almost certain to occur. It was to such a conversion in detail, in the experience of Peter, Jesus alluded when, with reference to that disciple's sin of moral cowardice in denying his Master, He said, "When thou hast turned, strengthen thy brethren."[1] And we can hardly bring ourselves to believe that Jesus seriously considered anything more than such a conversion necessary in the case of men who had been so long with Him, even when their sin was not, like Peter's, one of infirmity due to a surprise, but a rooted evil disposition breaking out into unseemly manifestations. And yet we may not shut our minds to the graver alternative. Christ speaks too strongly to have in view merely the correction of a particular fault. He obviously regards childlikeness not as a graceful accomplishment of the citizen of the kingdom, but as an indispensable requirement. In saying, Be childlike, He is only saying in a new way, Give the kingdom the first place. And when we consider the matter, we see that ambition for distinction in the kingdom is only another way of committing the common sin of putting the kingdom in the second place. The many do this by giving food and raiment the first place in their thoughts. The disciples, in forsaking all for the kingdom, rose above the vulgar form of worldliness. But when they became supremely concerned about their place in the kingdom, they were guilty of worldliness in a more refined form. They made the interests of the kingdom second, and their own standing therein first. Thus we see that Christ's demand for the unpre-

[1] Luke xxii. 32.

tentiousness of childhood is only a new proof that in His view repentance consisted in a change of mind, to the effect of exalting the kingdom to the place of supremacy. We may also find in it a significant hint as to the true nature of the kingdom and its righteousness. A kingdom of God so conceived of as to give rise to ambitious passions is not such in reality, but a kingdom of this world. The utmost devotion to such a counterfeit does not amount to compliance with the demand, Seek first the kingdom. For that there is needed not only zeal but pure motive; and the kingdom is there only where zeal and motive coalesce, zeal excluding impurity of motive, and purity of motive guaranteeing the due measure of zeal. The kingdom of God is a kingdom of love from which selfishness in every form is excluded; not merely the mitigated selfishness of concern about animal wants, but the intenser though subtler selfishness of egotism and vainglory. Hence it follows that there may be much religious activity, making a great display of zeal and gaining golden opinions, which has no relation to the kingdom of God, except it be one of antagonism, and no more makes us children of the kingdom than does the struggle for existence amid the secular callings of life. The struggle for religious name and church place and power may be more respectable than the struggle for physical livelihood, but it is not less, but rather more, ungodly. It deepens our reverence for Christ as a spiritual Teacher that He said this quite plainly, and even with passionate emphasis; not slurring over the vices of disciples, while loudly denouncing the vulgar worldliness of the multitude.

THE CONDITIONS OF ENTRANCE.

Of this also, however, He was wont to speak faithfully, as we learn from His bitter complaint against the inhabitants of the towns lying along the shores of the Galilean lake among whom He mainly exercised His ministry. It was to the effect that they *repented* not, though such mighty works had been done among them as might have moved even Tyre and Sidon and Sodom to repentance.[1] The charge is significant as confirmatory of the view I have given of the sense in which Christ used the word. The inhabitants of the plain of Gennesareth are not accused of being sinners like the men of Sodom; that ancient city is rather referred to as the extreme instance of sensual wickedness, in comparison with which the people by the Galilean Sea might justly deem themselves exemplary. What then was their fault? It was that the mighty deeds of the Christ had not led them to give the kingdom its place of supremacy. They had been much interested in these deeds; they had followed the Doer with eager curiosity and intense admiration; they had even been willing, according to an intimation in the fourth Gospel, to make Him their King, and so set up the Messianic kingdom.[2] Still they remained essentially as they had been before, greatly more concerned about food and raiment than about righteousness and the kingdom of God in the true sense of the words. Their state was that so graphically depicted in the words Christ is represented as addressing to the multitude at Capernaum by the fourth evangelist: "Ye seek me, not because ye saw the signs, but because ye did eat of the loaves and were filled;" "Busy not yourselves about the

[1] Matt. xi. 20–24.   [2] John vi. 15.

food that perisheth, but about the food that endureth unto eternal life."[1] From such words, as from those addressed to the disciples at a later date, the plain inference is that repentance as preached by Jesus was a very high requirement indeed, with which few complied in a manner He deemed satisfactory.

Though mentioned here in the second place, after repentance, *faith* was in reality the first and chief condition of admission to the kingdom in the teaching of Jesus. Faith was a great word with Him, and through Him it became a great word in the New Testament literature, the watchword of the era of grace, so that it might also be called the era of faith. Christ was Himself emphatically a man of faith. He lived a life of perfect holiness by faith in His heavenly Father. He wrought His miracles by faith. He demanded faith in others as the condition of His ability to work miracles for their benefit. He regarded faith as an almighty power by which not only He but any of His disciples could do wonders, and without which nothing great could be accomplished. He was grieved by manifestations of unbelief or weak faith; from exhibitions of strong faith He derived intense pleasure. He had unbounded confidence in faith's virtue within the moral sphere as a recuperative influence, raising the fallen, sanctifying the sinful, restoring peace to the troubled conscience. He commended trust in their heavenly Father to His followers as the best religious service they could render, and as an infallible specific against fear and care.

[1] John vi. 26, 27.

All this was significant of a new departure. The prominence given to faith denotes a new way of conceiving the kingdom. "Repent," the Baptist's watchword, suits one idea of it. "Believe," Christ's watchword, suits and implies another and very different one. "Repent" is the appropriate word when the kingdom is conceived of as the reward of legal righteousness; "believe" is the more appropriate word when the kingdom is conceived of as a gift of grace to be conferred on all who are simply willing to receive it. In the one case the message to be delivered to men is, "Conform your lives to the law, that you may hope to obtain the honours of membership in the holy commonwealth;" in the other it is, "The kingdom of grace is here, God is come to dwell among men in the plenitude of His love; make the kingdom welcome, and it will make you welcome." To comply with this invitation, and to receive the kingdom as offered, is to believe; faith needs no better definition: it consists in spiritual receptivity. And the kingdom being such as described, not a mere kingdom of law in which God appears making demands, but first of all, a kingdom of grace in which God appears freely bestowing benefits, it is clear that receptivity is not only a suitable attitude, but an indispensable one. The kingdom being a gift, the one thing needful is that it be received. This indispensable requirement is happily one within the reach of all. The gospel of a kingdom so conceived as to require only faith, is a gospel for the million. The announcement that the kingdom was approaching, made by the Baptist, was a gospel or good tidings only to the few who were righteous, or who had strength of will to reform their lives in obedience to a mere legal demand. Christ's announcement of a kingdom that had simply to be received, was a gospel for all; for sinners not less than for saints, for them even chiefly or very expressly. He came, as He Himself said, signalizing this fact, "not to call righteous ones, but sinners;" He came calling sinners, not "to repentance" merely, according to the expanded form of the saying as given by Luke,[1] but generally to participation in all the benefits of the kingdom. If we must add an interpretative gloss to the original word, the more appropriate one would be "to faith." For the kingdom of Christ's Evangel was such that what men had to do first of all was to receive it as a boon, and sinners had the best reasons for being ready to do that.

The adoption of faith as the new watchword was, moreover, a prophecy of Christian universalism. A Divine kingdom addressing itself to faith is likely not only to go down to the lowest moral depths of Jewish society that it may raise the low and lost to heavenly heights, but also to overleap the geographical boundaries of Palestine and become a world-wide phenomenon. The word "repent" holds out little hope to those outside the pale. It is spoken most fitly to a covenanted people for whom God had done much, and from whom therefore He demands much. The preacher of repentance by the banks of the Jordan thinks naturally only of the children of Abraham, and his summons refers exclusively to theocratic privileges and obligations. But when one comes preaching *faith*, He may readily have the Gentiles

---

[1] Luke v. 32. The εἰς μετάνοιαν of Luke's text is a false reading in the other Gospels introduced for the purpose of assimilation.

in view. For though they too have abundant cause for repentance, they have sinned in ignorance, and are more fitly objects of compassion than of wrath. They need grace, and if they are to have any part in the kingdom, their first duty will be to believe in grace, and possibly they may develop no mean capacity for believing. Why should not the Preacher of a kingdom addressing itself to faith have these thoughts present to His mind? Nay, how could He fail to have the Gentiles in His view if He realized the import of His own programme?

The Gospel history supplies abundant evidence that Christ fully understood the scope of His doctrine of faith in all directions. Specially significant in this connection are the three narratives, of the woman "who was a sinner," the Roman centurion, and the woman of Syro-Phœnicia.[1] The first shows Christ's estimate of the power of faith as a redemptive force; the other two reveal His consciousness that before faith all barriers of race, rite, or election must go down. The woman who entered into Simon's house Jesus assumed to be a great sinner; nay, held her proved to be, by the very intensity of her love to Himself as exhibited in her remarkable behaviour. From the great love He inferred a great need of forgiveness. Yet He had perfect confidence in the power of faith to "save" her, to make her happy and good. "Thy faith hath saved thee," He said to her at parting; "go into peace." In what had just taken place He saw the process of salvation begun, and even virtually completed. Faith in the good tidings we may

[1] Luke vii. 36-50; Matt. viii. 5-13; Luke vii. 1-10; Matt. xv. 21-28; Mark vii. 24-30.

assume she had heard Him preach, for "faith cometh by hearing," had led her to believe in the forgiveness of sins, and to cherish hope of being able by Heaven's help to live a useful, pure life for the future. The very sight of Him had been a gospel to the heart of this fallen one, revealing an infinite depth of tender, pure sympathy with the like of her which touched the remnants of true womanhood in her, and made sensual impulses seem hateful. And now here she was in His presence, suitable occasion offering, her heart bursting with gratitude for benefit received, and demonstrating by a series of extraordinary actions her pure though passionate affection for her Saviour. What better evidence could one desire of faith's power than the moral transformation actually effected: a sinner turned into a penitent, a harlot into a devotee; the shameless one raised above the shame which keeps men from doing noble actions, and become a heroine who can defy conventional proprieties at the bidding of the heart? Here was a last one become first: in the very first passages of her new life leaving Simon the Pharisee far behind—his behaviour towards his guest, compared with hers, seeming cold and mean. It was with these things in view that Jesus declared, surely not without reason, that faith had saved that woman. True, the new life was only begun, and there were many risks ahead. Many conversions are only temporary, and early enthusiasms are too often followed by lamentable falls. Jesus knew all that full well; but He was not a Pharisee, therefore He deemed it better to speak a generous word than to offer cold advices, to sympathize than to caution. He believed that faith, and what faith feeds on, redeeming love in God and man, is the best preservative against apostasy, and that when it fails no other influences will be of much avail. Nor did He send the penitent away with that cheering sympathetic word, from mere motives of prudence. He spoke from conviction, as cherishing strong hopes for the future of the erring one. He saw no reason in the evil past for despair. He believed it possible for great offenders permanently to forsake wicked ways and rise to great heights of sanctity. He even expected such, once changed, to rise highest. Therefore it was that He spent so much of His time among the outcasts. He expected to find there the best citizens of the kingdom. The motto, "Much forgiveness, much love," was part of His apology for His sympathetic relations with the class of which the woman "who was a sinner" was a sample. The confidence He expressed in her case was not the result of a momentary generous impulse. It embodied a fixed principle on which He acted all through His ministry. "It is faith that saves, it can save the lowest, it can save them most conspicuously,"— such was the cheering, hopeful creed of Jesus Christ.

In the light of that creed we understand why Jesus said so much less about repentance than about faith. He believed that faith would do the work of repentance, that indeed it bore repentance in its bosom. And when we recall His definition of repentance, we perceive that the fact is even so. Repentance means a change of mind consisting in the recognition of the kingdom as the chief end of man. But faith, we have found, means the reception of the same kingdom as the highest good, the sum of all blessedness bestowed on men as a free gift from

God. Evidently, then, the reception of the boon by faith is the most direct way to the goal aimed at in repentance, the exaltation of the kingdom and its interests to the place of supremacy. And the repentance thus brought about is altogether wholesome; not legal but evangelic, not compulsory but spontaneous; not a habit of sadness as if doing eternal penance for the past, but a turning of the moral energies in a new direction in cheerfulness and hope, letting the dead past bury its dead. In this way, not after the rueful manner of the Baptist circle, would Jesus have His disciples repent. What He said to the palsied man, He virtually said to all: "Courage, child, thy sins are forgiven thee."[1] He summoned penitents not to fasting but to service, such as that of the women who followed Him and ministered to Him of their substance.[2] She that had been a sinner probably joined that company, and that was the way by which she entered into peace.

In the cases of the Roman centurion and the woman of Syro-Phœnicia, the faith manifested, though in both instances eliciting the admiration and praise of Jesus, was less obviously of the kind that "saves." The benefit sought in both cases was physical, and the faith exercised in seeking it seems rather a capacity for uttering bright sayings, and the eulogy called forth appears to be homage done to genius under another name. There is certainly something to be learned from these narratives concerning the *psychology* of faith as conceived by Jesus. Obviously He did not regard faith as an isolated faculty separate from reason, and still less as opposed to reason, but

---

[1] Matt. ix. 2.   [2] Luke viii. 1-3.

rather as a function of the whole mind exercised on religion. Those whom He accounted great in faith were thus likely to be interesting people, in all respects far from commonplace either intellectually or morally; and in fact it is evident that all the three chief characters in the incidents under consideration, the sinful woman, the centurion, and the Syro-Phœnician, were as far as possible from being commonplace. There was an element of genius and heroism in them all; a talent for doing uncommon actions, for thinking great thoughts, for uttering sparkling, witty words. And the truth is, whatever prejudice may exist to the contrary, faith is always a heroic quality, by no means a prosaic homespun virtue likely to be most conspicuous in persons of dull minds, and characterized by moral mediocrity. As to the physical nature of the benefit, Jesus did not view it in isolation any more than the faculty of faith. His idea seems to have been, that as faith in its acting maintains solidarity with all the mental powers, so all its acts are in solidarity with each other. Capacity to believe in one direction implies capacity to believe in all directions.

While intellect was conspicuously active in the centurion and in the Syro-Phœnician woman, faith in the ethical and religious sense also revealed itself in no ordinary degree. The saying of the centurion, besides indicating deep humility, showed strong faith in the power and the will of the Divine Being, as represented by Jesus, to interpose in the world's affairs as a helper of men in their needs. It is true, any one not inclined to think well of Pagans might very easily detract from the merit of the striking word which compared Christ to a general or imperator, by representing it as the combined product of Roman military discipline and Roman religious superstition.[1] But the centurion's faith is thus made less remarkable in one aspect, only to become more significant in another direction. If Christ's praise was exaggerated, it but the more conspicuously evinces his *philo-Pagan* spirit, and raises the hope that the generous eye of Heaven may detect traces of faith in the hearts of benighted heathens dimly groping after the true God, where narrow-souled men judging by dogmatic tests would discover none. We may safely assume, however, that the praise, while generous, as was always Christ's way, was in the main deserved. In that case the centurion's faith, as that of a Pagan,—for such we may regard him, even if, as is probable from Luke's narrative,[2] he had become a Jewish proselyte,—possesses peculiar value as foreshadowing the universal destination of the kingdom. Here on heathen soil, so to speak, is a faith which on Christ's own testimony eclipses any to be seen in Israel. It is a melancholy, although not a surprising fact, as it concerns Israel. Here is a people which has had a very long and careful training in religion, and has busied itself very much with religion. And the result is that the faith-faculty has almost died out within it; has been killed out by Rabbinism, which can believe in no new revelations, but only in old revelations overgrown by the moss of centuries. There is a better chance of learn-

---

[1] Weiss characterizes the centurion's idea as "certainly very superstitious" (*Leben Jesu*, i. p. 425).

[2] Luke vii. 5.

ing what faith can be and do by going outside the Jewish pale. Verily a thing of evil omen for the elect race. For if the kingdom addresses itself to faith, and if faith be forthcoming among Pagans more readily than among Israelites, will it not forsake the sacred soil and step forth into the Gentile world, going where it meets with a hearty welcome? The reflection forces itself on our minds, and it is nowise unlikely that it suggested itself to Jesus and found expression in the words: "Many shall come from the east and west, and shall sit down with Abraham and Isaac and Jacob in the kingdom of heaven; but the children of the kingdom shall be cast out."[1] The truth that the gospel is for the world is not expressed here as Paul expressed it. The kingdom does not go to the Pagans, the Pagans come to the kingdom, localized in the Holy Land. But the day-dawn of Christian universalism is manifestly here.

In the case of the Syro-Phœnician woman the dawn grows brighter. Here also there is a double interest, a personal interest connected with the unfolding of a striking human character, and the didactic interest connected with the fact that the heroine was a Pagan. We all feel the charm of the story. The pathos, humour, and meekness blended together in the pleadings of this Syrian mother for her afflicted daughter conquer every Christian heart. Had the narrative told that Jesus persisted in His refusal, it would have been hard for

---

[1] Matt. viii. 11. This saying is given by Luke in another connection (xiii. 28, 29), and we cannot be sure that Matthew places it in its original position. But as it stands in his Gospel it suits well the occasion.

us to have borne it. But there was no risk of that happening. Not that Jesus was not in earnest in the declaration made to His disciples that His vocation was to the lost sheep of the house of Israel. He meant that seriously, and then and always acted on it. But faith made all the difference. Faith anywhere and everywhere must be respected. Jesus accordingly did respect faith in this instance, and in the light of His ultimate compliance with the woman's request, His rule of conduct becomes modified thus: Israel my ordinary care, with exceptions made in favour of faith. In Christ's own lifetime the exceptions were few, but these exceptions, and the one before us in particular, were prophetic of a time when the exception would become the rule. For Christian universalism was immanent in the Syro-Phœnician's faith; therein lay its profound religious significance. When she said meekly and wittily, "We are Gentile dogs, yet there is a portion even for the dogs of the household crouching below the family table," she expressed by implication her belief that the barrier between Jew and Gentile was not insurmountable, that election did not exclude the outside world from all share in Divine compassion, that Heaven's grace could not possibly be confined within certain geographical boundaries. She said in effect what Paul said afterwards, "God is not the God of the Jews only, but of the Gentiles also;" with him, she ascribed to God's love a length and breadth wide as the world. Her faith filled up the deep ravine of Pagan unworthiness, and levelled the mountain range of election which separated Jews from Gentiles, and made a straight way for the kingdom with its blessings even into Syro-Phœnicia. All this Jesus understood, and all this He had in view in granting the request. His ultimate compliance was not a merely exceptional favour to a Pagan out of regard to a most unusual spiritual insight. It was a virtual proclamation that before faith all partition walls must fall, that wherever there is recipiency the blessings of the kingdom must be communicated, irrespective of race, rite, or peculiar privilege. It was an anticipation of the position taken up by the Apostolic Church in Jerusalem, when, in deference to undeniable facts, its members said, "Then hath God also to the Gentiles granted repentance unto life." In their case it was a reluctant acknowledgment in which deeply-rooted prejudice yielded to the force of events. One may feel disappointment that in this respect there is the appearance of a resemblance between their attitude and that of Jesus on this occasion. It is natural to wish that His universalism had been as pronounced and as undeniable as that of Paul, by the side of which his reluctant yielding to the pressure of importunate faith wears an aspect of provincial narrowness. But that could not be. However like Paul in spirit and conviction, Jesus could not but be more reserved in utterance and in action. Respect was due to the law of development. Bright day is ushered in by the grey dim dawn. It was good and wholesome that the day of grace should thus gradually steal on. The public action of Jesus was guided by this consideration. In confining His activities to Israel, He was exercising a self-restraint which was a veritable part of His earthly humiliation. How real the self-restraint was, appears from the heartiness and even eagerness with which exception was made on good cause shown. In the case of the Syro-Phœnician woman, as in the case of the Roman centurion, it would have been very easy for an illiberal churlish Jew to have minimized the merit of the words spoken. It is always easy to put a sinister construction on the conduct of people we dislike. Good qualities may be turned into their opposites: humility into impudence, genial wit into mere pertness. Christ saw in that woman nothing that was not there; nevertheless He saw what He was very willing to see; what no scribe, rabbi, or Pharisee would ever have discovered. It was once asked with reference to Himself, "Can any good thing come out of Nazareth?" That He was not inclined to ask, "Can any good thing come out of heathendom?" His admiring exclamation, "O woman, great is thy faith!"[1] very sufficiently demonstrates. Though He did not say it, He doubtless felt that here again was a faith the like of which was not to be found in Israel. The remark might have been made with even more justice than in the case of the centurion. Faith was a scarce commodity in Israel in any form; and what there was of it was of a homeward-bound character—faith in a grace available for the chosen race, but not for those beyond the pale. Here, on Pagan soil, on the

---

[1] Matt. xv. 28. Mark's version is less gushing: "For this saying go thy way" (vii. 29). The meaning is the same. The gush comes out in action: "The devil is gone out of thy daughter." It is noticeable that the harshness of Christ's refusal is softened in Mark's account by the introduction of the words: "Let the children first be filled" (vii. 27). This sounds like an echo of Paul's: "To the Jew first, and also to the Gentile."

contrary, was a faith remarkable not only for its brightness and strength, but for its spiritual enlightenment and width of horizon; accepting as a truism what to the ordinary Jew seemed all but incredible, that there was hope in God even for Gentiles.

After the foregoing observations, it can hardly be necessary to point out that, in the view of Christ, faith was not only the necessary but the sufficient condition of admission to the kingdom. "Faith alone" was a motto for Christ not less than for Paul. Faith alone with reference to repentance, because including it; faith alone with reference to circumcision and the like externalities, because rendering them utterly meaningless. Faith alone sufficed in the case of the Syro-Phœnician mother and her daughter. The mother came to Jesus a Pagan, and she returned to her home a Pagan, yet with a blessing for herself and for her afflicted child. It is true, indeed, that faith obtained, apparently, only the dog's portion, a crumb of healing for a diseased body. Might it not suffice for that, yet fail to obtain the full benefits of citizenship in the holy commonwealth without the aid of some supplementary qualification, such as, for example, circumcision? No, for there is solidarity in the benefits procurable by faith, as well as in faith's actings. The law of solidarity prevails all round. The soul exerts all its energies in believing; faith's individual acts all hang together; God's gifts to faith go in a body. If anything is given, all is given. Faith makes the dog a child, and gets a share not only of the crumbs below the table, but of all the viands on the table. That is the law of the kingdom. Recipiency is the sole requirement. External conditions can have no place in reference to the Highest Good. Existing restrictions are only economical and temporary, and a sign that the era of spiritual reality is not yet come. The behaviour of Jesus towards the Pagans mentioned in the Gospels shows that He was of this mind.

CHAPTER IV.

CHRIST'S DOCTRINE OF GOD.

IN passing from the Old Testament to the Gospels, we find God spoken of under a new name. The Jehovah of Israel is replaced by the Divine Father of men. An ancient reading of Matt. xi. 27, of earlier date than the oldest of extant manuscripts, made Jesus claim to be the revealer of God in His paternal character. "No man *knew* the Father save the Son." The claim is valid, independently of doubtful readings of evangelic texts. The "only-begotten" was the first effective *exegete* of God as Father. He declared Him so that the name Father took its place in human speech as the Christian name for the Divine Being. The declaration was an essential part of the doctrine of the kingdom. The title Father is the appropriate name of God in the kingdom of grace, for it is the kingdom of fatherly love.

The doctrine was not absolutely new; like every other Christian doctrine, it had its root in the Old Testament. But it was new in emphasis. It was also new in respect to the relation the name Father was employed to express. In Old Testament dialect the epithet expressed a relation of God to the chosen nation, or to its earthly sovereign, Jehovah's vicegerent. Israel or Israel's King was God's

Son. But Christ placed God in a paternal relation to individuals, and represented Him as the Father of the human spirit. It was in one sense a doctrine as old as Genesis, where it is taught that man was made in God's image. But it was the old doctrine with a marked difference. The man made in God's image, of the Book of Origins, is an ideal man untainted by moral evil. But Jesus said: God is the Father of men, sin notwithstanding.[1] He said this not merely with reference to the best men in whom moral evil appeared in the most mitigated form, the people of culture and character, but even with reference to the most depraved and degraded. The God He preached is Father not only of those who by His grace have become citizens of the Divine kingdom, but also of those who are without. The doctrine concerned both sinners and saints, and was proclaimed to all on highway or in market-place, irrespective of social or moral antecedents.

But the Fatherhood of God, as announced by Jesus, while having reference to all, does not necessarily mean the same thing for all. God cannot, any more than an earthly parent, be a Father to His prodigal children to the same effect as to sons who dwell in His house and regard Him with trust, reverence, and love. The full benefit of Divine Fatherhood can only be experienced where there is a filial attitude and spiritual receptivity. The will to bless may be in the Father's heart, yet be

---

[1] The idea that God is the Father of the just man occurs in the Wisdom of Solomon ii. 16-18: "He blesseth the end of the just, and boasts that God is his Father. Let us see if his words be true, and let us try his end. For if the just be the son of God, He will take his part, and deliver him from the hands of his foes."

frustrated by unbelief or alienation. Hence, in studying the doctrine of God's paternal love, we must have regard to moral distinctions. We must ask ourselves what it means for sinners, and what for saints; for men in general on the one hand, for the children of the kingdom on the other. We shall find that the words of Jesus supply us with materials for answering both questions.

The Fatherhood of God in both relations has two aspects, a providential and a gracious; the one referring to the temporal interests of men, the other to the higher interests of the soul. The paternal Providence of God over all is taught in that word in the Sermon on the Mount, in which the Father in heaven is represented as making His sun rise upon evil and good, and sending rain on just and unjust.[1] This part of Christ's doctrine is not so much a new revelation as a reversion to a simple truth of natural religion. Nature itself teaches men to think of the Maker and Sustainer of the world as a parent who gives to his children their daily bread. The Vedic Indians, with this thought in their mind, worshipped Dyaus-pitar, the heaven-Father. They felt their dependence for the things they chiefly sought after, food and raiment, on the elements; and without clearly distinguishing between creature and Creator, they looked up to the sky, and adored the Power that sent them sunshine and showers in due season.

On the other side of God's universal Fatherhood, Christ's teaching rises far above the level of man's unassisted thought. The natural man, because he seeks chiefly material good, does not much meditate on God's

[1] Matt. v. 45.

paternal care for his spiritual wellbeing. This aspect comes into full view only when men begin to seek the kingdom of God and His righteousness as the first goods of life. Jesus taught that God cares with paternal tenderness for the souls of those who utterly neglect the chief end and the chief good. His teaching on this subject is an essential part of His doctrine of the kingdom. It does not declare the truth concerning God's relation to the citizens of the kingdom which forms the crown of His theology, but it sets forth a truth the belief of which tends to make men become citizens. The *locus classicus* for this part of Christ's revelation of the Father is the fifteenth chapter of Luke's Gospel containing the parables concerning the finding of the lost, and especially the last of the three parables—the Prodigal Son. There God appears as One who takes pleasure in the repentance of sinners such as the reprobates of Jewish society, because in these penitents He sees prodigal children returning to their Father's house. By these parabolic utterances Jesus said to all, however far from righteousness, God loves you as His children, no more worthy to be called sons, yet regarded as such; He deplores your departure from Him, and desires your return; and He will receive you graciously when, taught wisdom by misery, you direct your footsteps homewards. It is not allegorizing exegesis to take this meaning out of the parables. Jesus was on His defence for loving classes of men despised or despaired of, and His defence in part consisted in this, that His bearing towards the outcasts was that of the Divine Being. He loved them as a Brother; God loved them as a Father.

Even if these parables had never been spoken, the fatherly love of God to the lost ones must still have appeared an obvious corollary from Christ's own behaviour towards them. The new doctrine of God was involved in the new line of conduct; and the three parables concerning finding the lost, even if not genuine, truly reflect the spirit of that conduct and its religious significance.[1] God was proclaimed to be the compassionate Father of the sinful by deeds more emphatically than by the most pathetic and beautiful words. The much-blamed sympathetic intercourse of Jesus with the publicans and sinners of Israel, said to all who could understand: "The most depraved of men is still a man, my brother, my Father's child; therefore I love him, and am fully assured that God loves him as I do." Doubtless converts to discipleship from these classes did understand. They felt instinctively that the God of Jesus was a different Being from the God of the Pharisees, who scorned and repelled them; not a God of merely negative holiness keeping aloof from the sinful, but One who desired to make others partakers of His holiness; not a merely righteous God, but good as well as righteous, the one absolutely Good Being, benignant, gracious, delighting to bestow favours; not the God of a clique or coterie, the head of the Pharisaical party or of

---

[1] Weizsäcker (*Untersuchungen*, S. 177) regards the parables in Luke xv. and xvi. as an appendix to the first of the group, that of the *Lost Sheep*, which Luke has in common with Matthew (xviii. 12, 13). In proof he points to the fact that in chap. xvii. Luke goes on to Christ's discourse on *Offences*, the connection in which the parable occurs in Matthew's Gospel. This is a shrewd observation.

the Rabbinical schools, but the God of the populace and the profane rabble, with whom a penitent publican had a better chance of acceptance than a self-complacent religionist who studied the law day and night and scrupulously observed all prescribed rules. "These things," this Father-God, was revealed to the "babes," though hidden from the wise and understanding; hidden from them because they desired not such a divinity, but rather one like unto themselves, priding himself on his holiness, and jealously guarding it from tarnish by isolation.

This Father-God who loveth even the unholy, whom Jesus preached by word and still more impressively by action, is another sign that the coming kingdom is not national but universal. This God cannot be the God of the Jews only, any more than He can be the God of a Pharisaic party within the Jewish nation. The Gentiles also are His children. He may seem to have neglected them hitherto, but the neglect can only have been comparative. Now that Jesus has come revealing the Father, the period of neglect manifestly draws to a close; the time of merciful visitation for the Gentile world is at hand.

Passing now from the universal aspect of Divine Fatherhood to the more special, we find that a paternal Providence for the citizens of the kingdom was very strongly asserted by Jesus. He told His disciples that they need have no concern about temporal interests; their Father in heaven would take charge of these; their part was to devote themselves in filial dutifulness and trust to the service of the kingdom. "Be not anxious," He said to them, "saying, What shall we eat, or what shall we drink, or wherewithal shall we be clothed? For after all these things do the Gentiles seek, for your heavenly Father knoweth that ye need all these things. But seek ye first His kingdom and His righteousness, and all these things shall be added unto you."[1] That is, Let your care be the kingdom, you yourselves will be your Father's care. It is a distribution of duties between a Father and His children. The children are to devote themselves to the *kingdom and righteousness of their Father*, for so these are named in the reading adopted above, which is intrinsically probable though found only in the Vatican manuscript. Devotion to the kingdom so conceived becomes an easy task. For children love to serve their Father; subjects who are also sons do the King's will with enthusiasm. On the other hand, they are relieved from all anxiety concerning themselves. For the Divine Father and King will provide for His children. He careth for all, even for His prodigal children who are unthankful and evil; how much more will He care for dutiful children who do His will, and devote themselves to those interests which He regards as of supreme importance!

The same distribution of duties between Father and children underlies the Lord's Prayer. First come petitions for the advancement of the kingdom, implying that that is the main object of solicitude for the petitioners; then follow petitions for personal wants—daily bread, pardon of shortcomings, and protection from evil, springing not out of anxiety, but out of an assured confidence that these boons will be granted. The import of the

[1] Matt. vi. 31-33; Luke xii. 29-31.

prayer is: Father in heaven, our heart's chief desire is that Thy name be glorified, and we give ourselves to the service of Thy kingdom, and the doing of Thy will, trusting that Thou wilt remember all the wants of us Thy children.

This paternal care of God for His servants, so pathetically taught by Christ, is the necessary complement of the entire self-consecration which is the cardinal virtue in the ethical code of the kingdom. Those who are required to seek the kingdom and its righteousness with their whole heart are men living in the body, needing food and raiment and other things of like nature for the preservation of their natural lives; and if they are not to be preoccupied with cares about such matters, or to permit such sordid solicitudes to take their thoughts off higher concerns, there must be some one else to look after their physical needs. There must be a Providence over them taking charge of temporalities, even as in military organization there is a commissariat department whose business it is to find the soldier in food and clothing, while he does not trouble himself about the affairs of life that he may please him who hath enlisted him for military service.[1] Christ taught His disciples that the commissariat department was in the hands of their heavenly Father, so that they had but to play the part of soldiers found in everything they need. This doctrine, so clearly stated in the passage above quoted from the Sermon on the Mount, He repeated as occasion required. When, for example, He sent forth His disciples on the Galilean mission, He gave them instruc-

[1] 2 Tim. ii. 4.

tions which might be summarized in these two precepts, "Care not;" "Fear not."[1] Be careful about nothing, food, raiment, lodging, not even about a staff; be not anxious as to what ye shall say, or how to say it when placed in trying positions: it shall be given unto you in that hour what ye shall say. Fear not; ye will doubtless sometimes be in circumstances fitted to inspire fear, involving peril to your lives. Yet fear not for your bodily life; fear only one thing, the death of your souls through unfaithfulness in yielding to the tempter who whispers, "Save thyself; prefer personal safety to duty." As for your bodies, why fear for them? Should the worst come, you are not really harmed, and your Father will provide that the worst come not so long as you are needed for the work of the kingdom. The hairs of your head are numbered by Him who careth even for valueless sparrows. To this effect did Jesus exhort the apprentice evangelists. It is unnecessary to ask, Who is the unnamed object of fear who is distinguished from the foes that seek to stay the progress of the kingdom by killing the bodies of its apostles, as one who is able to destroy both soul and body in Gehenna? Who else can the ghostly foe be but the evil spirit who goeth about tempting men to prefer their personal interests to the Divine? But why then is he not named? That he may be all the more an object of dread. Fear ye, said Jesus in effect, the nameless secret foe who seeks your ruin by tempting you to play the coward and deserter instead of the man and the hero. God also might be described as the Destroyer, in so far

[1] Matt. x. 19, 28.

as He judicially gives over to perdition those who act the part of apostates and traitors. But so to have spoken of God would have been bad policy and bad rhetoric, when the Speaker desired to lodge in the minds of His disciples the idea of God as a Father, as the antidote to all fear. To exhibit God as an object of infinite dread is a poor way of preparing men to receive Him as an object of unbounded trust. Moreover, the proper object of fear is not the judicial damnation, but that which leads to it, temptation to apostasy. The point on which we are to bring to bear all our faculty of horror is that at which the first Satanic suggestion is whispered, "Save thyself: self-preservation is the first duty; why risk property, name, life, in a mad enterprise?"

During the time He was with them, Jesus found cause for renewing the exhortations, "Fear not," "Care not," to His disciples. In the twelfth chapter of Luke we find such a counsel against anxiety lying like a pebble on a gravel-bank which may have strayed from its original position in the evangelic history, but whose intrinsic value remains undiminished. "Fear not, little flock: for it is your Father's good pleasure to give you the kingdom."[1] The situation is so described as to make clear how great is the temptation to fear. The disciples are, in relation to the world, a small flock of sheep, few in number, insignificant in influence, and helpless as sheep in the midst of devouring wolves. Nevertheless, with reference even to such an apparently desperate situation, they are exhorted not to fear, but to be assured that their Father will not suffer them

[1] Luke xii. 32.

either to lose the kingdom, the chief object of their quest, or to fall victims to hostile powers.

These and other words of Jesus setting forth God's paternal care for those who serve Him, are utterances full of poetry and pathos, the bare reading of which exercises a soothing influence on our troubled spirits in this world of trial, sorrow, and care. Yet we are tempted to regard them as a romantic idyll having the rights and value of poetry, but standing in no relation to real life. Christ's whole doctrine of a Father-God may appear to us the product of a delicate religious imagination and a child-like loving heart which went through life dreaming a pleasant dream, and scarce conscious of collisions with hard unwelcome experiences. Some may think the world has outgrown the doctrine. "We are of age," writes one, " and do not need a Father's care."[1] Others, the majority, little inclined to adopt this haughty tone, find the doctrine very welcome, if only it were true. It is a spring in the desert of life, nevertheless is not life a desert all the same? It may be; but whatever the facts are which seem to justify this pessimistic view, they were perfectly familiar to Jesus. His doctrine of Divine Fatherhood did come from the heart; it was as far as possible from being the dry scientific utterance of a scholastic theologian, and scholastic theology has shown its consciousness of the fact by treating the doctrine with neglect. But Jesus uttered the doctrine with full knowledge of all in experience that seemed to contradict it, and earnestly believed it, all that notwithstanding. He knew how much there is to tempt men to say: Provi-

[1] Heine, *Sämmtliche Werke*, v. 140.

dence is anything but paternal, if indeed there be a Providence at all; for has not every man to be his own providence, finding for himself food and raiment and all things needful as best he can, and endeavouring the while not altogether to forget higher matters? And He spoke words fitted to lay such doubting thoughts arising out of sombre experience. How vividly He conceived the mental state of the careworn, appears from Luke's version of the counsel against anxiety, which might be thus paraphrased: "Seek not what ye shall eat or what ye shall drink, *neither be ye as a ship raised aloft on the billows of a troubled, tempestuous sea.*"[1] But it was not alone by a stray word such as this, preserved by the third evangelist,[2] that Jesus showed His intimate acquaintance and deep sympathy with the trials of faith to which the servants of the kingdom are liable. From the lessons He taught His disciples on *Perseverance in Prayer*, it appears how well aware He was that God often shows Himself so little like a Father, that those who trust in Him are tempted to think Him rather like a man of selfish spirit who cares only for his own comfort, or like an unjust judge who is indifferent to right. Such precisely are the representations of God *as He appears* in the two parables of the *Selfish Neighbour* and the *Unjust Judge*.[3] The relevancy of the parables requires that these characters should be regarded as

---

[1] Luke xii. 29, καὶ μὴ μετεωρίζεσθε.

[2] It is impossible to decide whether we have here an explanatory gloss on the counsel against anxiety, or an utterance of Jesus in its original form. The striking character of the expression is in favour of the latter view.

[3] Luke xi. 5-8, xviii. 1-8.

representing God, not as He is indeed, but as He seems to tried faith. It is thus tacitly admitted by Jesus, that far from giving His children what they need before they ask or when they ask, God often delays for a lengthened period answers to prayer, so as to present to suppliants an aspect of indifference, heartlessness, unrighteousness. The didactic drift of the two parables is: You will have to wait on God, to wait possibly till hope deferred make the heart sick, but it is worth your while to wait, "for the Lord is good to them that wait on Him, to the soul that seeketh Him." Man can be compelled to hear by importunity and incessant knocking. God is not a man to be compelled, yet it may be said that the apparent reluctance of Providence can be overcome by persistent prayer which refuses to be gainsaid or frustrated, continuing to knock at the door with an importunity that knows no shame,[1] and assailing the ear of the judge with outcries in a temper that will not be trifled with, and an attitude almost threatening.[2] In other words, with full consciousness how much there is in the world which seems to prove the contrary, Jesus asserted the reality of a Paternal Providence continually working for the good of those who make the kingdom of God their chief end. And this faith is the distinctively Christian theory of the Universe. Christians believe that the kingdom of heaven is a chief end for God as well as for themselves, and that He makes all things subservient to its interests.

---

[1] $\dot{\alpha}\nu\alpha i\delta\epsilon\iota\alpha$, shamelessness, is ascribed to the petitioner in the earlier parable.

[2] The unjust judge affects to be afraid lest the widow at last should strike him: $\H{\iota}\nu\alpha\ \mu\dot{\eta}\ \dot{\upsilon}\pi\omega\pi\iota\acute{\alpha}\zeta\eta\ \mu\epsilon$.

This faith gives them victory over all sordid solicitudes, and enables them with cheerfulness and hope to leave all their personal concerns in the hands of their Father.

While assuring His disciples of God's care for their temporal wants, Jesus did not neglect to teach them the still more important truth that their spiritual wellbeing was an object of tender solicitude to their heavenly Father. This indeed hardly needed to be taught expressly. The higher care is implied in the lower. God cares for the bodies of His children, that they may give themselves without distraction to that service of the kingdom which is the very life and health of the soul. Nevertheless, Jesus deemed it expedient to make the higher aspect of God's paternal providence the subject of special declarations. One such may be found even in the promise that food and raiment would be provided, which is so expressed as to include a reference to the higher goods of life. "All these things shall be *added* unto you." If food and raiment be an addition, there must be a portion to which they are added. That portion consists of the kingdom and its righteousness, chiefly sought, and surely to be found. What Jesus thus taught indirectly though most forcibly, He directly declared when He said: "Fear not, little flock, it is your Father's good pleasure to give you the kingdom." He gave a similar assurance by introducing into the model prayer petitions for the pardon of sin, and for protection from temptation and from the power of moral evil.[1] The two parables already

---

[1] It seems best to take τοῦ πονηροῦ as referring, not to the Evil One, but to evil in the abstract. The petition thereby gains the widest comprehensiveness.

referred to bear, if not exclusively, at least inclusively, on spiritual interests. The later parable relates to the public interest of the Divine kingdom. The earlier must be supposed to embrace within its scope all the petitions of the Lord's Prayer to which it is appended, the petitions relating to pardon and protection from evil, not less than that relating to daily bread. From the sentence with which the lesson on prayer, recorded in the eleventh chapter of Luke, ends, we should naturally infer that the *Holy Spirit* as a sanctifying power is supposed to be the chief object of desire. Criticism may indeed find in the remarkable expression a tinge of Paulinism. But granting that we have here a Pauline modification of Christ's words, the promise of the Holy Spirit put into the mouth of Christ by Luke is nothing more than an assurance that the prayer for protection from temptation[1] shall be answered. The temptations chiefly to be dreaded are those which solicit us to sacrifice primary interests for secondary, righteousness for physical wants; and we are kept from yielding to such by the Divine Spirit dwelling in us, and imparting to us a single eye, a pure heart, a generous, noble devotion to the kingdom and its interests.

It is important to observe, that while giving these various assurances to His disciples that God would attend to their spiritual welfare, Jesus did not lead them to expect that in this sphere there would be no occasion for exercising the virtue of patience. On the contrary, it is

---

[1] In the best texts of Luke's version of the Lord's Prayer, the clause ἀλλὰ ῥῦσαι ἡμᾶς ἀπὸ τοῦ πονηροῦ is wanting. It qualifies the previous clause by explaining in what sense temptation is to be deprecated, and is therefore implied even when not expressed.

clearly implied in the parable of the selfish neighbour, that the delays which make God assume so untoward an aspect take place in connection with all the objects referred to in the Lord's Prayer: the advancement of the kingdom, daily bread, the personal spiritual necessities of disciples. Hence we learn that even the Holy Spirit may not be given at once in satisfying measure to those who earnestly desire it, though sure to be so given eventually. The heavenly Father may for a season appear unwilling to grant to those who seek first the kingdom, even that which they most value—righteousness, sanctity, complete victory over evil. This is a familiar fact of Christian experience, and the fact imports that personal sanctification is a gradual process. The Holy Spirit is given in ample measure to all earnest souls, but not even to the most earnest without such delays as are most trying to faith and patience. This fact, plainly implied in the lessons on prayer recorded by Luke, is directly recognised in the parable of *the Blade, the Ear, and the Full Corn*,[1] preserved by Mark alone. The parable may be held to refer in the first place to the Divine kingdom viewed collectively, and in that view it has an important bearing on the question whether Jesus expected the kingdom to pass through a lengthened period of development. But nothing forbids us to regard the parable as applicable likewise to individual experience. The kingdom comes in the individual as well as in the community; and the lesson we learn from the parable, is that the kingdom comes as ripe grain comes—gradually passing through stages analogous to

---

[1] Mark iv. 26-29.

those in the growth of corn: stages that cannot be overleapt, that no amount of earnestness will avail to supersede; that are indeed most marked in those who are most earnest, and who ultimately exhibit the Divine life in its highest measure of energy and beauty. This is a great truth still not well understood, which it much concerns earnest seekers after God to lay to heart.[1] Some insight into it is needful to enable Christians at the critical period of their spiritual life, that of the green ear, to believe in the Fatherhood of God in its highest aspect. Failing to grasp the law of gradual sanctification, they will be tempted to think that God does in the highest sphere what Jesus declared no earthly father would do in the lower sphere of physical life, viz. mock His children by giving them stones when they ask for bread, and so prove to be in truth no Father at all. And if we doubt the reality of God's Fatherhood in the realm of grace, what will it avail us to believe in His Fatherhood in ordinary providence? If we doubt His willingness to give us the bread of eternal life, what comfort can it afford us, who desire that bread above all things, to believe that He is willing to give the bread

---

[1] The parable above referred to contains the clearest statement of the truth that the law of growth obtains in the kingdom of God to be found in the New Testament. It is very doubtful whether this truth, in relation either to the individual or to the community, was grasped by the apostles (not excepting Paul), not to speak of the Apostolic Church in general. This consideration is the best guarantee for the genuineness of this logion recorded by Mark alone. Its absence from the other Gospels may be due to the fact that it teaches a truth in advance of the ideas both of the evangelists and of those for whose benefit they wrote. Pfleiderer (*Das Urchristenthum*, S. 370) recognises the originality of the parable.

that perisheth? Nay, if we let go the one faith, how can we retain the other? If we deny the Fatherhood of God in grace, how shall we believe in a paternal Providence? Along with faith in God as the Father of our spirits, will not faith in Him as the Provider for our bodies fade out of our hearts, and leave us with no better creed than that of a godless world—every man for himself?

That the kingdom of God comes as a spiritual possession, only gradually, even when earnestly sought as the highest good, the history of Christ's disciples suffices to prove. The devotion of these men to the kingdom was intense from the beginning, but it was ignorant and impure. Even at a late period they were so unacquainted with the nature of the kingdom that they could quarrel about places of distinction in it, and their motives were so corrupt that their Master found it necessary to speak of conversion as a condition of their obtaining the humblest place in the Divine commonwealth. The initial ideas of the Twelve were conventional. They accepted current ideas of the kingdom, and of righteousness, and of God; and poured the new wine of their enthusiasm into old bottles. This is ever the way with religious novices. There is plenty of zeal, but little spiritual discernment. Conventional orthodoxy is implicitly adopted as the truth, all conventionally holy causes are fervently espoused, and all current religious customs are scrupulously observed. The Twelve were sincere seekers of the kingdom; but they had to seek it not merely in the sense of serving its interests, but in the sense of striving to find out its true nature, and the nature of its laws, and of its Divine Ruler. They were Jews to begin with, and the task before them was to become Christians in their thoughts of God, and of all things Divine. It was for this end that "Jesus ordained twelve, that they should be with Him."[1] He invited them to take His yoke upon them, that He might teach them the mysteries of the kingdom, and reveal unto them the Father. The former function He performed by uttering deep truths, many of which are recorded in the Gospels; the latter not so much by word as by life. He showed the Father by unfolding Himself. To see Him was to see the Father, to understand His spirit was to know the Father's inmost heart. According to the testimony of the fourth Gospel, the companions of Jesus were slow learners in this department of their spiritual education. "Show us the Father, and it sufficeth us,"[2] Philip is made to say on the eve of the Passion. It seems a libel on a fellow-disciple. Yet, after all, the alleged ignorance is perfectly credible. Has not Christendom been slow to learn the revelation of the Father? Have we not yet to learn it, by accepting the Jesus of the Gospels as an absolutely true and full manifestation of the Divine Being, and believing without reserve that He and God are in spirit one? A thoroughly Christian idea of God is still a desideratum, and when the Church has reached it, the kingdom of God shall have come in power.

[1] Mark iii. 14. [2] John xiv. 8.

CHAPTER V.

CHRIST'S DOCTRINE OF MAN.

EVERY doctrine of God has its congruous doctrine of man. A consistent pantheism, for example, regards man as insignificant, not distinguishable from nature, not generically different from the beasts. The Christian idea of God, on the contrary, is naturally associated with high views as to the dignity and worth of human nature in its ideal, if not in its actual condition. For as God cannot be the God of the dead but of the living, so neither can He be the Father of beings not intrinsically superior to the brutes. His children must be made in His own image, and possess the inalienable dignity of personality constituted by the possession of reason and freedom. Accordingly Jesus taught a high doctrine concerning the dignity of man. He said with unexampled emphasis: A man is a man, not a mere human animal; he is a being of infinite importance to God, and ought to be such also to himself and to his fellows. He quaintly hinted the deep truth by asking such thought-provoking questions as these: Is not the life more than meat?[1] How much is a man better than a sheep?[2] What shall a man give in exchange for his soul?[3]

[1] Matt. vi. 25.   [2] Matt. xii. 12.   [3] Matt. xvi. 26.

Jesus taught His new doctrine of man more emphatically by His public action than by these or any other kindred words. In His invitations to enter the kingdom, He addressed Himself very specially, as I have already had occasion to remark, to the poor, to those who were in bad social repute, to the labouring and heavy-laden, the children of sorrow and care. This did not mean that He was animated by class partialities, and desired to set one part of society against another; the destitute against the wealthy, the profligates against well-conducted citizens. As little did the new interest in people of humble rank signify that Jesus regarded poverty as a virtue, of itself a passport into the kingdom of heaven. Some indeed have thought otherwise. "Pure Ebionism," says Renan, "that is, the doctrine that the poor alone shall be saved, that the kingdom of the poor is about to come, was the doctrine of Jesus. . . . Poverty remained an ideal from which the true lineage of Jesus never broke away. To possess nothing was the true evangelic state; mendicity became a virtue, a holy state."[1] This may be a slightly plausible, but it is certainly a mistaken judgment. With equal plausibility might it be maintained that, according to Christ's teaching, publicans and harlots were as such fit subjects of the divine kingdom. The truth is that poverty and sorrow were not, any more than bad character, positive qualifications for citizenship, but merely conditions that were likely to act as predisposing causes, preparing men to listen with interest to the announcement that the kingdom was at hand.

The prominence given to the *poor* in the Gospel of the

[1] *Vie de Jésus*, pp. 179, 183.

kingdom, in so far as it had theoretic significance, and was not the spontaneous expression of compassion, marked the value set by Jesus on man as man. The poor represent man stripped of all extrinsic attributes of honour, and reduced to that which is common to all mankind. On this naked humanity the world has ever set little value. It begins to interest itself in a man when he is clothed with some outward distinction of wealth or birth or station. A mere man is a social nobody. Christ, on the other hand, highly valued in man only his humanity, accounting nothing he could possess of such importance as what he himself was or might become. "What is a man profited," He asked, "if he shall gain the whole world, and lose his own life?"[1] The life declared to be so precious is that in man which makes him a man—the life of a spirit conversant with things divine and eternal. For the preservation and health of this higher life, Jesus taught, the lower animal life and all possessions should, if need were, be sacrificed.

By the interest He took in the *depraved*, Jesus still further accentuated His doctrine as to the value of human nature. "Honest poverty" has a certain worth appreciable even by those who set their hearts on possessions. But what shall be said of humanity stripped not only of outward goods but even of character? That it is still humanity, replied the "friend of publicans and sinners," with latent spiritual powers capable of development, with the solemn responsibilities of moral agents, with features of the divine image not yet wholly effaced

[1] Matt. xvi. 26.

and that may be restored. He did not deny the degradation, or utter sentimental apologies for the sin; but He did deny the irrecoverableness. He hoped for those of whom the world despaired, the world of culture as represented by philosophers like Aristotle and Celsus; the world of sanctity as represented by contemporary Pharisees. And because He hoped, He laboured, seeking as a physican to heal sick souls, as a shepherd to recover straying sheep.

Out of this high doctrine of the dignity of human nature springs the doctrine of immortality. That doctrine needed no separate announcement. Man in Christ's teaching is so great a being that he inevitably projects himself into eternity. The present world cannot hold him. The anthropology of Jesus also contains the germs of all manner of social improvements in the earthly life of man. It has been alleged, indeed, that by its otherworldliness Christ's teaching breeds indifference to temporal interests. "The aim of Christianity," remarks Renan, "was in no respect the perfecting of human society, or the increase of the sum of individual happiness. Men try to make themselves as comfortable as possible when they take in earnest the earth and the days they are to spend on it. But when one is told that the earth is about to pass away, that this life is but a brief probation, the insignificant prelude of an eternal ideal, to what good embellish it? One does not think of decorating the hovel in which he is to remain only for a moment."[1] But connect the doctrine of the life to come with its proper root, man's dignity as possessor of

[1] *Marc Aurèle*, p. 605.

personality and filially related to God, and there is no risk of the present life being overlooked. Man's dignity holds true in reference to both worlds, and must be respected in all relations. Each man must treat himself now as becomes a man, and must be so treated by his fellow-man. *Noblesse oblige.* The "children of the resurrection" must conduct themselves as becomes the heirs of a great destiny. It is therefore to be expected that, except when under the influence of morbid moods such as manifest themselves occasionally in all religions, believers in a future life will be as mindful of present human interests, physical and social, as the adherents of the modern religion of humanity, in which the divine Father and the heavenly home are discarded, and only earth and man retained. It does seem indeed as if a creed which says, "This life is all, therefore make the most of it," ought to make the most of it. But there is no small risk under this new creed of men growing weary in well-doing, through deadly doubt as to the worth of human life. While one generation says, "This life is all, let us make the most of it for ourselves and others," the next may go on to say, "This life is all, therefore it does not much matter how it is spent. Misery, vice, injustice—society is full of them; but no matter, it will all soon end for any individual victim."

The tendency of Christ's doctrine of man to make for social improvement is apt to be overlooked because of the indirectness of its method of working. The method of Christianity is to work by idealism, not by agitation; as a regenerative influence, not as a movement of reform. It does not say slavery is wrong, and follow up the assertion by an agitation for abolition and by stirring up servile insurrection. It says: "A slave is a man, and may be a noble man," and leaves the idea to work as a leaven slowly but surely towards emancipation and freedom. To ardent reformers the method may appear slow, and those who use it chargeable with apathy. On this very account the Baptist doubted the Messiahship of Jesus. Jesus was in no hurry to renovate the world. He let it go on in its bad way, and meantime did all the good He could. To the fiery reformer, the slow, indirect method of the Regenerator seemed most unsatisfactory. Nevertheless the slow method turned out in the long-run to be the surest.

To value human nature in its ideal is one thing, to take flattering views of its real state as seen in the average man is another. Jesus did the former; He did not do the latter. The interest He took in the poor, the suffering, the depraved, was not sentimental. These classes were not pets of whose condition He took an indulgent, partial view, deeming the poor the victims of wrong, and the sinful good-hearted, though weak-willed people. He was under no illusion as to the average moral condition of mankind. He saw clearly that few realized their moral responsibilities, and conducted themselves as became sons of the Father in heaven; and He spake as one well aware of the fact. He compared men as He found them to wandering sheep, lost coins, prodigal sons:[1] expressions certainly implying grave departure from the requirements of the moral ideal. It is therefore a serious mistake to suppose that Christ's view of human

[1] Luke xv.

nature in its actual condition was, to use a theological term, Pelagian. Baur puts a strained meaning on certain of His words, when he says that, according to the teaching of the parable of the sower, it lies with man himself to come into the kingdom of God, in his own will, his own natural capacity and receptivity.[1] A similar false impression, formed from stray utterances, seems to have dictated the remark made by Mr. Mill in his *Essays on Religion:* "According to the creed of most denominations of Christians (though assuredly not of Christ), man is by nature wicked."[2] Christ's authority might be cited for much that is said in the creeds on the subject of human depravity. He saw in human lives all around Him the evidence of sin's corrupting, deadening, enslaving power.

Yet it must be admitted, on the other hand, that Christ's way of speaking concerning human depravity was in important respects unlike that of scholastic theology. The way of this theology is to take all Bible terms as used with scientific strictness, and thereon to build the edifice of dogma; forgetful that the Bible to a large extent is literature, not dogma, and that its words are fluid and poetic, not fixed and prosaic. Thus the natural man is held to be "dead" as a stone is dead. Christ's view was more sympathetic, hopeful, and kindly. He saw in the sinful something more than death, depravity, and bondage—some spark of vitality, some latent affinity for good, an imprisoned spirit longing to be free, a true self victimized by Satanic agency, that would fain escape from thrall. On this better element

---

[1] *Geschichte der Christlichen Kirche*, i. 34.
[2] *Three Essays on Religion*, p. 10.

He ever kept his eye; His constant effort was to get into contact with it, and He refused to despair of success. Most significant in this connection are the words in which He compared the multitude, whose spiritual destitution moved His compassion, to an abundant harvest waiting to be reaped.[1] The comparison implies not only urgency, but *susceptibility*. The grain is ready to be reaped. The people are ready to receive any one who comes to them in God's name with a veritable gospel on his lips, and an honest human love in his heart; the evidence being the way they crowded around Jesus Himself. A recent writer on the life of Jesus remarks that the words are parabolic, and that the term harvest was not applicable to the spiritual sphere; in that region it was seed-sowing, not harvest-work, that was in request.[2] This is simply a superficial explaining away of the words. The very point of interest in the saying is that Jesus does mean to say there is an abundant harvest waiting to be reaped among the masses. Doubtless it was a harvest not visible to the professional religious guides of Israel, any more than to modern commentators. What was apparent to them was merely the ignorance, the vice, the sordid misery of the million; not a harvest, but a heap of rotting weeds exciting aversion. The harvest existed only for the eye of a faith whose vision was sharpened by love. Therein precisely lay the difference between Jesus and the Rabbis. Where they saw only useless noxious rubbish, He, with His loving, hopeful spirit, saw useful grain; not mere sin, but possibilities of good; not utter hopeless depravity, but

[1] Matt. ix. 37.   [2] Weiss, *Leben Jesu*, ii. 119.

indefinite capabilities of sanctity. There an extensive harvest for the kingdom might be reaped, in conversions of profligates into devotees, of moral outcasts into exemplary citizens, of ignorant men into attached disciples. No wonder the religious guides of Israel misunderstood the sinner's Friend! How could they fail to misunderstand the conduct of a man whose thoughts of the people they heartlessly abandoned to the fate of an untended flock were so generous and hopeful? It was so much easier to call Him a bad man than to comprehend a love in which they had no share!

Sympathy and hope were expressed in the very terms which Jesus employed to describe the moral degeneracy of those whose good He sought. The remark specially applies to the term "lost" so often used by Him with that view. It is a word expressive of compassion rather than of judicial severity. It points to a condition falling far short of final irretrievable perdition. To express that state the middle voice of the verb ἀπόλλυμι is sometimes used;[1] but the neuter participle τὸ ἀπολωλός, applied by Jesus to the objects of His loving care, denotes rather a condition of peril like that of a straying sheep, or of waste like that of a lost coin, or of thoughtlessness ending in misery like that of a wayward youth. The lost ones have wandered unwittingly from the fold; they are living in forgetfulness of the chief end of man; they are children of passion, obeying fitful impulse, and impatient of moral restraints. But they are lost *sheep* that may be brought back to the fold; they are lost *coins* possessing value if only they could be found; they are

[1] *Vid.* John iii. 16.

lost *sons of God*, with filial memories and filial feelings buried in their hearts which will rise to the surface when want and woe have brought them to their senses.

In the story of Zacchæus [1] the epithet seems to express a relation to society rather than a moral condition. As applied to the chief publican, it describes the state of one who is a victim of social ostracism. There is nothing in the narrative to show that he was a bad man. They called him a "sinner," but that was due to popular prejudice. He was a publican, and rich; and no further evidence of guilt was needed. What he states concerning himself is very much to his credit. For one occupying the position of a tax-gatherer to give half of his goods to the poor, and to restore fourfold what he may have taken from others in excess, argues no ordinary virtue. It has indeed been supposed that Zacchæus spoke of what he meant to do in future, rather than of what he had been in the habit of doing. But he spoke in self-defence against evil insinuations, and his words would carry weight only if they not merely expressed purposes formed under a sudden impulse, but stated actual undeniable facts. That they did so is a natural inference from his eager desire to see Jesus. Evidently his remarkable behaviour springs from something deeper than curiosity. He has a history which explains the interest he feels in the Man who has the courage to be the publican's friend. He sees in Jesus one who does not believe all the evil things said of an unpopular class, and regards it as possible that good may be found even among publicans. Not that he claims to have a faultless

---

[1] Luke xix. 1.

record; he admits that he has sometimes yielded to the strong temptations connected with his calling. But he has repented of the wrong, and has made strenuous efforts to do justly and to love mercy. This man is not a lost sheep in the moral sense; in love of righteousness he is one among a thousand. But he is still a social outcast, and the Son of Man saves him by giving him brotherly recognition, going to be the guest of one whom most shunned as a leper.[1]

Sometimes Jesus used the term "lost" as a synonym for "neglected." So, for example, in the instructions to the disciples in connection with the Galilean mission, in which they were told not to go into the way of the Gentiles, or into any city of the Samaritans, but to go rather to the *lost sheep of the house of Israel*.[2] The mission had its origin in compassion for the multitude, who appeared to the eye of Jesus as a flock of sheep without a shepherd, scattered and faint. The pathetic description implies blame, but blame not of the people but of their professional religious guides, who had neglected their duty and had laid themselves open to the charge brought by the prophet Ezekiel against the shepherds of Israel in his day: "The diseased have ye not strengthened, neither have ye healed that which was sick, neither have ye bound up that which was broken, neither have ye brought again that which was driven away; neither have ye sought that which was lost."[3] Their neglect made the mission necessary. The harvest was great, but the labourers were few. Of professional

---

[1] *Vid.* Sermon on *Zacchæus* by Robertson of Brighton, 1st series.
[2] Matt. x. 5, 6.   [3] Ezek. xxxiv. 4.

religious officials—priests, scribes, rabbis—there was no lack; and if they had been counted, the number of labourers would not have been small. But they had no sincere human sympathy with the people, and therefore Jesus left them out of account as not available for the harvest work; thus by implication pronouncing a very severe censure on them. It was a very significant judgment as coming from Him. On some men's lips such a judgment would not amount to much. It is not unusual for enthusiastic promoters of special movements to ignore all but their own associates, and practically to limit what they call "the Lord's work" to that which is being carried on under their direction. This way of speaking is often the utterance of an offensive egotism, and it is always indicative of weakness. But in Christ were no egotism and vanity such as too often reveal themselves in the character of religious zealots. He was ever ready to recognise work done for the good of men, even when the agents stood in no close relation to Himself. His disciples might wish to reserve a monopoly of casting out devils for such as belonged to their company; but if devils were indeed cast out He was satisfied, it mattered not by whom. "Forbid him not,"[1] He said, with reference to an attempt to establish such a monopoly, so throwing His shield over all whose aims are good, however eccentric their methods. Yet He who spake that tolerant word said also "the labourers are few," so virtually asserting that the whole established machinery for the cure of souls in Israel was useless. It was a just judgment, however severe. The parties animadverted on did

[1] Mark ix. 39.

not even pretend to be labourers in Christ's sense. Their business was to attend to the sacrificial ritual, to copy and comment on the Scriptures, to study and teach the law. Those who neglected the feasts, and were ignorant of the law, they dismissed from their thoughts with a malediction. Reflecting on these false shepherds of Israel and their heartless indifference, we perceive that the prayer Jesus exhorted His disciples to offer up for the increase of labourers cannot have had in view the mere multiplication of persons professionally occupied with religion. It is rather a prayer for increase of the number of men imbued with the Christian spirit of hopeful, helpful love, and might be paraphrased thus: "Father in heaven! pour out on the world the spirit of sympathy. Now that spirit is rare. In this land of Israel it is almost confined to the little company gathered around the Son of Man. We believe that Thou takest pleasure in the moral recovery of the lost, that the fortunes of the poor, the suffering, and the erring are not indifferent to Thee. In this faith we rejoice, by this faith we are impelled to seek those who have strayed, and to do good to all as we have opportunity. Let this inspiring faith, and this enthusiasm of love, prevail more and more, till all men believe in the heavenly Father, and sin and misery have been banished from the earth."

The prayer, thus interpreted as involving a hidden allusion to the prevailing inhumanity of those who passed for good, implies a new idea of holiness, and throws light on the nature and extent of human depravity. "True holiness," it virtually teaches, "consists in love. Negative holiness, which carefully keeps aloof from the unholy, is a counterfeit. Selfishness is the root of sin; and it reaches the lowest degree of turpitude when it is associated with religion. To be religious without love is to be at the farthest possible distance from God and true righteousness. Therefore the shepherds of Israel who pride themselves on their virtue and sanctity, and despise the sensual irreligious multitude, are more truly lost than the sheep they neglect, by reason of that very neglect."

Tested by the law of love, all men come grievously short. The term "lost" embraces the whole human race. All have gone astray, each one in his own way and in his own measure. Selfishness is universal, and men are so accustomed to it that it hardly appears to them evil. How different was the view of Christ! In one of His most striking parables a rich man is sent, at his death, to the place of torment for no other apparent reason than because he lived in this world a selfish life, enjoying his comforts and heedless of the misery of his fellow-mortals.[1] The epithet $\pi o\nu\eta\rho\acute{o}s$ in another part of His teaching is applied to the average earthly father viewed simply as one who falls short of the divine standard of charity, and allows a certain measure of selfishness to enter into his dealings with his children.[2] ‘Ο $\pi o\nu\eta\rho\acute{o}s$ was His name for the Evil One, Satan;[3] yet He deemed it not too strong a term to apply to men who, while incapable of diabolic wickedness such as giving their children a stone for bread, are not always proof against the temptation to sacrifice their children's interests to their own pleasures. Nothing could more clearly show

---

[1] Luke xvi. 19.   [2] Luke xi. 13.
[3] Matt. xiii. 19, 29.

how serious was the view Jesus took of human depravity, than the application of so strong a term to a form of selfishness not uncommon.

The fact that Jesus, while acknowledging that His mission was to the whole of Israel, yet addressed Himself specially to the humbler classes, points to a policy deliberately adopted for definite reasons. These reasons were chiefly two: belief in the greater receptivity of those classes to the blessings of the kingdom, and expectation of intenser devotion to its interests. Jesus took into account the tendency of wealth, happiness, and moral respectability to hide from their possessors their true character, to fill them with self-complacent thoughts, and to make them indifferent or contemptuous towards the grace of God. Therefore He turned to those who were exposed to no such temptations, in hope to find among them less pride, prejudice, self-delusion, more insight into the truth of things, a deeper sense of the need of pardon, a hunger of the soul for righteousness worthy of the name. That such considerations influenced Him, we learn from certain of His sayings. In explaining the parable of the Sower, He mentioned the deceitfulness of riches as one of the hindrances to fruitfulness.[1] After His interview with the young ruler who inquired concerning eternal life, He sadly remarked, "How hardly shall they that have riches enter into the kingdom of God!"[2] He meant to express a similar feeling in reference to the "righteous" when He said, "I came not to call the righteous, but sinners." On His defence for the crime of consorting with those whom the exemplary shunned, He thereby intimated to

[1] Matt. xiii. 22.   [2] Mark x. 23.

His accusers that He called "sinners" because they were more ready than the righteous to acknowledge their faults, and to welcome the good news of God's pardoning love.

That Jesus also called the sinful because He expected converts from that class to make the best citizens, we learn from the parable of the *Two Debtors* viewed in connection with its historical setting.[1] On that occasion, also, He was on His defence for His sympathetic relations with social reprobates, and the gist of His apology was—the greater the forgiveness, the greater the love, and therefore the better the citizen, the test of good citizenship being devotion. "Which of them will love him most?" He asked; and his host, on principles of common sense, could only reply: "I suppose that he to whom he forgave most." Then said He in effect: "That is why I have relations with such as this woman. I seek such as will love me, not with cold civility as you have done, but ardently after the manner of this penitent. Such I find not among the 'righteous,' but among the 'sinners.'"

This policy of Jesus, to be fully understood and appreciated, must be looked at in connection with the peculiar religious condition of Jewish society in His time. Viewed in the abstract, and conceived of as applicable indiscriminately to all communities, it may appear well intended, but mistaken. One may not unnaturally ask, "Is it to be inferred that had Christ lived in our day and country, He would have expected to find the best disciples among what we are accustomed, from the ecclesiastical point of view, to call the 'lapsed masses,' composed largely of persons who, without any breach

[1] Luke vii. 36-50.

of charity, may be described as weeds? That they should not be neglected is of course right; that converts may be, and have been made among them, even in large numbers, cannot be denied; that a few very exceptional Christians, like Bunyan, have come from their ranks is cheerfully admitted; but surely the action of Jesus does not imply that it is the duty of the Church deliberately to turn its attention to that part of society as the most hopeful field?" I do not care to answer these questions too confidently in the negative, lest the judgment should be but the superficial verdict of Pharisaism in a modern guise. I certainly believe that there are many more unpolished diamonds hidden in the churchless mass of humanity than the respectable church-going part of the community has any idea of. I am even disposed to think that a great and steadily increasing portion of the moral worth of society lies outside the Church, separated from it not by godlessness, but rather by exceptionally intense moral earnestness. Many, in fact, have left the Church in order to be Christians. I also believe in an indefinite power of moral reaction even in the most depraved, though it is unhappily only too rarely exemplified. Christ has taught us to hope for wells of water springing up unto everlasting life from below the rocky surface of inveterate evil habits. Yet, withal, there is a wide difference between Britain in the nineteenth century and Judæa in our Lord's day. In the professedly religious portion of society there is more of the salt of real righteousness, and in the outer fringe of the churchless probably less susceptibility to good influence. The strictly religious Jews in Christ's time were a comparatively small coterie. Their righteousness was, moreover, as we shall see, a thoroughly artificial system, too elaborate and too unreasonable for ordinary mortals to practise. The Pharisees stood in a relation to the populace somewhat similar to that of the monks in the Middle Ages to the laity. To the esoteric brotherhood, in both cases, the world without appeared very unholy. And there was, in truth, much licentiousness among the uninitated; for an artificial system of morals is ever very demoralizing, not only among those who accept it as their rule of life, but among those also who refuse to be bound by it. The latter deeming themselves fully justified in disregarding its arbitrary requirements, do not stop there, but indulge in indiscriminate transgression. But the Jewish populace who knew not nor kept the precepts of the scribes, *Am Haarez*, "the people of the land," as they were contemptuously called, were by no means so bad as their self-righteous censors accounted them.[1] Among them probably were many who were not Pharisees, mainly because they were comparatively simple and unsophisticated, who were therefore not the worse but the better men because they had remained inaccessible to Pharisaic influences. Such might be open to influence of a truly wholesome kind like that which Jesus brought to bear on the "lost," and might supply the raw material

[1] According to the tradition of the scribes, the *Am Haarez*, like the Samaritan, was a person with whom no dealings should be had. They said: "Bear no witness for him, take none from him, reveal to him no secret, entrust nothing to his charge, make him not treasurer of monies for the poor, associate not with him on a journey." He was excluded from sharing in the resurrection. *Vid.* Weber, *System der altsynagogalen Palästinischen Theologie*, p. 43.

out of which could be formed excellent citizens of the divine commonwealth. It was with this conviction that He devoted so much of His time and attention to them. His example is fitted to inspire a most hopeful view of the redeemableness of mankind. Apart altogether from His teaching, His public action is itself a gospel of hope, rebuking cynical despairing views of human depravity, saying to us: "Give up no man as irrecoverably lost," reminding us that much spiritual susceptibility may slumber in most unexpected quarters, and bidding us look for the most aggravated types of moral degeneracy from the divine ideal of manhood, not among the irreligious, but among the inhumanly religious.

CHAPTER VI.

THE RELATION OF JESUS TO MESSIANIC HOPES AND FUNCTIONS.

Not less important than the question as to the attitude of Jesus towards the Mosaic Law, is the inquiry in what relation He stood to the Messianic hopes current among the Jewish people in His time. The inquiry has two aspects, one referring to the extent of our Lord's sympathy with prevailing Messianic ideas, the other to His claim to be the Messiah. The two topics are closely related, but they may, to a certain extent, be looked at apart. Even if Jesus had not claimed to be the Christ, He would still have had to adjust Himself to a conception shared by nearly the whole of His countrymen, based on Hebrew prophecy, and received as a sacred inheritance from the Fathers.

A priori it was to be expected that Jesus would have His Messianic idea. For the ideas of a Messiah and a kingdom of God were kindred, and one who made the latter theme the burden of his preaching could not fail to have a Messianic theory and belief. The two subjects were closely associated, not only in Hebrew prophecy, but in the nature of things.

What, then, was the position taken up by the Herald of the kingdom on this burning question? The opinion of Dr. Baur on the point is well known. In his view, the Messianic idea had no vitality for Jesus. The prophet of Nazareth was a purely ethical teacher, who would gladly have ignored a hope with which at heart He had no sympathy, and which He knew to be a delusion. But being a Jew, He was obliged to recognise the national expectation, however distasteful to His own feelings, and speak as if He regarded it as important; nay, He was compelled reluctantly to let Himself be taken for the Messiah, as the indispensable condition of success on Jewish soil in an attempt to introduce a new universal religion.

The truth of this view must be acknowledged to the extent of admitting that there was much in the conventional Messianic idea with which Jesus was not in accord. His habitual reticence regarding His own claims to be the Christ is sufficient evidence of the fact. That reticence might be adduced as a proof that His conception of the kingdom was peculiar; for King and kingdom correspond, and divergent thoughts as to the nature of the one imply an analogous divergence in reference to the other. It shows that Christ's idea of the kingdom must have been different even from that of the Baptist; for the preacher of repentance practised no reserve on the subject, but spoke openly of a Coming One whose shoe-latchet he was not worthy to unloose. But the point insisted on now is the significance of that reticence as an index of Christ's position in reference to the Messianic hope. It betrayed a consciousness that His thoughts thereon were not those of the Jewish people, giving rise to a natural unwillingness to say much on a subject on which it was difficult to speak without being misunderstood. It did not, however, imply, as Baur imagined, that Jesus had no Messianic convictions, but merely adapted Himself prudentially to those of others. It is not credible that He would be guilty of such insincerity, any more than that such a policy, if adopted, could be successful. Had the Messianic idea in every form been void of all validity for His mind, He would certainly have discarded it and taken the consequences. For the sincere man, religious beliefs current in his time, which he cannot accept, must either be rejected or transformed. The Messianic faith of Israel could not be absolutely rejected, because it contained elements of truth, and therefore the only possible alternative was transformation. Christ's position in reference to it can be partly understood through our own in reference to an idea of vital significance in Christian piety. It is essential to a religion bearing Christ's name that it be *evangelic*, for that is only to say that it must conform to the teaching and spirit of our Lord as exhibited in the Gospels. Yet the term has been so often associated with a legal spirit in theology and life, that one earnestly minded to follow the Master feels the need either of a new word or of a very discriminating use of the old one. Even so was it with the Master Himself in regard to the Jewish hope of a Messiah. The word expressed a faith in a bright future for the world, which no one not given over to atheistic pessimism would consent to part with. Nevertheless, in current use it was so mixed up with idle dreams, ambitious passions, false opinions, and sham sanctities, that one wishing to hold fast his belief in the divine reality was under the necessity of breaking with tradition, and rediscovering the truth for himself; and having found it, of uttering his thoughts concerning it, as one conscious of isolation.

We may conceive of Jesus as going forth to His public ministry with transformed ideas both of the Messianic office and of the Messianic kingdom. His spiritual nature determined the form of the Messianic idea, gathering up as by elective affinity the congenial elements of Old Testament prophecy. Ample materials for such a transformation were to be found in texts which suggested the notion of a gentle, missionary, suffering Messiah gaining power by meekness, by His wisdom giving light to the world, bearing the sins and miseries of men by sympathy as a burden on His heart. The first evangelist, who has taken pains to illustrate his narrative by prophetic citations, quotes some of these texts, giving prominence to that which describes the Messiah as one who shall not strive nor cry, and who also shall not break the bruised reed or quench the smoking flax.[1] The oracle is introduced in connection with directions given by Jesus to the sick people whom He healed, that they should not make Him known. This retiring habit in one possessing such powers seemed to the evangelist very remarkable. And so indeed it was. It was utterly contrary to the spirit of the world, which pursues the policy of self-advertisement and self-assertion with a view to gratify personal ambition, and works by ostentation and

[1] Matt. xii. 18–21. The quotation is from Isa. xlii. 1–4.

conflict; by the one seeking public applause, by the other striving to overcome obstacles. It was this way the brethren of Jesus desired Him to adopt when they counselled Him to go up to Judæa to show His works, reckoning it foolish in one who had it in His power to become celebrated to remain in obscurity.[1] But such counsel, whether given by the god of this world or by its children, Jesus ever declined to follow. He would not strive, but when His acts or words provoked hostility, as in the instance recorded by Matthew before citing the prophetic oracle, He withdrew from the scene. Neither would He cry or lift up His voice in the streets, following the methods of those who hunt after fame; He rather took as much pains to hide His good deeds as others took to make theirs widely known. Yet He was ever willing to do deeds of kindness; when suffering multitudes gathered around Him in season or out of season, He healed them all. His was a spirit of gentleness, humility, and sympathy: of gentleness towards opponents, of humility in shunning vainglorious display, of sympathy shown in pity for the sick and in patience with spiritual weakness. Such were the attributes of Jesus. Such were the attributes of the Servant of Jehovah, as described by the prophet, which made Him God's well-beloved and elect One, and proved that God's Spirit was in Him. The evangelist was struck with the correspondence; and with true insight discerned in the character of Jesus, as revealed in His actions, the fulfilment of the oracle. We cannot doubt that the significance of the prophetic utterance was as apparent to Jesus Himself as to His disciple,

[1] John vii. 3, 4.

and that it was one of the ancient texts from which He drew His idea of the Messiah.

In a Messiah of the type therein sketched Jesus could earnestly believe. No other type of Messiah could have any attractions for Him: not the political Messiah of the Zealots, whose one desire was national independence; not the Messiah of common expectation, who should flatter popular prejudices and make himself an idol by becoming a slave; not the Messiah of the Pharisees, himself a Pharisee, regarding it as his vocation to deliver Israel from Pagan impurity;[1] not even the austere Messiah of the Baptist, who was to separate the good from the evil by a process of judicial severity, and so usher in a kingdom of righteousness. The Messiah devoutly to be longed for, and cordially to be welcomed when He came, in His view, was one who should conquer by the might of love and truth; who should meet the deepest wants of man, not merely gratify the wishes of Jews, and prove a light and a saviour to the whole world; who should be conspicuous by patience and hopefulness rather than by inexorable sternness,—a humane, universal, spiritual Messiah, answering to a divine kingdom of kindred character,—the desire of all nations, the fulfilment of humanity's deepest longings, therefore not destined to be superseded, but to remain an Eternal Christ, the same yesterday, to-day, and for ever.

[1] Montet (*Essai sur les Origines des Partis Saducéen et Pharisien*, p. 247) remarks of the Messiah described in the Psalterium Salomonis, which was purely Pharisaic in spirit: "We are tempted to say that he (Messiah) is a separatist Pharisaic king, who will deliver Israel from Pagan uncleanness." The remark rests on the words: ῥύσεται ἡμᾶς ἀπὸ ἀκαθαρσίας ἐχθρῶν βεβήλων (xvii. 51).

Such a Messiah Jesus not merely believed in, but claimed Himself to be. The claim finds expression in many of His recorded words, and underlies the whole evangelic history from beginning to end. It is implied in the announcement of the kingdom as *present*. It is implied also in the titles Son of Man and Son of God, which, as we shall see, sprang out of a Messianic consciousness. It is indirectly asserted in such sayings as these: "I say unto you, that in this place is One greater than the temple;"[1] "Behold, a greater than Jonas is here;"[2] "Behold, a greater than Solomon is here."[3] It lurks in the title "Bridegroom"[4] applied by Jesus to Himself, a title applied by the prophets to Jehovah in relation to the covenant people, and teaching that in Him to whom it is given the soul finds its Lord and the fulness of spiritual bliss. It was involved in the tacit acceptance by Jesus of the epithet "the Coming One" employed by the Baptist in his doubting message to describe the Christ.[5] It found utterance in the prophetic discourse on the παρουσία in the solemn declaration, "Heaven and earth shall pass away, but My words shall not pass away."[6] Specially significant is the text in which, after condemning the Pharisaic lust for titles of honour, Jesus gives His disciples the counsel: "Be not ye called Rabbi, for one is your Master, and all ye are brethren."[7] There can be no doubt who the διδάσκαλος is: the word finds its interpretation in the

---

[1] Matt. xii. 6.
[2] Matt. xii. 41.
[3] Matt. xii. 42.
[4] Matt. ix. 15.
[5] Matt. xi. 3.
[6] Matt. xxiv. 35.
[7] Matt. xxiii. 8. The words ὁ Χριστός are a gloss.

fact that the Speaker stood in the relation of Master to His hearers. This claim to be the one Master, taken in connection with the condemnation of pretensions to Mastership, can escape the charge of inconsistency only on the supposition that He who makes the claim is conscious of being an exceptional person who without arrogance may say to men: "Learn from Me,"[1] take Me as your supreme teacher and guide in religion. Similar reflections apply to Christ's mode of enforcing lessons of humility by prescribing Himself as an example; as on the occasion when the sons of Zebedee advanced their ambitious request, when He said: "Whosoever will be chief among you, let him be your servant; even as the Son of Man came not to be ministered unto, but to minister."[2] This was spoken out of the consciousness of being the first in the kingdom—king by right, though servant by choice; and the implied claim is accentuated from being uttered in connection with a rebuke of ambitious passions. In one notable instance Jesus asserted His superhuman greatness even in the very act of limiting it, viz. when He declared His ignorance of the last day, saying, "Concerning that day, or that hour, no one knoweth, neither angel in heaven, nor the Son, absolutely no one, save the Father."[3] Nescience is here professed in a manner involving a claim to a very high position in the scale of being, superior to that of angels, subordinate only to that of the Supreme.

Jesus proclaimed Himself to be the Messiah by ascribing to Himself Messianic functions. Thus we find

---

[1] Matt. xi. 29. μάθετε ἀπ' ἐμοῦ.
[2] Matt. xx. 28.   [3] Mark xiii. 32.

Him in many utterances representing Himself as the *Judge* of the world; as in the saying, "The Son of Man is about to come in the glory of His Father, with His angels, and then shall He give to every one according to his works."[1] Baur, while admitting the fact as indisputable, resolves the judicial action of Jesus into a purely ethical process. Jesus judges men by His doctrines, which are the fundamental laws of the divine kingdom, because according to the attitudes they assume towards these, men divide themselves into two morally distinct classes. He judges them by His own person, because He is the concrete embodiment of the absolute worth of His teaching. Baur doubts whether Jesus ever spoke of His judicial function in such terms as those in which He appears promising to the twelve seats of judgment beside Himself in the παλιγγενεσία, discovering in the words an eschatological colouring arising out of gross popular ideas of the coming Messianic kingdom. In the representation of the judgment in Matt. xxv. he finds simply a parabolic embodiment of the judicial power of Christ's doctrine. The good *per se* is personified in Jesus, and men who do the good for its own sake, living loving lives, are represented as unawares doing kind actions to Him. Be it so; what a high claim even this view of Christ's judicial function involves! It implies that Jesus regarded Himself as the moral idea realized.

[1] Matt. xvi. 27. This is a new feature in the conception of Messiah. In pre-Christian Jewish literature the function of judge is not ascribed to the Messiah. Such an ascription does indeed occur in a certain part of the Book of Enoch. But this part is by many scholars regarded as of post-Christian date. *Vide* next chapter.

Jesus advanced His claim to Messiahship in a more genial way by proclaiming Himself to be the *Saviour* of men. This He did under various forms of representation; at one time announcing Himself as the Shepherd of Israel, sent to seek the lost sheep; at another as the Physician of souls, whose vocation it was to heal the spiritually diseased; on other occasions exercising saving power by forgiving sin. The whole ministry of miraculous healing may be regarded as an exhibition of Messianic resources brought into play for the good of men. It was the saving grace of Messiah active in the physical sphere, and giving to His work as Redeemer a comprehensiveness and completeness answering to the requirements of the Messianic ideal. It was meet that there should be a wealth of salvation, a plenteous redemption, in the promised Deliverer, and the presence of these in the ministry of Jesus pointed Him out as the fulfiller of the promise.

Once more, Jesus declared Himself to be the Messiah by claiming to be the *Revealer* of God as Father, as in the memorable words: "No man knoweth the Father, save the Son, and he to whomsoever the Son is pleased to reveal Him."[1] By the solemn affirmation Jesus raised Himself, not only above rabbinical teachers, whose chief function, in effect, if not in intention, was to hide God from men, but even above the prophets, through whom God made a partial, fragmentary, piecemeal revelation of His nature and will. He claimed to be in possession of a full, adequate, absolutely true knowledge of God, for all this is implied in knowing the Father;

[1] Matt. xi. 27.

and He represented Himself as possessing this knowledge in virtue of His relation to God as a Son. The Son knows the Father's heart, and can reveal its inmost thoughts. Jesus offers Himself to the world as one occupying this unique position, the complete final exegete of the Divine Being. He could not advance a more imposing claim, neither could He offer Himself as a Messiah in a more acceptable form. A Messiah who can reveal God must ever be welcome, for the knowledge of God is man's supreme need. A Christ who tells us of a Divine Father will never go out of fashion or be superseded; for "to-day, to-morrow, and for ever, we can know nothing better than that God is our Father, and that the Father is the rest of our souls."[1] This is a Christ for all the world, as well as for all time, a universal human Messiah, in whom all the nations gladly put their trust.

Jesus asserted His Messiahship in yet another way, viz. by demanding or accepting Messianic honours. Meek, humble in spirit, He nevertheless ever assumed the position of Lord. "Follow Me" was the word of command He addressed to those whom He desired to become disciples, at the very commencement of His public ministry.[2] And the conditions of service He imposed on His followers were very exacting. He required them to leave all for His sake,—dearest friends, most valued possessions; such as shrank from the sacrifice He deemed unworthy of the name of a disciple. He put Himself on a level with the kingdom; whatever men were required to do out of regard to its interests,

[1] Keim, *Geschichte Jesu von Nazara*, ii. 385.   [2] Mark i. 27.

they must be ready to do for Him. "For the kingdom's sake," and "for My sake," He treated as expressions of equal value. In other words, He claimed to be the Messianic King: not merely the Herald of the kingdom, but its highest personage.

That Jesus habitually, and from the first, regarded Himself as the Messiah, is thus beyond all reasonable doubt. How did He arrive at this view of His vocation; what was the genesis of His Messianic consciousness? No answer to the question can be accepted which does not respect the humility of Jesus. He certainly did not elect Himself to this high career. "No man taketh this honour unto himself, but he that is called of God;"[1] no man such as Jesus of Nazareth, absolutely free from self-seeking and ambitious passions. It is not credible that He set Himself to invent a new idea of Messiah, combining in one the gentle and warlike elements in prophetic representations, and then going forth to try by experiment how the new scheme of a Messiah conquering by patience would work.[2] He entered on His Messianic vocation simply as one obeying a divine summons.[3] How the call was communicated we can only conjecture. We may think of the secret of His birth revealed to Him by His parents, of His Davidic

---

[1] Heb. v. 4.

[2] So in effect Mr. Arnold. *Vid. Literature and Dogma*, p. 96.

[3] This must ever be borne in mind when we speak of Christ's *claim* to be Messiah, a word which readily suggests the idea of ambitious pretensions. On this point it has been well remarked by a recent writer: "It is not a question of the claims of Jesus and their validity. The question which presented itself to Him was whether He could righteously withdraw from the clearly discerned will

descent, of His significant name Jesus, as suggesting the thought that God had appointed Him to a unique career. But these alone would hardly suffice to give the necessary assurance. Probably the chief guidance came from within, from the spiritual endowments wherewith the soul of Jesus was richly furnished. In this connection stress has been laid on His perfect holiness. In that sinless life the kingdom of God as a kingdom of righteousness was realized in germ. The kingdom which had been long looked for was at length come in the person of the Holy One, and He Himself must be the Messiah.[1] Doubtless moral purity was one source of the Messianic consciousness. But one shrinks from the thought of Jesus arriving by reflection on His own personal holiness at the conclusion that He was the Messiah. It gives to His Messianic consciousness an aspect of self-righteousness. The inference from the spotless life to the Messianic vocation is just, but it seems one more appropriate for us to draw than for Jesus. I prefer therefore to look in the direction of the deep intense human sympathies with which the heart of Jesus was filled. Love is the fulfilling of the law, and the destined Messiah was conscious of His sinlessness in the form of a consuming passion of filial love to His Father, and of

---

of God. His coming forth as Messiah was not usurpation, but obedience; not free choice, but inevitable divine necessity." Baldensperger, *Das Selbstbewusstsein Jesu im Lichte der Messianischen Hoffnungen seiner Zeit*, 1888, vid. S. 191. In his account of the development of the Messianic consciousness of Jesus, Baldensperger lays stress, as is done in the text, on His intense sympathy with His oppressed brethren and fellow-countrymen.

[1] So Weiss, *Das Leben Jesu*, i. 290.

compassionate love for men. And it was under the impulse of that mighty love that He went forth to do His work, scarce daring to think Himself the Christ, yet knowing full well that the work to which His love impelled Him was just the work Messiah had to do. Through that love His Father seemed to say to Him, Go forth to heal the world's woes, and He loyally obeyed the call, walking by faith, and expecting confirmations that He had rightly interpreted the divine will.

This view is in accordance with the account given by Luke of our Lord's appearance in the synagogue of Nazareth.[1] The text on which He discoursed there represents Messiah's outfit as consisting in an abundant anointing with the Spirit of love. If the text was given to His hand in the lesson of the day, He accepted it as a most congenial one wherefrom to discourse on the Messianic vocation. A sceptical criticism may indeed doubt whether any reference was made by Jesus to the prophetic oracle quoted by the third evangelist, tracing its presence in the Gospel to the Pauline bias of the writer leading him to select it as a motto. The scepticism is excessive, for even Mark's narrative implies that a very remarkable discourse had been delivered by Jesus to His fellow-townsmen;[2] but even granting it to be well founded, one can only say that Luke has shown excellent judgment in the selection of his motto. No Old Testament text could more felicitously interpret the Messianic consciousness of Jesus, or more faithfully express the general drift of His ministry. This assertion

[1] Luke iv. 14-20. [2] Mark vi. 2.

rests on His own testimony, as contained in the well-authenticated account He gave of His own work in His reply to the doubting message of the Baptist. "Art Thou He that should come, or do we look for another?" asked John. What was the answer of Jesus? "Go and show John again those things which ye do hear and see. The blind receive their sight, and the lame walk, the lepers are cleansed, and the deaf hear, the dead are raised up, and the poor have the gospel preached to them."[1] He expected the report of such events, duly weighed, to solve John's doubts. It is reasonable to assume that what He regarded as good evidence for John He had found helpful to Himself. The love out of which the healing miracles and the evangelizing of the poor had flowed had been to Him the token of His Messianic vocation.

There is no indication in the records that Jesus was ever visited by doubts concerning His Messiahship, such as those which distracted the mind of the Baptist. His path as the Christ appears ever to have been illumined by the light of faith. Nevertheless it was a path of faith, of a faith subject to trial, and standing in need of confirmation. The whole life of Jesus is represented in the New Testament as a walking by faith wherein He is our example, and it could not be appropriately so characterized if so momentous a matter as His Messianic consciousness were exempted from faith's scope. The experiences of His ministry supplied material for severe trials of His faith in reference thereto. There were temptations to entertain false views of Messiah's office,

[1] Matt. xi. 4.

arising out of the popular enthusiasm awakened by His words and deeds; temptations to distrust His own true conception, arising out of the antagonism of the wise and religious, and the sincere doubt of such a man as John; temptations springing from the prospect of a tragic end to regard His whole career as a gigantic mistake and failure. These temptations were successfully resisted, but not without moral effort. The Messianic consciousness advanced onwards from the morning twilight to the perfect day; but it remained unclouded through strenuous use of aids to faith. The chief aid was habitual close fellowship with the Father in heaven. In the healing miracles, wrought in a spirit of dependence, and "by the finger of God,"[1] the Worker had sensible evidence that "God was with Him,"[2] and was owning Him as the Christ. Special aids were not wanting at critical periods. The incidents connected with the baptism supplied one at the commencement. The voice from heaven, however viewed, points to confirmation needed and given to the purpose already formed to enter on a Messianic career. Jesus came to the Jordan thinking of Himself as the well-beloved elect One of Messianic prophecy,[3] and after His baptism He felt assured that in this He was not mistaken. The temptation in the wilderness immediately following supplied

---

[1] Luke xi. 20. Matthew's expression (xii. 28) is "by the Spirit of God." On the two expressions, *vide Introduction*, p. 17.

[2] Acts x. 39.

[3] The voice from heaven at the Jordan, repeated at the Transfiguration, is an echo of Isa. xlii. 1, cf. Matt. xii. 18. This points to that prophetic passage as an important factor in the formation of Christ's Messianic idea.

another important aid. Whatever conception we form of that mysterious experience, we must hold that it involved at least a mental process through which Jesus gained a clear view of the true vocation of Messiah as opposed to the false. He left the wilderness understanding well that the genuine Christ of God could not be a self-pleaser either in spirit or in lot.

The connected scenes at Cæsarea Philippi and on the Mount of Transfiguration had an important bearing on the self-consciousness of Christ. At that late time it was becoming increasingly apparent that the career of the Prophet of Nazareth was to terminate tragically. Judged by the vulgar test of success, it might already be pronounced a failure, and looking forward ignominy and death seemed probable. Could He be the Christ who had such a prospect before Him? The question, it cannot be doubted, exercised much the thoughts of Jesus in those days. From the outset He understood that sorrow awaited Him; but when the cross stared Him in the face, it needed a firm grasp of truth to enable Him to meet His fate calmly. It was a time demanding earnest meditation and prayer. Through these Jesus arrived at a clear conviction that the cross, instead of being a sign of mistake or failure, was the inevitable goal for all who were loyal to the kingdom and to righteousness, and in a superlative degree for the Messianic King. This view had full possession of His mind when He made His Messiahship a subject of conversation with His disciples at Cæsarea Philippi. He therefore took that step, not so much with a view to confirmation of His own faith, as to confirm the faith of His companions.

He desired to elicit from them a confession of His Messianic claims before speaking to them of His approaching sufferings. Yet we cannot doubt that He found comfort in the hearty, unhesitating response of Peter speaking in the name of all. As at a former time the attachment of the " babes " was a solace to His heart in presence of the unbelief of the wise and understanding, so now the earnest faith of the twelve consoled Him under the prospect of unbelief speedily ripening into deadly hatred. In view of that faith He felt sure of the future, whatever might happen. Out of it would spring a Church strong as the gates of Hades.

In the Transfiguration scene Jesus received a second consolation, made necessary by the failure of the disciples to comprehend the law of the cross. He obtained the assurance that by willingness to become a sacrifice He gained the approval of His heavenly Father, With this faith He went cheerfully on His way with His face stedfastly set towards Jerusalem, finding in the certainty of death the most convincing evidence that He was indeed the Lord's Anointed. Henceforth unwavering confidence might go hand in hand with deepest lowliness. I said that no explanation of the Christ-consciousness of Jesus could be accepted which did not respect His humility. For this reason I hesitated to regard the sense of sinlessness as the origin of that consciousness, and preferred to find it in the Messianic charism of love. Impelled by love, Jesus could wear His honour meekly. Still more effectually was His meekness guarded when the Messianic vocation was associated with the spirit of self-sacrifice. Then Messiahship appeared not as an honour, but as a service, and as a service involving humiliation and pain. "No man taketh this honour unto himself," writes the author of the Epistle to the Hebrews, with reference to the priestly office. Ambition might seize the position when priest and sacrificial victim were distinct, as under the Levitical system; but there was no fear of that happening when, as in the case of Jesus, priest and victim became one. Then the wearer of the sacerdotal robes, instead of proudly arrogating office, rather humbly submitted to be made a priest. Even so was it with the vocation of Messiah. The dignities of a Messiahship honoured by the world's homage vanity might covet, but the office of a suffering Messiah no one would undertake unless his motto were, "Not My will, but Thine be done."

CHAPTER VII.

THE SON OF MAN, AND THE SON OF GOD.

Both these titles were applied by Jesus to Himself, the former the more frequently, and by preference; the latter, though seldom so far as the synoptical record is concerned, on important occasions which invest its use with deep significance. Both sprang out of His Messianic consciousness, and gave expression to it under different aspects. Both marked Him out as in some sense an exceptional man, and tended naturally to provoke the inquiry, Who is this who designates Himself in this unwonted fashion?

With reference to the former of the two titles, *the Son of Man*, the question has been asked, Was it current as a Messianic name among the Jews in our Lord's time? This question is not foreclosed by the statement that the name had Messianic significance for Jesus Himself. It might have a private meaning for Him which it did not bear to the public; it might even conceivably have been employed to serve the purpose of an incognito. On the other hand, there is no antecedent improbability in the supposition that the name had gained currency in the popular religious dialect, as a Messianic title, through the influence of the book of Daniel. That it had actually obtained this position might even be regarded as a probable inference from the use made of it in the apocryphal book of Enoch, assuming—what, however, is much disputed—that the date of that writing, or of the whole of it, is earlier than the Christian era.[1] But that it had not in fact become fully naturalized as a title of the Messiah in the time of our Lord appears from two circumstances. One is that He employed it freely, while practising reserve in regard to His claims to be the Christ. The other is the peculiar form in which Matthew gives the question addressed by Jesus to his disciples at Cæsarea Philippi: "Whom do men say that I, the Son of Man, am?"[2] Even if the original form of the question were that given in Mark, "Whom do men say that I am?"[3] the insertion of the explanatory clause

---

[1] There is little doubt that a part of the book is of pre-Christian origin. The uncertainty as to date concerns chapters 37–71, called the book of Parables or Similitudes, in which the title "Son of Man" is of frequent occurrence, and which is generally regarded as of later date than the rest of the book. Scholars are much divided in opinion as to whether this portion of the book of Enoch came into existence before or after the Christian era. Drummond, in his work on *The Jewish Messiah*, thus expresses his opinion: "I fear we must rest in the conclusion that we cannot rely upon the integrity of the present book of Enoch; that the Messianic passages in the Similitudes are of unknown but probably Christian origin; that therefore we cannot safely appeal to them as evidence of pre-Christian Jewish belief." In a note he states: "This conclusion is accepted, in addition to Hilgenfeld, by Holtzmann, Keim, Oehler, Volkmar, Kuenen, Tideman, Colani. On the other side are Anger, Schenkel, Schürer." Among the most recent writers the same diversity of opinion prevails. Baldensperger claims a pre-Christian date (the Herodian period) for the Similitudes. On the other hand, Stanton (*The Jewish and the Christian Messiah*, 1886) believes them to be post-Christian.

[2] Matt. xvi. 13.   [3] Mark viii. 27.

by the first evangelist is significant, as showing that at the time when his Gospel was written the name "Son of Man" was not regarded as a synonym for Christ. In that case the proper form of the question had been: Whom do men say that I am? do they take me for the Son of Man?

To whatever extent the book of Enoch may have influenced contemporary opinion, it may be taken for granted that Jesus did not simply adopt traditional notions of Jewish theology respecting the Son of Man. He borrowed from the past as Shakespeare borrowed, transmuting traditional data into a new conception bearing the stamp of his own genius. An apocalyptic element is indeed traceable in His use of the designation now under consideration. But in how purified a form does that element appear! What simple dignity characterizes the solemn declaration made before the Sanhedrim: "Hereafter shall ye see the Son of Man sitting on the right hand of power, and coming in the clouds of heaven"![1] Such an utterance stands in the same relation to corresponding passages in the book of Enoch, that the cosmogony of the book of Genesis bears to the Chaldæan myths regarding the creation. But, in truth, it is very questionable if the words of Jesus have any connection whatever with that apocryphal book, and are not rather to be directly affiliated to the oracle concerning the Son of Man in the book of Daniel, whereof the relative parts of the book named after the ancient patriarch are a coarse sensuous expansion. It has even been disputed whether Christ's use of the title had any

[1] Matt. xxvi. 64.

conscious reference to that oracle, and is not rather to be accounted for by some other Old Testament texts in which it occurs. Schleiermacher, *e.g.*, reckoned the derivation of the title from Daniel as an odd fancy, remarking in proof of its untenableness that the prophet does not call the Messianic King the Son of Man, but simply represents Him as *manlike*, in contrast to the kings of the other kingdoms previously mentioned, of whom beasts were the appropriate emblems.[1] The words spoken by Jesus at His trial, however, correspond so closely with those of the prophet as to make it almost certain that He had the latter in His mind, and an echo of them may be recognised in other sayings recorded by the evangelists, in which the same apocalyptic colouring appears.[2] And we can easily imagine how Daniel's prophecy might have its attractions for the mind of Jesus. Specially congenial to His spirit, doubtless, was the description of the Messianic kingdom as one in which humanity was to replace the ferocity characteristic of the great monarchies symbolized by the winged lion, the bear, the leopard, and the beast with ten horns. It was such a kingdom, wherein wisdom and love bore sway, whose advent He proclaimed, and of which He claimed to be King. In adopting the style and title of "the Son of Man," as the Ruler of that kingdom, it was not alone the halo of apocalyptic glory that He had in view; it probably lay nearer His heart to accentuate His human sympathies.

Another possible source of the title is the saying in the Psalter: "What is man that Thou art mindful of

[1] *Christliche Glaube*, ii. 91.   [2] Matt. xvi. 27, xix. 28, xxv. 31.

him, or the son of man that Thou visitest him?"[1] It expresses the humility of the Psalmist by contrasting God's favour to man with man's intrinsic insignificance. It also expresses his sense of the dignity of man as by the grace of God placed at the head of creation, and crowned with glory and honour. If Jesus borrowed the designation from the psalm, we might expect to find in His use of it both of these sentiments reflected. Keim, accordingly, who adopts this view, ascribes to the name the twofold sense—the humble poor man, and the man who in lowliness is highly exalted; to which he adds a third meaning, due to the passage being transformed from a statement about mankind into a Messianic text—the man organically united to humanity.[2] As used by the prophet Ezekiel, the title seems to bear a meaning kindred to that of the Psalmist. It expresses the humility of one who, notwithstanding his intimate relation to God, was ever mindful of his human weakness. But from the simple circumstance of being applied to a prophet, it might become in course of time a name of dignity, denoting the prophetic vocation, and asserting a claim to exercise the highest prophetic functions. Accordingly it has been maintained that the title was actually so used by Jesus, and that some of the most characteristic instances of its use in the Gospels, are cases in which it is associated with the exercise of the higher prophetic rights, such as the forgiving of sin, in connection with the healing of the paralytic, and the claim of lordship over the Sabbath. This usage, it is held, was intended as an education of the disciples for ultimately recognising in their Master

---

[1] Ps. viii. 4. [2] *Jesu von Nazara*, ii. 75.

something more than a prophet like Ezekiel, even the Messiah.[1]

Yet another theory as to the Old Testament origin of the title has been advocated, which for the sake of completeness may here be referred to. It finds the source in the Protevangelium, in which it was promised that the seed of the woman should crush the head of the serpent, and which led Eve on the birth of her first-born son to exclaim, "I have gotten a man from the Lord!" On this view, Jesus, by calling Himself Son of Man, claimed to be the promised seed of the woman, the man from the Lord, the Son of Adam by whom the race of Adam was to be redeemed, the title being thus made to have reference not merely to the person, but more particularly to the work of Christ. The Son of Man is thus "the man to whom the whole history of humanity points as its end, and in whom the hope of humanity is fulfilled."[2]

None of these views can be regarded as established, or at least as exclusively true, and in the midst of uncertainty we must turn to the actual use of the title as recorded in the Gospels, as our best guide to its meaning. And in doing so I am inclined to dismiss at once, as improbable, any explanation which gives to Christ's favourite self-designation a prosaic or dogmatic character. I assume that in this as in all His utterances, He was like Himself, and spake not as a rabbi, or a theological doctor, but as a prophet and poet whose words came from the heart charged with emotion. This principle excludes almost without examination several theories as

---

[1] Weizsäcker, *Untersuchungen*, S. 430.
[2] Hofmann, *Schriftbeweis*, i. 54.

to the significance of the title, such as that of Hofmann above explained, or that which interprets it to mean *the ideal man*, or that which finds in it a hint of Christ's divinity, and would paraphrase it: the man who is more than man, and who therefore needs to say that He is man; and even that of Weizsäcker, according to which it is to be interpreted: the man who is a great prophet, and possibly something still higher. These theories are very ingenious, but they are too far-fetched to commend themselves to approval. A sense which is simple, spontaneous, and natural is much to be preferred.

The texts in which the title occurs admit of being gathered into groups. There is a large group, which readily suggests the thought that the "Son of Man" means for one thing the man of sorrow and acquainted with grief. The typical text of this class is that containing the saying: "The foxes have holes, and the birds of the air have nests, but the Son of Man hath not where to lay His head,"[1] which declares the Speaker to be emphatically an unprivileged man, whatever would-be disciples might imagine. To the same class belongs the saying: "Whosoever speaketh a word against the Son of Man, it shall be forgiven him."[2] This does not mean that the blasphemer of the Son of Man shall with difficulty be forgiven, as if the design were to indicate the limit of forgiveness. It signifies rather that this kind of blasphemy is of course pardonable, as being only an instance of a common offence committed by men against each other through misunderstanding of each other's characters and motives. The Son of Man is not exempt

[1] Matt. viii. 20.   [2] Matt. xii. 32.

from the common lot; He is liable to be misunderstood and maligned like other men, and He accepts that as part of His experience. Blasphemy against the Holy Ghost is another matter altogether. It is to speak against Christ, or against any other servant of God, not under misapprehension, but knowing full well that they are the agents of the Divine Spirit. To this group also belong the texts in which the coming sufferings of the Son of Man are predicted, such as these: "As Jonas was three days and three nights in the whale's belly, so shall also the Son of Man be three days and three nights in the heart of the earth;" "Elias is come already, and they knew him not, but have done unto him whatsoever they listed. Likewise shall also the Son of Man suffer of them;" "The Son of Man shall be betrayed into the hands of men."[1]

As this first group of texts proclaims the Son of Man to be the unprivileged Man, so a second group signalizes Him as the *sympathetic* Man. Of this class we may take as the type: "The Son of Man came eating and drinking,"[2] in which the reference is to the social sympathetic relations into which Jesus entered with the outcasts with a view to their spiritual benefit; with which may be associated, "The Son of Man came to seek and save the lost,"[3] which states the philanthropic aim of Christ's mission, as the other states its method. Under this head also may be included, most legitimately, the two remarkable sayings in which Jesus claimed for the Son of Man power to forgive sins, and lordship over the Sabbath.[4]

[1] Matt. xii. 40, xvii. 12, 23. [2] Matt. xi. 19.
[3] Luke xix. 10. [4] Matt. ix. 6, xii. 8.

The key to the meaning in both cases is the deep human sympathy of Jesus, in virtue of which He can declare with effect the divine forgiving love, and is the best interpreter of the Sabbath law, and the best judge as to the wisest mode of observing it. The claim advanced is in both cases directed against Pharisaic notions. The Pharisees viewed God's relation to sin from the side of His majesty; Jesus, on the contrary, viewed it from the side of His grace. God, He says to His critics, is not such as ye imagine—severe, slow to forgive, and jealous of His prerogative; He is good, and ready to forgive, and has no desire to monopolize the privilege of forgiving. He is willing that it should be exercised by all on earth in whom dwells His own spirit; and My right to forgive rests on this, that I am a sympathetic friend of the sinful, full of the grace and charity of heaven. The Pharisaic view of the Sabbath was kindred to their view of forgiveness. They regarded the institution not as a divine gift for man's benefit, but as a divine exaction; and hence they hedged the weekly rest about with innumerable vexatious restrictions. Jesus regarded the institution from a philanthropic point of view, and He claimed lordship over it for the Son of Man on the ground of His sympathy with mankind, which He deemed a far more reliable interpreter of the divine purpose and guide in observance, than the merciless rigour of the rabbis.

In a third group of texts the apocalyptic element is more or less prominent. In all these there are allusions to a future coming of the Son of Man, and in some to the accompanying circumstances of the coming: the appearance in the clouds, the throne, the glory, the escort of angels. In a number of the texts there is an implied contrast between a present full of trial and the future glory which lends pathos to the words recorded, making the bright hope of the Son of Man appear as His consolation amid the sorrowful experiences of earth. Thus, when Jesus told His disciples at Cæsarea that the Son of Man should come in the glory of His Father with His angels, to reward every man according to his works, it was in immediate connection with an announcement of His approaching passion.[1] When at Peræa He promised to His faithful companions, in the regeneration, thrones beside the Son of Man, the promise was made by one who knew that He should soon have to lay down His life for the kingdom, to men who had left all that they might follow Him.[2] The solemn declaration before the high priest concerning the session on the right hand of power, was made by one who at the moment was a prisoner at the bar on His trial, and it meant: "Ere long you and I shall change places."[3]

In one remarkable instance, the parabolic representation of the judgment, there is not merely an implied contrast, but an express blending of the future glory with present humiliation. He who shall come in His glory accompanied by all the holy angels, and take possession of His judicial throne before an assembled world, is one who can say: I have been an hungered, thirsty, a stranger, naked, sick, a prisoner. The fact of His having such a history throws a deep pathos into the judgment programme, and divests it of every semblance of vainglory or arrogant pretension. No one grudges this

[1] Matt. xvi. 27. [2] Matt. xix. 28, cf. 27. [3] Matt. xxvi. 64.

Man of Sorrow His judicial honours; He has fully earned His throne, and His competency for the task is beyond question. His verdict will be according to truth if the treatment given to the natural objects of pity is to be the supreme test of character, for He has become an expert in applying the test. And that this is to be the principle of judgment is solemnly announced: "Inasmuch as ye did it unto one of these least ones, my brethren, ye did it unto Me."[1] The Judge regards the children of sorrow everywhere as His vicars, and takes what is done to them as done to Himself. In this part of the parable the human sympathy of the Son of Man becomes conspicuous, so that in the delineation as a whole all the attributes denoted by the title, majesty, humility, love, are united, presenting together an imposing picture. By this feature, moreover, Christianity is adapted to be the basis of equitable judgment of all men irrespective of time and place. Men can be approved or condemned for their attitude towards Christ who have never heard His name. The essence of Christianity is placed in love, and love is made the touchstone of character and the arbiter of destiny. A loftier ideal of judge and judgment it is not possible to conceive.

It thus appears that the title "Son of Man" expressed the Messianic consciousness of Jesus in three distinct directions. It announced a Messiah appointed to suffer, richly endowed with human sympathy, and destined to pass through suffering to glory. In all three respects it pointed at a Messianic ideal contrary to popular notions. For that very reason Jesus loved the name, as

[1] Matt. xxv. 40.

expressing truth valid for Himself, as fitted to foster just conceptions in receptive minds, and as steering clear of current misapprehensions. With reference to these it served the purpose of an incognito, making it possible for Jesus to declare Himself to be the Christ to those who were in the secret, and yet remain an unknown stranger to the outside world. In adopting the name "Son of Man," Jesus as it were spoke in parables, teaching much to prepared hearers, little to the unprepared. The twelve, to whom it was given to know the mysteries of the kingdom, penetrated gradually into the hidden import of the pathetic mystic name, inductively gathering impressions from its daily use. But the incidents at Cæsarea show that even then they had not divined all its meaning. Peter declared *ex animo* his belief that his Master was the Christ; but that his Messianic creed had not yet undergone complete transformation, appeared from his vehement resistance to the announcement of the coming passion. He now fully understood that the Son of Man was the Christ, but he did not yet understand that the Christ was the Son of Man. He had probably mastered some of the lessons the title was fitted to teach, but he had failed as yet to master the most abstruse, and the most remote from prevalent notions, the idea of a suffering Messiah. That thought was not to be communicated by mere names, or even by the plainest pre-intimations; the event alone could open the eyes of the disciples. Minor incidents in the Master's curriculum of trial, such as already lay behind them, they could easily reconcile themselves to, but death by violence to the last must remain incredible.

The title *Son of God* expressed the Messianic consciousness of Jesus God-wards. It might conceivably have been used by Him in four distinct senses: as expressing a relation to God common to Him with other men, and based on the simple fact of being a man; as a Messianic title of dignity; as denoting moral likeness to and intimate fellowship with God; and as implying possession of the divine nature. The four senses may be discriminated as the human, the official, the ethical, and the metaphysical. Of the first sense no example can be cited. We do not anywhere find Jesus calling Himself Son of God merely in virtue of His being a son of man. Neither do we find Him referring to God in terms suggestive of a relation to Him common to Himself with others, using *e.g.* the expression "our Father in heaven" in addressing an audience as a modern preacher might, or as the prophet Malachi did when he asked his countrymen guilty of a wrong against their brethren, "Have we not all one father?"[1] He said "My Father" and "your Father." Only once does the expression "our Father" occur, viz. in the Lord's Prayer, and it is far from certain that Jesus meant to include Himself in the "our," albeit the prayer was given for the use of His own disciples; though the supposition is not in itself inadmissible, sonship in a most real sense being common to Him with them.

Three instances of the official sense occur. The first is in the confession of Peter as given in the first Gospel: "Thou art the Christ, the Son of the living God." There is room for doubt which of the two forms of the con-

[1] Mal. ii. 20.

fession, that of Matthew or the shorter one given by Mark, "Thou art the Christ,"[1] is the original. In the latter case we should merely have in the words an instance of the use of the name as a Messianic title of honour by the evangelist, or by the Apostolic Church whose faith is reflected in his narrative; in the former we should be entitled to cite the passage as an instance of its use in that sense by Jesus Himself, seeing He emphatically approved the solemn declaration made by His disciple. The second instance occurs in the parable of the wicked vinedressers, in which, under "the son" whom they slew, Jesus doubtless made a veiled allusion to Himself as the Messianic Son of the Most High.[2] The third occurs in the question put by the high priest to Jesus before the Sanhedrim: "I adjure Thee by the living God, that Thou tell us whether Thou be the Christ, the Son of God."[3] The affirmative reply of Jesus homologated the double title as applicable to Himself. As understood by both parties, the second name was a synonym for the first. The Christ was regarded as *ex officio* Son of God. In all three cases the obvious Old Testament basis of the title is to be found in the two texts: "Thou art my Son, this day have I begotten Thee;"[4] "I will be His Father, and He shall be my Son."[5]

Of the use of the title in the ethical sense we have a peculiarly instructive example in the saying, "No man knoweth the Son, but the Father; neither knoweth any man the Father save the Son, and he to whomsoever the Son is pleased to reveal Him."[6] This notable word

[1] Mark viii. 29.   [2] Matt. xxi. 37.   [3] Matt. xxvi. 63.
[4] Ps. ii. 7.   [5] 2 Sam. vii. 14.   [6] Matt. xi. 27.

points to a very intimate fellowship based on moral affinity. The text as used by Gnostics ran, "No man knew the Father save the Son, and no man knoweth the Son save the Father," and in this form amounted to little more than a claim advanced by Jesus to be the historical revealer of the Fatherhood of God, the religious teacher who first gave prominence to that aspect of the divine character. But the text as it stands in our Gospels, which we have every reason to regard as the authentic form of the saying, points to something deeper, even to intimate personal relations between Father and Son. The word flowed out of the hidden fountain of the Son's heart. Through it, as through all kindred sayings, the Messianic consciousness of Jesus found utterance. This is not to be understood, however, in the sense that Jesus inferred His Sonship from His Messiahship, and called Himself Son of God because He believed Himself to be the Christ. On the contrary, the filial consciousness was the source of the Messianic. The love Jesus bore to His Father, and the love He bore to men, together gave birth to faith in His Messianic vocation, even as they also aided Him to hold fast that faith through all the trials of His public life.

The filial consciousness of Christ blossomed into rich and varied expression at the time when the memorable word above quoted was spoken, supplying materials from which we can learn the outstanding characteristics of the spirit of sonship. The sayings recorded by the evangelist reveal a spirit of loyal devotion and humble submission to the Father's will, of unlimited confidence in the Father's love, of intimate fellowship with the Father fruitful in peace and joy, and of liberty and self-reliant independence in reference to the world. The first of these four qualities found expression in the words: "I thank Thee, O Father, Lord of heaven and earth, because Thou hast hid these things from the wise and understanding, and hast revealed them unto babes."[1] There were both resignation and thanksgiving in the utterance —resignation in view of the unbelief of the wise, thankfulness for the faith of the babes. Both were possible only through single-hearted, self-effacing devotion to the service of the Father in the work of the kingdom. Jesus could leave the results of His ministry in His Father's hands, content that they should be great or small as Providence appointed, because in all His efforts He sought not His own glory, but the glory of Him who sent Him. His intense interest in the progress of the kingdom might tempt Him to regret that so few received His message, but the disciplined spirit of filial devotion replied: "It is my part to labour with all my soul and strength; it is my Father's to determine the issue. Far from me be the thought of shaping my conduct so as to ensure popularity. Let me be faithful to truth, and satisfied with such disciples as I can get on these terms."

Christ's filial trust found emphatic expression in the words: "All things are delivered unto me of my Father."[2] This was a remarkable statement in the circumstances. For one who found Himself distrusted or repelled by the great mass of his fellow-countrymen, and especially by such as possessed social influence, and believed in only by a small band of insignificant persons, to say, "All

[1] Matt. xi. 25. [2] Matt. xi. 27.

things are delivered unto me," was surely to walk by faith. To the eye of sense, that little band of disciples was a niggard gift. The world in its heartless way would call it ignominious failure. From that company to "all things," what a leap! It was a leap possible only to a faith which was the evidence of things not seen, to a confidence in a Father's goodwill and purpose so absolute as to be unassailable by adverse circumstances, and able to say: "The future, the world, universal lordship are mine, though this motley group are all that can be seen of my inheritance."

It was out of the blissful consciousness of a serene joyful fellowship with His Father that Jesus uttered the third filial word recorded by the evangelist: "No man knoweth the Son but the Father, neither knoweth any man the Father save the Son." The reciprocal knowledge alluded to is not of the theoretic sort, but such as springs out of a loving, confiding intimacy. It is the good understanding that subsists between bosom friends in full accord in sentiments, sympathies, and aims. The Gospel history supplies numerous illustrations and evidences of such an understanding between Jesus and His heavenly Father; as in the narratives of the Baptism, the Transfiguration, the choice of the Twelve, and the preaching of the Sermon on the Mount. At critical times it was the habit of Jesus to spend hours in devotional converse with Heaven, meditating over and speaking about His plans in presence of His Father. After such seasons of solitary communion with God, He went forth to action or suffering with cheerful resolute step, assured that He was about to do or endure what was well-pleasing in God's sight. In such communion He experienced a peace and gladness which were but accentuated by adverse circumstances. Misunderstood by men, much even by friends, totally and fatally by foes, it was an abundant consolation that He was perfectly understood by His Father. Left absolutely alone at the last, He did not feel lonely, because the Father was with Him. His lot was hard; poverty, social contempt, and other ills of life pressed heavily on Him; yet amid all His spirit was irrepressibly buoyant and gay. The Lord God was His joy and strength: communion with Him made His feet like the feet of the hind of the dawn, and He could walk, yea leap, securely on the rocky Alpine heights.

The same words in which Jesus revealed the deep tranquillity of His heart in fellowship with God, also gave forcible expression to the free, self-reliant spirit which animated Him in His whole bearing towards the world. In this aspect they meant: "My Father knows Me, and I can dispense with the recognition of the wise and learned. I can do without them, though they cannot do without Me; for no man knoweth the Father save the Son, and he to whomsoever the Son is pleased to reveal Him." This independent attitude was a true victory of faith for the Son of Man in His state of humiliation, wherein no virtue could be practised without moral effort. One confronted with so imposing an array of antagonists might well be dismayed. He would be greatly tempted to think He must be wrong when so many men, and of such weight and quality, disapproved. If He still continued to believe in Himself and in His

Messianic mission, He could hardly escape being discouraged by prevalent coldness and hostility. Neither effect was produced on the mind of Jesus. In spite of the disapproval of the sages He was sure He was right, and being sure of that He could bear isolation, though valuing sincere appreciation. This self-certainty was another fruit of a fellowship with the Father which made Him independent both of the world's guidance and of the world's friendship. Through that fellowship He knew the truth concerning Himself and the Kingdom at first hand, by direct unerring intuition, and needed not the guidance of the world's oracles or of the traditions of men. When the divine spirit of truth led Him into non-conforming paths, censuring voices scared Him not; for the inward voice told Him that He was in the right way, and He could confidently declare the customs with which He was expected to comply to be plants which His Father had not planted.[1]

In all these respects Jesus exhibited a type of sonship which may be and ought to be repeated in Christians, so that their Lord should be only the first-born among many brethren. Are there no respects in which He was unique, Son of God in a sense predicable of no one but Himself? In reply, I have to admit that there are no texts in the synoptical Gospels in which Divine Sonship in the metaphysical sense is ascribed to Jesus in a perfectly clear, indisputable manner. But there are some texts in which a mysterious incommunicable relation to God seems darkly hinted at. One is that on which I have already commented at some length, in

[1] Matt. xv. 13.

the closing words of which Jesus claims to be sole revealer of God: "No man knoweth the Father save the Son, and he to whomsoever the Son is pleased to reveal Him." This is a claim almost as absolute as that made for the Logos in the prologue of the fourth Gospel to be the light of every man that cometh into the world. The claim is not meant to exclude from saving knowledge of God all who are ignorant of the historical Christ. It is meant rather to teach, that whoever has such knowledge, whether within Christendom or without, gets his illumination from the Son who perfectly knows the Father. Does not this point to a being of the Son independent of space and time? In the present connection, the epithet "living" applied to God in Peter's confession is not without significance. It seems to indicate a consciousness on Peter's part, that in calling Jesus the Son of God he was saying a very daring thing, not merely repeating one of Messiah's conventional titles. Specially important is the saying in the eschatological discourse in which Jesus disclaimed even for the Son knowledge of the day and hour.[1] It gives to the Son a very lofty place in the universe, superior to angels, second only to the Father. From the point of view of anti-Arian controversies, it may seem to teach a low doctrine as to Christ's divinity; but considered as an authentic utterance of Jesus concerning Himself, its significance is great. Finally, I need only allude to the question put by Jesus to His adversaries amid the conflicts of the passion week: "What think ye of the Christ? Whose Son is He?"[2] He did not then reveal all that was in

---

[1] Mark xiii. 32.   [2] Matt. xxii. 42.

His thoughts, but He hinted at a deep truth when, in reply to the answer of the Pharisees to His first question, He propounded the second, "How can David's son be also David's Lord?" It was an allusion to something more than a merely official Messianic Sonship, which could hardly have puzzled experts in Rabbinic lore.

After the foregoing discussion the significance of the two titles, *Son of Man* and *Son of God*, in reference to the doctrine of the kingdom, will be apparent. As *Son of Man*, Jesus stood in a relation of solidarity and sympathy with men. As *Son of God*, He stood in a similar relation to God. As bearing both titles, He was in intimate fellowship with both God and man, and a link of connection between them. In His person the kingdom was thus realized in germ, as a kingdom of grace in which God is related to men as *Father*, and men are related to God as *sons*.

CHAPTER VIII.

THE RIGHTEOUSNESS OF THE KINGDOM—NEGATIVE ASPECT.

"SEEK ye the kingdom of God and His righteousness," said Jesus to His hearers in the Sermon on the Mount, co-ordinating righteousness with the kingdom as fundamentally important. What is the nature of the righteousness which the preacher thus commended as an essential part of the highest good?

Christ's doctrine of righteousness has two sides, a negative and a positive. The negative aspect, with which we are now to be occupied, consists in a criticism of current ideas and practices in ethics and religion. Such criticism was an unavoidable task for Jesus, however uncongenial. The Jewish mind was not a *tabula rasa* in reference to righteousness. A very definite and elaborate system of thought and action was in full possession, with the rights of prescription and the prestige of authority on its side, and one who came with a doctrine of his own must of necessity compare it with the one in vogue, assuming towards the latter a polemical attitude in so far as he deemed it erroneous. For similar reasons every great ethical teacher has been compelled to be more or less controversial. Moral polemics form a conspicuous feature in Hebrew prophecy. From Isaiah to John the Baptist the prophets cried aloud and spared not, showing the people of Israel their transgressions, whether consisting in counterfeit forms of piety, or in deeds of flagrant wickedness. If an ordinary prophet could not shirk the duty of censure, still less could the Christ. He must come with the fan of moral criticism in His hand, separating wheat from chaff. The Baptist was not wrong in assigning to Messiah a sifting function; his only error lay in a too crude conception of the process. As the Christ, Jesus was the bearer of the moral ideal in its purity, and it was incumbent on Him to use all possible means to make that ideal appear in all its divine beauty before the eyes of men. It was not for Him to ignore prevalent caricatures and perversions, saying in effect: I am not responsible for them, and would rather not speak of them. He was no mere private individual, who might mind His own business and leave the world to go its own way. He was the servant of God and of mankind for righteousness' sake, His very vocation being to be the light of life to the world. Men were entitled to look to Him for guidance, saying: Lead us in the path of true righteousness; show us the by-paths of error, that we may not wander therein to our hurt.

Jesus loyally recognised moral criticism as one of the perilous tasks connected with His Messianic calling. He knew that it was urgently needed; that the ideas current among His people concerning righteousness were even more widely divergent from truth than their ideas concerning Messiah and the kingdom of God; and that their errors on all these subjects formed together an intricate network of delusion. And He performed the difficult duty faithfully, throughly purging the threshing-floor; yet in a manner to which no exception can be taken. The manner of His censure we do well to note before entering on the matter of it, as it may help us to appreciate a part of His teaching with which the average Christian only imperfectly sympathizes. His exposure of Pharisaism or Rabbinism, while severe, is free from violence, bitterness, or undue emphasis. There is, on the one hand, no hesitation: the critic, even at the early period of His ministry, speaks as one who has decidedly and finally made up His mind that the system He criticises is incurably bad; as in the solemn declaration in the Sermon on the Mount, "Except your righteousness shall exceed the righteousness of the scribes and Pharisees, ye shall in no case enter into the kingdom of heaven," which in effect pronounces pharisaic righteousness to be wholly chaff. Yet, on the other hand, there is no unworthy passion or spasmodic effort in utterance; the description of the system condemned is characterized by self-possession, dignity, easy mastery and felicity of style. "All their works they do to be seen of men. They make broad their phylacteries, and enlarge the borders of their garments, and love the uppermost rooms at feasts, and the chief seats in synagogues, and greetings in the markets, and to be called of men, Rabbi, Rabbi."[1] In such simple terms is pharisaic vanity depicted. It is the style of one to whom the whole subject is familiar, and who contemplates it with an artist's placid penetrating eye. How much this calm bearing imports, we feel

[1] Matt. xxiii. 5-7.

when we compare it with the temper in which men of noble spirit are wont to utter their "everlasting no" against the moral and religious counterfeits of their time. How the protestant labours in utterance, as if he could not find words strong enough to say all he feels, striving by spasmodic speech to clear his sick soul of falsehood; how by every gesture he seems to say, "Get thee behind me, Satan;" how long it is before, satisfied with truth found, he can speak of lies renounced in measured terms, as of something external! Of these agonies of "honest doubt" there is no trace in the life of Jesus. If they had any place in His religious experience, it was before He left the retirement of Nazareth to enter on His public ministry.

The judgment of Jesus on the moral and religious life of His contemporaries was not only calm in tone, but discriminating. While pronouncing unqualified condemnation on the system, He was ready to acknowledge that those who were associated with it might be, in the conventional sense, exemplary, likely to pass in all religious societies for "good" people. He described them as "righteous,"[1] as men who (by comparison) needed no repentance,[2] as dutiful sons who did their father's commandments, and shunned lawless, foolish ways.[3] He made the typical Pharisee describe himself as innocent of vices—extortion, injustice, impurity, and the like, and scrupulously attentive to all religious duties, such as fasting and tithe-paying, the pretensions of the self-satisfied worshipper being tacitly allowed.[4] Even with

[1] Matt. ix. 13.
[2] Luke xv. 7.
[3] Luke xv. 29.
[4] Luke xviii. 11, 12.

reference to the system condemned, He seems to have made the admission that it was the degenerate issue of a movement which at its commencement had an aim deserving of respect. So we may understand the words which form the preface to the great anti-pharisaic discourse: "The scribes and the Pharisees sit in Moses' seat; all therefore whatsoever they bid you observe, observe and do."[1] He could not mean thereby to recommend indiscriminate compliance with all Rabbinical prescriptions, but He probably did mean to acknowledge the legitimacy and utility of the original design from which Rabbinism took its rise. That design is explained in the opening sentences of the collection of sayings by Jewish scribes called the Pirke-Aboth. "Moses," we read, "received the Torah from Sinai, and delivered it to Jehoshuah, and Jehoshuah to the elders, and the elders to the prophets, and the prophets to the men of the Great Synagogue. They said three things: Be deliberate in judgment; and raise up many disciples; and make a fence to the law." The three sayings ascribed to the ancient sages signify: "Be careful in deciding what the law requires or forbids; teach as many as possible the knowledge of the law; and surround the law with additional rules, as safeguards against transgression through ignorance or inadvertence." Beforehand one would pronounce these good and wholesome counsels. Afterhand, in view of what came out of them, one might very reasonably hesitate; yet even then it would be only fair to admit good faith and good intention at least. This much, as I have already indicated, Jesus appears

[1] Matt. xxiii. 2, 3.

to have conceded, and He doubtless made all parties connected with the system—Pharisees, scribes, Rabbis—welcome to the benefit of the concession. All were equally entitled to the benefit, for all were alike zealous for the law, and theoretically or practically concerned about its observance. The Pharisee, as such, made it his business to keep the law blamelessly in his own conduct. The scribe was originally one who made copies of the law, but gradually he added to the work of copyist the higher function of interpretation. Hence arose a large body of opinions as to the meaning of the law uttered by successive generations of scribes, referred to in the Gospels as "the traditions of the elders."[1] He was the wise man in Israel who was acquainted with these legal opinions, and could cite them appositely. Lovers of wisdom desired to know such a sage and to hear him speak of the law, giving his own thoughts and quoting those of others. Out of this desire sprang the Rabbinical schools. The Rabbi was the master of such a school. The same man might be Rabbi, scribe, Pharisee, all in one. The title Rabbi, in our Lord's time, was probably of recent origin. Lightfoot conjectures that it was first used in connection with the disputes between the schools of Hillel and Shammai.

The reforming zeal for the strict observance of the Mosaic law, which began with Ezra, was very liable to degeneracy in many ways. The process of degeneracy had reached an advanced stage in our Lord's time, and the gravest of the evils resulting are noticed in His

[1] Mark vii. 3.

teaching. In the first place, the movement inevitably led to an enormous multiplication of rules to make the written law cover the whole ground of human conduct, —a huge development of what may be called scribe-made law; a burden even to think of, how much more to practise![1] However minute the civil and ritual laws contained in the Pentateuch may seem, many points are nevertheless left ambiguous or indeterminate. The rule might indeed be sufficiently definite to guide one who aimed at rendering a reasonable obedience, free from scruples as to insignificant minutiæ. So, for example, in the case of the law of tithes. But as time went on, the Jews came to be more and more of opinion that a more rigorous kind of obedience was required of them. Then it became necessary to fix many points which in the Mosaic statute were left vague. The result in reference to the law of tithes was, that to make sure that a tenth of one's possessions was given, it was ruled that even garden herbs, mint, anise, and cummin, etc., must be tithed.[2] Such was the hedge set around that particular law. In Deuteronomy it is written: "Hear, O Israel: the Lord our God is one Lord: and thou shalt love the Lord thy God with all thine heart, and with all thy soul, and with all thy might. And these words, which I command thee this day, shall be in thine heart; and thou shalt teach them diligently unto thy children, and shalt talk of them when thou sittest in thine house, and when thou walkest by the way, and when thou liest down, and when thou risest up."[3] The passage does not

---

[1] Lightfoot, *Horæ Hebraicæ*, notes on Matt. xxiii.
[2] Matt. xxiii. 23.   [2] Deut. vi. 4-7.

contain a law in the strict sense meant to be literally kept; it is rather a prophetic exhortation whose general spirit is to be observed. But the scribes interpreted it rigidly, and drew from it the rule that the *Shema*, so called from the first word of the passage in the Hebrew text, should be recited morning and evening. And legal pedantry did not stop there. There were anxious discussions of the question when precisely the morning and evening began. Some said it was day when one could distinguish blue from white; others, blue from green, which is more difficult. With reference to the evening, it was agreed that the sign of its coming was the appearance of the stars, it being written in Nehemiah: "So we laboured in the work, and half of them held the spears from the rising of the morning till the stars appeared."[1] But Rabbinical doctors differed on the momentous question how many stars made night. One Rabbi in high repute said: If only one star was visible, it was still day, for the text in Nehemiah says "stars;" if two stars only were visible, it was doubtful, for the first star did not count; but when three were seen, night had certainly arrived.[2]

These examples show what fencing the law meant, and how inevitably it led to indefinite multiplication of rules. We can faintly imagine the burdensomeness of the vast mass of Rabbinical prescriptions for those who thought themselves bound to obey them in order to please God. Jesus alluded to this evil feature of Rabbinism when He said: "They bind heavy burdens [and grievous to be

---

[1] Neh. iv. 21.
[2] Schwab, *Le Talmud de Jérusalem; Traité des Berachoth*, i. 1.

borne], and lay them on men's shoulders;"[1] and also when He described His own yoke as easy and His burden as light.[2] In inviting men to take His yoke upon them, He meant to suggest a contrast between it and another well-known yoke that was not light, and said in effect: "Galling is the yoke of the Rabbis, heavy the burden of legal duties they impose. Farewell to peace, rest, and freedom, when ye enter their school. Sunless gloom, hopeless bondage, incessant irritation to reason and conscience, is the lot of their hapless disciples. Come to Me, ye who are weary of that lot, or who dread it; come to Me, and find rest from all that soul-misery. For My yoke is easy. The commands I teach are not grievous." It was the one true Master offering deliverance from an oppressive spiritual tyranny. But we may not forget that, while in one aspect tyrants over their disciples, the scribes were themselves slaves of the system they represented and helped to perpetuate. They were to be pitied as well as condemned. Masters and scholars were both in the same hapless predicament. Jesus recognised this when, not without a touch of compassion, He called the teachers of the law "blind leaders of the blind."[3] Yet it is noticeable that in all His allusions to the "blind guides,"[4] a tone of severity predominates; not without reason. The disciples of the scribes were merely victims, sinned against rather than sinning, but the masters were willingly the slaves of a system which gave them despotic power over the consciences of others.

[1] Matt. xxiii. 4; the words within brackets are a doubtful reading. The idea expressed is implied in the epithet "heavy."
[2] Matt. xi. 30.   [3] Matt. xv. 14.   [4] Matt. xxiii. 16, 19, 24, 26.

Whenever burdens become oppressive, the overburdened, whether man or beast, instinctively seek relief. When rules of conduct are unduly multiplied and made vexatiously minute, there inevitably springs up a desire to evade them. So it happened under the reign of Rabbinism. Relief was sought from irksome statutes by the invention of other statutes virtually cancelling them. As those who make laws are likely to be the most expert in the arts of evasion, we are not surprised to find our Lord hinting that the Rabbinical law-makers were the greatest law-breakers: "They themselves will not move them (the burdens) with one of their fingers."[1] The scribes were as fertile as the Jesuits in evasive inventions for releasing themselves and others from the obligations they had created, loosing where they had already bound, so making life a constant game of fast and loose. In His anti-pharisaic discourse Jesus cited instances of this hypocritical casuistry in connection with the subject of oaths, representing the "blind guides" as teaching that an oath by the temple or by the altar was not binding, and that a man must swear by the gold of the temple or by the gift upon the altar in order to be bound.[2] The examples selected are by no means extreme. Multitudes of cases could be cited from the Talmud, showing the system to far greater disadvantage. Most striking illustrations might be taken from the numerous devices for mitigating the rigour of the Sabbath law as fenced by the scribes. The burden of Rabbinism reached its maximum in connection with the fourth commandment. It was a saying current in the schools, that the rules for the

[1] Matt. xxiii. 4.   [2] Matt. xxiii. 16-22.

observance of the weekly rest were a mountain suspended by a hair, the meaning being that the rules were very many, and their connection with Scripture very slight. Many of them were ridiculously minute, carrying the prohibition against work and bearing of burdens the length of absurdity. The rubbing of the ears of corn by the disciples was reckoned a sin against the Sabbath law, because it was a species of thrashing. A tailor might not go out with his needle near dusk on Sabbath eve, lest he should forget he had it, and carry it out with him on the Sabbath day. For the same reason the scribe might not go out at that time with his pen behind his ear. A man might not wear on Sabbath sandals weighted with nails. It was not agreed whether a cripple might on that day wear his wooden leg. A thing might be moved within a house from one end to the other, but only four ells in a public place. An endless series of rules, conceived in this spirit, was fitted to make the day of rest an insupportable horror. But mitigations were ingeniously provided. A whole treatise of the Mishnah is devoted to contrivances for easing the pressure of the Sabbatic yoke, especially in reference to the length of a Sabbath-day journey, and the distance to which things, such as articles of food, might be carried. This was achieved by the method of connections, in Rabbinical dialect *Erubin*. Several houses standing in one court, *e.g.*, might be formed into one house by the separate householders agreeing to deposit an article of food at a certain spot in the court. One desirous of making a journey longer than two thousand paces might lawfully do so by depositing food for two meals near the legal limit, whereby the spot where the food was deposited became his domicile, so that after having travelled already the legal distance, he might set out from that point and travel as far again, and so on *ad libitum*.[1]

Except as fostering the spirit of chicanery, the cancelling of one set of Rabbinical rules by another may appear no great evil. A much more serious mischief flowing from the multiplication *ad infinitum* of petty precepts, was the neglect and transgression of the great commandments of God. Rabbinism began by making a hedge about the law, and it ended by substituting the hedge in place of the law. The means supplanted the end. So complete was the process, that the abuse was accepted by public opinion as the right order of things. The superiority of the tradition to the law was openly proclaimed. They compared the law to salt and the traditions to pepper, the law to water and the traditions to wine. They spoke of the study of the law as a matter of indifference, but of the study of the traditions as a duty and a virtue. Jesus pointed at this evil when He described the Pharisees as paying tithes of mint and anise and cummin, and omitting the weightier matters of the law, judgment, mercy, and faith; and as straining out a gnat and swallowing a camel.[2] He gave a special example of this tendency when, to substantiate the charge of making the commandments of

---

[1] *Vide* Schwab, *Le Talmud de Jérusalem*, tome 4ième; *Traités Schabbath et Eroubin*. In Edersheim's *Life and Times of Jesus the Messiah*, vol. ii. appendix xvii., English readers will find a full analysis of the Sabbath law as set forth in the Mishnah and the Jerusalem Talmud.

[2] Matt. xxiii. 23, 24.

God of none effect by their traditions, He alluded to the Rabbinical maxim, that merely to call a thing *corban* made it impossible for a man to use it even for the most benevolent purposes, such as rendering assistance to his parents.[1] It was only one of many ways in which the evil genius of Pharisaism brought about a most disastrous divorce between religion and morality.

Kindred to the foregoing evil in nature and tendency was the *externalism* of Pharisaism. This was an inherent vice of the system. The whole attention was fixed on the outward rule: that complied with, the requirements of Rabbinical righteousness were satisfied. Hence it was possible for a man to regard himself and be regarded by others as righteous, while in spirit he was far from God and goodness. As the little commandments of the scribes made men forget the great commandments of God; so the external rules of the scribes made them overlook the world within, the heart and its dispositions. In point of fact, the righteousness of the scribes very often coexisted with many base affections. This combination, patent to the eyes of the discerning, Jesus exposed in some of His most pungent sayings, as when He compared the scribes and Pharisees to whited sepulchres which appeared beautiful without, but within were full of dead men's bones and all uncleanness;[2] and represented them as making clean the outside of the cup and of the platter, while within they were full of extortion and excess.[3] The words may seem severe, but

---

[1] Matt. xv. 4-6.   [2] Matt. xxiii. 27.
[3] Matt. xxiii. 25, 26.

they are only a graphic description of the actual fact. Pharisaic righteousness, through its externalism, not only coexisted with, but even tended to produce, certain vices of the spirit. Conspicuous among these was vanity or ostentation, the moral feature of Pharisaism on which Jesus chiefly remarked in the Sermon on the Mount. "They do their works to be seen of men," He said over and over again, in reference to such duties as almsgiving, praying, and fasting.[1] It was the most obvious moral characteristic, thrusting itself on the observation of all, therefore specially fit to be mentioned in a popular discourse. It was, moreover, a very significant characteristic. It was the natural outcome of the Rabbinical system. The whole superstructure of scribe-made law rested on opinion. The traditions of the elders were the dicta of individual scribes. How natural that those who practised a righteousness based on opinion should make their appeal to opinion, study appearance, and almost regard ostentation as a duty! Thus they justified themselves before men,[2] and sought honour one of another. And they had their reward. Mutual admiration and flattery became the order of the day. Disciples did homage to their masters by calling them Rabbi, and receiving their sayings as oracles. Masters rewarded with an approving smile disciples who strictly observed their precepts.

Along with ostentation goes self-complacency. He who loves the praise of men praises himself. Self-flattery found in Rabbinism a congenial atmosphere. To become eminently righteous a man had but to be an

[1] Matt. vi. 1-18. [2] Luke xvi. 15.

extremist in opinion and practice, following the straitest sect. The more absurdity, the greater sanctity. The novice might find some difficulty in believing that there could be any merit in compliance with ridiculous rules. But that initial difficulty once overcome, fanaticism could feed pride by going in for the strictest style of observance. Judging from the parable of the Pharisee and the publican, there seems to have been no lack of self-admiring devotees in our Lord's day. The typical representative of Pharisaism thanks God he is so good a man, and enumerates with complacency his virtues, prominent among which is strictness in fasting and tithe-paying, belonging to the artificial region of will-worship.

The natural companion of self-esteem is censoriousness. To lower others is an easy way to exalt ourselves. Besides, the Pharisee could hardly help thinking ill of ordinary men. The devotee despises the man of the world quite as naturally as the man of the world despises him. If goodness consist in cultivating artificial virtues, then certainly the greater part of the world lies in wickedness. How could a Pharisee fail to have a low opinion of "publicans and sinners"? and in what other aspect could the pagan world appear to his eyes than as a vast territory full of darkness and uncleanness? Accordingly, in the Gospels, inhuman contempt for others not of his coterie appears as an outstanding trait in the character of the Jewish religionist. The typical Pharisee thanks God he is not as the rest of men, who are conceived to be given up to the grossest vices; adding, "or even as this publican," as if a publican were an epitome of all the sins. The pharisaic party sneered at Jesus Himself as "the friend of publicans and sinners,"[1] not deeming it possible to say a worse thing of Him. The self-styled saints and sages of Judæa, who prided themselves on their wisdom and their goodness, regarded with sanctimonious abhorrence the people who lacked legal lore and neglected Rabbinical traditions. "I hate," said they in their hearts, "the profane rabble." Jesus had this haughtiness in His view when He described Himself as "meek and lowly."[2] With pity in His heart for the neglected multitude, who were as a flock of sheep without a shepherd, the true Shepherd of Israel said: "Come unto Me, all ye burdened ones, whether laden with ignorance, social degradation, or sin; come unto *Me*, for I am not haughty, like these wise and holy men who scorn and repel you. However unlearned or unholy, come unto Me, for I am meek and lowly in heart, and will *not* cast you out."

These vices of the spirit, vanity, self-complacency, contemptuousness, appeared in the characters even of sincere Pharisees. They were inseparable from the system. In some the fashionable piety was associated with baser passions, and served as a cloak for iniquity. The third evangelist remarks of the Pharisees generally that they were covetous,[3] and Jesus repeated the charge in an aggravated form when He represented the scribes as devouring widows' houses, and for a pretence making long prayers.[4] He gave to the grave accusation a still

---

[1] Matt. xi. 19.   [2] Matt. xi. 29.   [3] Luke xvi. 14.
[4] Mark xii. 40; Luke xx. 47. The passage as found in Matt. xxiii. 14 is not genuine.

wider scope when He compared the hypocritical Pharisees to cups clean without, and within full of extortion and excess.[1] What a character for apparently holy men: wearing an aspect of austere unworldliness, yet all the while robbers and libertines! But surely these were merely accidental monstrosities, of no significance in reference to the system? Not so; the system by its externalism made the occurrence of such characters not only possible but certain. It gave bad men a tempting opportunity to use religion not only as a mask, but even as a means for promoting nefarious designs. A man could comply with all Rabbinic requirements, and even gain golden opinions by his public profession of piety, and yet be an utter miscreant. The worse the man, the more religious he was likely to be, because he found it profitable. The righteousness in vogue put a premium on hypocrisy, and by that fact it was hopelessly condemned. The hypocrite, consummate at once in "righteousness" and in iniquity, was the *reductio ad absurdum* of Rabbinism, as he was its ripe fruit.

We are now in a position to judge with what truth Jesus taught that pharisaic righteousness lay entirely outside the kingdom of God. It is in connection with the externalism of that righteousness that the truth of the allegation becomes most apparent. Pharisaism laid exclusive stress on the outward act; whence it came to pass, as we have seen, that legal piety might be associated with various evil dispositions. In the kingdom of God, on the contrary, no action has value except in connection with motives and dispositions. One great aim of the

[1] Matt. xxiii. 25.

Sermon on the Mount is to proclaim this great principle in opposition to current notions. Hence the unfavourable verdict on Pharisaism is placed near the beginning of the discourse. It is the thesis which the Preacher means to illustrate, by setting the outward righteousness of the Pharisee and the inward righteousness of the kingdom over against each other. The contrast is so drawn as to bring into prominence the virtues opposed to the most characteristic pharisaic vices. First, in a series of examples, the inwardness of true righteousness is opposed to the outwardness of the counterfeit.[1] Then over against pharisaic ostentation is set the grace of modesty.[2] Single-minded sincerity is next commended in opposition to the double-heartedness so often exhibited in the pharisaic character through the combination of religion with worldliness.[3] Then the odious pharisaic vice of censoriousness is animadverted on, and by implication it is taught that the genuine citizen of the kingdom judges himself rather than others.[4]

In its other leading characteristics—the burdensomeness of its innumerable enactments, the chicanery to which it had recourse to ease the self-made burden, and its tendency to neglect great duties in zeal for trifling observances—Pharisaism was equally alien from the kingdom of God. That kingdom is a kingdom of liberty; it abhors tyranny and oppression; Jesus, the living embodiment of its spirit, said truly: "My yoke is easy, and My burden is light." It was His passionate love of spiritual freedom that constrained Him to denounce the evil thing,

---

[1] Matt. v. 21–42. [2] Matt. vi. 1–18.
[3] Matt. vi. 19–24. [4] Matt. vii. 1–5.

and for this brave deed humanity owes Him a deep debt of gratitude. It is further a kingdom of truth; not of "the truth," or of religious orthodoxy, that is the theological perversion—Rabbinism *redivivus* under new conditions; but in the sense of moral simplicity. Sophistry can find no harbour within its borders. Its yea is yea, and its nay, nay. Finally, it is a kingdom in which the moral ideal in its purity reigns supreme. It values not a fear of God taught by the traditions of men. It requires of its subjects only that they do justly, love mercy, and walk humbly with God. In all these respects Pharisaism was without the kingdom. And it shut the kingdom against those who, but for its influence, might have entered in.[1] For one Paul who escaped, as if by miracle, from its malign thraldom, many were enslaved and perverted for ever. In view of this melancholy fact, the sombre declaration of Jesus concerning the straitness of the gate and the narrowness of the way leading to life becomes intelligible.[2] The gate is strait and the way narrow, because the righteousness of the kingdom is spiritual, and the majority prefer the beaten path of legalism. If any one, weary of the Rabbinical yoke, seek admittance, he will find the gate wide enough. The road indeed has all the breadth required for a world's highway; for it is important to observe that the spirituality which contracts the entrance to the kingdom is precisely that which fits Christianity to be a universal religion.

It remains to add that, apart from abuses, the method of Rabbinism, however natural in the circumstances amidst which it took its rise, was alien from the kingdom of God

---

[1] Matt. xxiii. 13.   [2] Matt. vii. 13, 14.

It fenced the law against violation by an immense mass of precautionary rules. The method of the kingdom is to have the law written on the heart. Thereby the keeping of all that is essential is effectually provided for. What cannot be protected in that way is of only secondary and temporary significance.

CHAPTER IX.

THE RIGHTEOUSNESS OF THE KINGDOM—POSITIVE ASPECT.

HAVING ascertained what the righteousness of the kingdom is not, we have now to consider what it is.

Jesus called it *the righteousness of God*.[1] In absence of evidence, we are not justified in assuming that He used this name in the technical and peculiar sense which it bears in the Pauline theology. We may, however, take for granted that He meant thereby a righteousness of which God is the centre. That will imply: right thoughts about God, without which it is impossible to be righteous in our highest relations; likeness to God in that which is most characteristic of Him as revealed to our faith in the doctrine of the kingdom, viz. charity, our righteousness towards men; realizing the ideal of man as God's son, our righteousness towards ourselves; imitation of Christ, the Son of God and Son of man, in whom the divine and human meet, the righteousness of discipleship; devotion to the interests of the kingdom, which is an end for God, and which ought to be for us at once chief end and chief good—the righteousness of citizens.

---

[1] Matt. vi. 33. I do not forget the critical doubts which have been expressed regarding the originality of this clause in Matthew's version of the saying. It is enough for my purpose that Jesus might have used the expression, it being congruous to His teaching.

Right thoughts of God are at once the beginning of true righteousness, and that on which the quality of all the other elements depends. In other words, ethically right conduct has its foundation in true religion. A wrong idea of God was the secret of all Rabbinical errors. The scribes believed in a far-off God. This fact Jesus pointed at when He quoted the words of the prophet Isaiah as applicable to them, "This people honoureth Me with their lips, but their heart is far from Me."[1] His immediate intention, doubtless, was to suggest a charge of insincerity, as the epithet "hypocrites" applied to the same persons shows; but we may legitimately give to the prophetic words a wider scope, so as to make it contain a description of Rabbinical piety even at its best, and in its essential character as the worship of a far-off God not revealing Himself directly to the heart, but only through an ever-lengthening chain of legal tradition. So understood, the words declared the truth very exactly. The God of Jewish theology at the beginning of our era stood at the remote end of a long series of mediators through whom the law was handed down. The Deity, too exalted to have direct dealings even with the greatest of mortals, first gave it to angels,[2] angels then gave it to Moses, then Moses gave it to Joshua, then Joshua to the elders, then the elders to the prophets, then the prophets to the men of the Great Synagogue, from whom it passed through successive generations of scribes to the contemporaries of Jesus. How feeble the sense of the divine presence in

---

[1] Mark vii. 6.

[2] For references to the mediation of angels, see Acts vii. 53; Gal. iii. 19; Heb. ii. 2.

the law must have been after so lengthened a process of transmission, and how degenerate the type of reverence whereof the divinity at the far-off end could be the object! Even the God of Sinai was an awful Being who influenced His worshippers mainly through fear, and upheld His majesty by keeping sinful mortals at a respectful distance. But He could at least inspire wholesome dread by His thunders and lightnings, and so compel a rude people to yield at least an outward obedience to His behests. But the sombre accompaniments of the lawgiving lay far back in history, and the God of the scribe, divested of Sinaitic terrors, had sunk into a very ancient Rabbi, who supplied the original text whereon the commentators exercised their wits. Such a God could awaken neither fear nor respect. He must be the object either of an imbecile superstition, or of utter contempt.[1]

This Rabbinical idol Jesus replaced by God the Father. He is not a far-off God; for though He be the Father in heaven, He is also near at hand speaking to men in their hearts, and through their family relations; not far from any one of them, even the most wayward, seeking their good always. He was not without a witness even in the hearts of the Rabbis, as is proved by this saying ascribed to one of them: "Be bold as a leopard, and swift as an eagle, and fleet as a hart, and

---

[1] The rabbinizing of the idea of God came about gradually. The older Rabbinism of the Targums insisted on the unity and transcendence of God, jealously guarding against anthropopathism. The later Rabbinism transformed God into a Rabbi who studied the law in heaven with other beatified Rabbis, and carefully observed all Rabbinical rules. *Vide* Weber, *System der Altsynagogalen Palästinischen Theologie*, pp. 146-159.

strong as a lion, to do the will of thy Father which is in heaven."[1]

The change introduced by Jesus in the way of thinking concerning God was of infinite practical consequence. It altered the whole character of religion and life. Belief in the Father-God makes child-like trust and rational reverence possible and even inevitable. From the heart one can desire that the name of this God may be hallowed and that His will may be done. "All that is within" a man blesses the Benignant One. Worship becomes eloquent and obedience spontaneous. Faith in the Divine Father hath, moreover, a magic power to emancipate from the yoke of man-made ordinances. Faith in a far-off Rabbinical God, Himself a Rabbi in temper, enslaves to tradition which thereby becomes the real deity. Faith in the God who reveals Himself to the heart instinctively understands that this God desires spiritual worship — the free rational homage of mind, heart, and conscience. From the moment one knows this truth he is free; the grievous burden of ordinances drops off the shoulders, and the tyranny of tradition is at an end.

To him who believes in the heavenly Father proclaimed by Jesus it is counted for righteousness in the kingdom. His faith evinces a pure heart in which the divine image can mirror itself, and it will lead on to still higher measures of purity.

Right thoughts of God naturally lead to imitation of divine virtues. Now the most characteristic attribute of the God whom Jesus preached is charity; benignant gracious love of men, clear of all particularism or

[1] Pirke-Aboth.

partiality. Of course the Divine Father is holy, but to say of a god that he is holy is to say little, for holiness in some sense is predicated of all the gods by all peoples. The vital question is, What is the quality of the holiness? In this respect gods differ widely. The holiness of pagan gods was compatible with the grossest immorality. The holiness of the Rabbinical God was purely negative, consisting, like that of the Pharisees, in keeping aloof from the evil. Jesus ascribed to God a holiness of an essentially different character, by representing love as His most prominent moral attribute, thereby transforming the idea of holiness as completely as He transformed the ideas of the kingdom and of the Messiah. "Love your enemies," He said, and so shall ye "be the children of your Father who is in heaven."[1] He required such as would be citizens of the kingdom to love those they were naturally tempted to hate, and whom custom allowed them to hate, on the ground that thereby they should be imitators of God; so indirectly teaching that God loves those whom He is supposed to hate, pagans, publicans, sinners, nature's non-elect, society's reprobates, and that His holiness is a social sympathetic thing which is ever seeking to communicate itself to others who greatly stand in need of it. In giving this counsel He pointed out a way whereby His disciples might fulfil all righteousness towards men, and be perfect even as their Father in heaven is perfect.[2] If they could love their enemies they would, of course, love their friends, as even publicans and pagans did,[3] their fellow-countrymen, and their fellow-disciples. The

[1] Matt. v. 44. [2] Matt. v. 48. [3] Matt. v. 46, 47.

difficulty is to love one whose behaviour towards us provokes us to anger or hatred. Therefore Christ insisted mainly on the more arduous and heroic type of beneficence, saying: "Resist not evil; but whosoever will smite thee on thy right cheek, turn to him the other also; and if any man will sue thee at the law, and take away thy coat, let him have thy cloak also; and whosoever shall compel thee to go one mile, go with him twain."[1] The high doctrine thus taught in the Sermon on the Mount, Jesus repeated in the parable of *The Good Samaritan*.[2] In that parable the term "neighbour" is set free from all artificial or conventional restrictions, and made to mean: any one that needs help and whom it is in my power to help, even though it should turn out to be one belonging to a hated nationality whom all my religious and racial prejudices would tempt me to injure rather than succour. Love, humane, catholic, all-embracing, that cannot be overcome of evil, is thus declared to be the fulfilling of the law in so far as it requires us to do justly to others. At this point the righteousness of the kingdom is seen to be a synonym for goodness, which goes far beyond what men can demand as their legal due. It is a reflection of the righteousness of the Father, the absolutely, unapproachably good.[3]

---

[1] Matt. v. 39-41. These precepts of Jesus have received their most realistic interpretation in recent times from Count Tolstoi, for whose views, as expressed in *Ma Religion*, in point of sincerity and moral earnestness I entertain profound respect, though I cannot help finding in them a tinge of that ascetic rigour which is the natural reaction from an early life of pleasure, in the case of one so richly gifted in intellect and heart.

[2] Luke x. 30.   [3] Matt. v. 48, xix. 17.

Acceptance of Christ's doctrine of God involves acceptance of His kindred doctrine of man. The believer in the Father becomes conscious of his vocation to the privileges and responsibilities of sonship. Out of this consciousness springs earnest endeavour to live under the influence of the filial spirit. Through a life so ordered is fulfilled the righteousness of sonship, which is a two-sided righteousness, having a relation to God on the one hand, and to the ideal of manhood on the other. What the component elements of this righteousness are I have already had occasion to point out in analysing the filial consciousness of Christ; for His Sonship and that of Christians are to a great extent identical in character, it being His will to reveal unto His disciples the Father as He Himself knows Him, and is known of Him.[1] First there is filial submission and devotion to the Father's will. In action and in suffering, in work and in lot, the motto of sonship is, "God's will be done." Its chief end is the divine glory; that secured, it is content to fill a little space or to bear a heavy cross. To be a son of God to this effect is not easy. It is possible only through a deadly struggle with, and victory over, self. To reach this higher life of sonship in which the ideal of our nature is fulfilled, we must lose the lower life of natural self-will. The spirit of sonship is a heroic spirit, seen at its best and purest in the pioneers of the kingdom whose lot it is to toil and endure; a career most honourable, but also arduous. The true sons of God are to be sought among those who are persecuted for righteousness' sake, in the glorious company of prophets,

[1] Matt. xi. 27. *Vide* pp. 180-4.

apostles, and martyrs. Self-seekers are never to be found in such company. They may enrol themselves among the servants of God, and profess to aim at the advancement of God's glory and the interests of His kingdom; but they seek these only when there is a prospect of personal advantage. Their place is not among the pioneers of a despised cause, but among the promoters of a movement which is already prosperous. They have their reward, but it is not to be reckoned among the genuine sons of God.

Next comes the spirit of confident trust in the Father's good-will, raising above all ignoble fear and sordid care, and making it possible to leave the morrow to take thought for the things of itself. To this life of noble carelessness Jesus exhorted His hearers when He bade them take no thought what they should eat or drink or put on; and He suggested two aids to its attainment, viz. consideration of the dignity of human life, and trust in the heavenly Father's care. "Is not the life more than meat?" He asked; and in proof of the reality of a paternal Providence He pointed to the fowls of the air and the flowers of the field. A man, He said in effect, has higher work to do than to win a livelihood, and he may safely leave these minor concerns in the hands of Him who feeds the birds and decks the lilies. Beautiful words, and not less noble the temper they inculcate! How great is the man who can really be, not by natural easy-mindedness, but by faith and devotion to the higher ends of life, as free from care as the birds or the unconscious wild flowers! Those who are incessantly distracted by secular solicitudes may more than doubt whether any such men ever existed. One at least did, even Jesus. And He has had genuine followers; probably many more than we know of. And such, wherever they are, are sons of God indeed, who by faith make their lives sublime, and in the spirit of Christian optimism say: "If God be for us, who can be against us?" "All things work together for good to them that love God;" "at the heart of this universe is One whose name is Love, and nothing in the universe can harm me."

The third element of filial righteousness is fellowship with God. Such fellowship as Jesus enjoyed is in measure possible for all Christians. He came into the world for the very purpose of making it a common good. It is part of the objective significance of the Christian era that it has abolished the distant relations between God and men characteristic of the old era, and introduced relations of a more familiar and intimate nature. And it is the duty of each individual Christian to realize the change subjectively. This the spirit of sonship does. It draws near to God with true heart and full assurance of faith. The legal spirit, on the contrary, stands afar off. It is content to fear, and aspires not to filial fellowship. It must have a veil between it and the Holy One; if the veil that could in its time claim for itself to be divinely appointed be removed or rent asunder by the advent of Christ, it will weave one for itself. It has been weaving a veil all through the Christian centuries, of varying material; before the Reformation, of priestcraft and sacramentalism; since then in the Protestant world, of orthodox opinions and time-honoured religious custom. Judaism dies hard, and Rabbinism is prone to reappear in new forms; therefore it is not enough to be objectively redeemed once for all: redemption from legalism must be wrought out in each generation, and in each individual heart. We to-day need to be redeemed, not less than the Jewish contemporaries of Jesus, from a vain religious conversation received by tradition from the fathers. The legal spirit resists the process, which threatens to rob it of the veil between it and God without which it does not feel comfortable. The spirit of adoption, on the other hand, eagerly assists, lending a hand to tear asunder the God-concealing screens that it may get into the Father's very presence, and doing its best to keep the king's highway open for all wayfarers to the Father's house on high. This part of filial righteousness may seem to be a purely religious virtue in which no one has any concern but the individual Christian. In reality it has most important bearings on morals, and very closely concerns the wellbeing of society. It is not good in any view that the righteousness of the scribes should reappear and gain the ascendency, and the only guarantee against so undesirable an occurrence is the prevalence of the spirit of sonship, as a spirit of direct personal, joyful communion with Heaven, without the mediation of either priest or Rabbi.

The last element of filial righteousness is spiritual liberty or independence, a virtue closely related to the foregoing, and already in part referred to. The significance of this attribute in the character of Christ has been indicated in a previous chapter. It remains now to add that it has similar significance in the character of the Christian. It imports a self-reliant attitude in reference to the world, religious as well as irreligious. The son of God is not dependent on public opinion for his knowledge of truth. He has an anointing of the Spirit of truth which makes him feel sure he is in the right path when a thousand voices declare he is in the wrong. He is not in the slippery, insecure position of those who know of no guide in religion, and to a certain extent even in morals, but custom, and the oracular utterances of men who make confident assertions, or who pass in the world for wise. He stands firm on the rock of personal conviction. Jesus indicated this as the desirable and normal state of mind when He described the people among whom He lived as a community of blind men, the majority being blindly led by a class of persons as blind as themselves.[1] What He desiderated was that men should know for themselves what was true and what false in religion. He regarded this as possible for all whose hearts were right. And He carefully trained His own disciples to regard independent thought and action as a duty, by accustoming them to do many things which were witnessed with pious horror by the abject slaves of custom.

The last observation conducts us by an easy transition to the fourth aspect of the righteousness of the kingdom, according to which it consists in the imitation of Christ. This is the righteousness of *discipleship*. In the Sermon on the Mount, Jesus did not directly adopt the style of one who summed up duty in likeness to Himself. He exhorted His hearers to be perfect as their Father in heaven was perfect. Even in the text in which He

[1] Matt. xv. 14.

describes spurious disciples as calling Him Lord at the judgment, He makes their fate turn not on the question whether they have done His will, but on the question whether they have done the will of His Father in heaven.[1] In the epilogue He represented hearers as wise or foolish according as they heard and did His sayings, or only heard without doing.[2] But thereby He only showed His perfect confidence as a religious teacher in the truth and vital importance of His doctrine. He took up a somewhat higher position when, at a later period, He claimed to be the exclusive organ of the revelation of the Father, and invited men to come and learn from Him.[3] Even then His claim formally was to be the supreme religious guide rather than the living law of life. "Learn from Me" signifies strictly, not take Me as an example, but take Me as the one great Master. But in the case of Jesus the latter claim includes the former. For He taught not by word only, but also and even more by action; and when by word, often by accompanying illustrative action. So, for example, in relation to the subjects of fasting, ritual ablutions, Sabbath-keeping, intercourse with social outcasts. So likewise in relation to the temper becoming disciples. Jesus taught His disciples to be humble by being Himself meek and lowly, and on suitable occasions He expressly invited them to take note of His behaviour with a disciplinary purpose.[4]

Learning from Christ thus virtually signifies imitating Christ. This imitation has a very wide range, covers

[1] Matt. vii. 21.
[2] Matt. vii. 24-27.
[3] Matt. xi. 27, 28.
[4] Matt. xx. 28.

indeed the whole ground of Christian duty. Jesus was a model in all things: in philanthropy, in sonship, in devotion to the kingdom, in temper. The following points, however, may here be specially mentioned. It behoves the Christian disciple to imitate the Master in His *sympathies* with the objects of pity, the poor, the sorrowful, the sinful; in His *antipathies* against the religious vices of Pharisaism; in His *lowliness;* and in His heroic *devotion* to duty at whatever cost of self-sacrifice. These four things stand out most prominently in the public ministry of Jesus. He was emphatically a philanthropist, a lover of men, a friend of such as most needed a friend; and no one can be a good Christian in whom the spirit of pity does not reign. He was not less emphatically a hater of all counterfeit sanctities. Nor were these anti-pharisaic antipathies of Jesus accidental: they formed an essential part of the religion He preached and practised. They cannot be regarded as now merely historical; they must be repeated in every generation. For the spirit of Pharisaism lives on through the ages, ever embodying itself in new forms, and growing like a fungus on every manifestation of the divine in human life, not excepting evangelic religion itself, which might be supposed to be its natural antithesis. The protest of the Founder of our faith did not slay the evil thing; it only clearly revealed its nature, and made manifest to the whole world that Christianity and it have nothing in common. Therefore the protest needs to be constantly renewed, and every sincere Christian will do his utmost to make it as effectual as possible for the benefit of the time in which he lives. No Christian worthy of the name will be ashamed of the antipathies of Jesus, or think it necessary to apologise for them or to throw them into the shade. He will rather take pains to evince his cordial sympathy with them that the world may not be misled into the deplorable mistake of confounding the piety of the scribes with the Christianity of Christ, and that those may be brought to Christ's school whose present religious position is merely negative, and whose only creed is utter disbelief in the type of religion which Christ so unreservedly condemned. A religious community which, while bearing Christ's name, leaves its attitude at this point in doubt, or, still worse, gives good reasons to suspect that its sympathies are on the wrong side, is a salt without a savour, and sooner or later will be trodden under foot of men.

On the other attributes of Jesus above mentioned it is not necessary to expatiate. However rare the spirit of lowliness may be, all acknowledge that it was conspicuous in His character, and that in this very specially He is to be regarded as our example. The greatest in the kingdom in a spirit of lowly love became the least. He was among His own disciples as the serving man. He held Himself up as a pattern in this respect to His disciples when in a spirit of ambition they disputed about places of distinction, and taught them the great truth, that honour in the kingdom of God comes by service.[1] Thereby He proclaimed one of the most characteristic laws of that kingdom, and indicated one of the most essential elements in its righteousness. No

[1] Matt. xx. 27, 28.

one has any part in the righteousness of the kingdom or any fellowship of life with Christ who does not loyally accept this law of greatness by service. Of Christ's heroic devotion to duty there is also no room to doubt, nor has He neglected to instruct His disciples that in this virtue He expects them to follow in His footsteps. The precept, "deny thyself," is one of the commonplaces in the doctrine of Jesus. In various forms of language and on several occasions He said : " Whosoever does not bear his cross and come after Me, he cannot be My disciple."[1] He even went so far as to prescribe hatred of the most dearly loved objects of affection as a qualification for true discipleship.[2] This is one of the sayings of our Lord which must be taken in the spirit and not in the letter. It presupposes the existence of the opposite affection to that enjoined, and requires disciples to subordinate the love of kindred and life to the duties of their spiritual calling, repressing all softheartedness as passionately as if they hated what in truth they intensely love.

We come now, in the last place, to the righteousness of *citizenship*. The cardinal virtue here also is absolute devotion. The complete self-surrender which Jesus in such strong terms demanded from disciples towards Himself, He also demanded towards the kingdom of God from all citizens. The two demands indeed are substantially one, for the interests of the kingdom and the service of the King practically coincide. The ground of

---

[1] Luke xiv. 27.
[2] Luke xiv. 26. On this saying as given by Luke *vide* Introduction, p. 19. Even in this strong form it might have been spoken by Christ.

the demand is that the kingdom is the chief good, and the chief end. It is represented as the chief good in the parables of *The Treasure hid in a Field*, and *The Pearl of Great Price*,[1] in both of which it is taught that the kingdom of heaven is of incomparable worth, so that a man who knows its true value will joyfully sacrifice all he hath for its sake. It is implied in the same parables that a man may reasonably be expected to make this sacrifice, because the kingdom is the chief end. What is there implied is in other texts expressly declared. Nowhere do we find the sovereign claims of the kingdom expressed in more peremptory terms than in two sayings reported by the third evangelist: "Let the dead bury their dead, but go thou and preach the kingdom of God;" "No man, having put his hand to the plough, and looking back, is fit for the kingdom of God,"[2]—the one spoken to a disciple who wished to bury his father before entering on the duties to which the Master summoned him, the other to a disciple who desired permission to go and bid farewell to his friends. The reply in either case was a refusal, and the terms in which it was expressed in both instances seem harsh and unreasonable. It does seem hard that a man enlisted for service in the kingdom cannot get leave to go home to pay the last duty to a parent, and little less hard that one cannot speak of bidding friends good-bye without incurring the suspicion of half-heartedness. But the very harshness and apparent unreasonableness of the sayings serve to show how exacting and inexorable is the demand of the kingdom for heroic devotion; and when we carefully consider

[1] Matt. xiii. 44-46.   [2] Luke ix. 60, 62.

the words, we see that they convey that idea in terms which, under a superficial appearance of extravagance, conceal principles on which Jesus seriously meant all disciples to act. Each of the three sayings, brought together by Luke in the place from which the above two are quoted, contains a distinct principle applicable to a particular type of character. The word spoken to the scribe: "Foxes have holes, and birds of the air have nests; but the Son of Man hath not where to lay His head," suggested to an inconsiderate enthusiast the lesson that one must count the cost before entering on the career of a disciple. The second word is adapted to the case of a man thoroughly in earnest, but distracted by a conflict of duties, and virtually enunciates the principle that in all collisions between the duties we owe to the kingdom and those arising out of natural relations, the former must take precedence. The third word meets the case of a divided heart. The ploughman who looks back does not give his undivided attention to his task, and therefore fails to drive a straight furrow. The man who desired to bid farewell to his friends was hankering after home enjoyments, and the reply to his request taught the lesson that no one who is drawn two ways by his affections is fit for the service of the kingdom, because it demands the whole heart and mind.

While pronouncing the man of divided heart unfit, Jesus reckoned the man who served the kingdom with singleness of heart *perfect*. It was in this sense He used the term when He said to the young ruler: "If thou wilt be perfect, go and sell that thou hast."[1] There are two

[1] Matt. xix. 21.

senses in which we may speak of perfection. There is a perfection of motive, which is equivalent to single-mindedness; and there is a perfection in conduct, freedom from fault in all parts of character. Both sorts of perfection are to be desired, and are possible here or hereafter. But when men are spoken of in Scripture as actually perfect, while still living in this world, the word is used in the first sense, not in the second. Noah and Job are called perfect in this sense,[1] and could not be in any other, for they were both faulty. Caleb and David are virtually described as perfect in this sense when they are said to have followed God fully or with all the heart,[2] and they deserved the praise, while David at least could not be characterized as perfect in the sense of faultlessness. Keeping in mind this distinction, we can understand how Paul could speak of himself as at once perfect and imperfect, as when he said, "Not that I have already attained or am already perfected,"[4] and immediately after referred to a class called the τέλειοι which included himself. In Paul's judgment the τέλειοι possessed two attributes —aspiration, implying a consciousness of yet unreached moral attainments, and single-mindedness, having for its motto: ἓν δέ,—one idea, one aim filling the whole mind. Such was the perfection Jesus demanded of the young ruler, and of all who undertook the responsibilities of citizenship in the divine kingdom. He did not require or expect perfection in the details of conduct, but He did demand a perfect heart. It was to this He pointed when He said, "Go and sell that thou hast." He did not

---

[1] Gen. vi. 9; Job i. 1.   [2] Num. xiv. 24; 2 Kings xiv. 8.
[3] Phil. iii. 14–16.

mean: "You have many virtues, it would seem, add yet one more—the renunciation of property, and then you will be a perfect man, a paragon of excellence without a single defect." Not one act or virtue more is exacted, but a state of heart, the presence or absence of which will be ascertained by the manner in which the advice is taken. Can the aspirant part with all, then he is perfect in the sense of caring supremely for the kingdom of God. Can he not part with his possessions, then his interest in eternal life or the divine kingdom is not a consuming passion, but simply one of many inclinations, and not the strongest. He is what St. James calls ἀνὴρ δίψυχος,[1] a two-souled man, with one soul loving the world dearly, and another loving somewhat, but not enough, the kingdom of heaven. Such two-mindedness Jesus looked on as a fatal defect. In His view the perfection of single-mindedness was not merely a desirable ornament, but an indispensable requisite of genuine citizenship.

The man of perfect heart is never self-complacent; he serves God devotedly yet humbly. This truth Jesus taught in the parable of *Extra Service*,[2] which depicts a labourer returning from the fields in the evening, weary and hungry, yet called on to serve his master at supper, before he can himself sit down to meat and rest. The parable conveys two lessons: one, that the service of the kingdom is of a very exacting nature, recognising no day's work of statutory length, and often summoning to extra tasks a servant who has already toiled many hours; the other, that the right-minded servant will perform

[1] Jas. i. 8.   [2] Luke xvii. 7–10.

these added tasks without a murmur, and without a thought that anything great or specially meritorious has been done by him. The temper equal to this is manifestly not that either of the slave who works as a drudge under compulsion, or of the Pharisee who sets a high value on his performance. It is the temper of devotion mellowed by the grace of humility.

Incapable of mean-minded self-satisfaction, the devoted man is still less capable of mercenariness. He serves generously in obedience to the impulses of a heart which loves the kingdom for its own sake, not for hire. Generosity enters as an essential ingredient into the righteousness of citizenship. This Jesus taught in the parable of *The Labourers in the Vineyard*.[1] The praise of generosity is not expressed indeed, but it is implied in the preference of the employer for those who entered at the eleventh hour, and worked without making a bargain,—a preference shown by paying them first, and by paying them a full day's hire. If the occasion of the parable was Peter's question, "We have left all, and followed Thee, what shall we have therefore?" the purpose to discourage a mercenary spirit becomes still more certain.

I close this exposition of the righteousness of the kingdom by three general observations.

1. In that righteousness as here exhibited religion and morality are blended. This is as it ought to be. Religion and morals may be separated in natural ethics, but not in the ethics of Christianity, which embrace the whole of human conduct under all aspects and relations.

[1] Matt. xx. 1–16.

The counterfeit righteousness of the scribes was also of this composite character. Hence in the Sermon on the Mount the term δικαιοσύνη is used in reference to such matters as almsgiving, praying, and fasting,—all three more or less of a religious character. "Take heed," said the Preacher, "that ye do not your righteousness before men, to be seen of them;"[1] proceeding thereafter to illustrate the counsel by describing the ostentatious manner in which the Pharisees performed the duties above specified.

2. It will have been observed that the diverse aspects under which the righteousness of the kingdom has been presented to a considerable extent overlap each other. This may appear a fault of method, but it is a fault which cannot well be avoided. This righteousness is a many-sided thing; it is like a rich landscape to which justice cannot be done by a single painting taken from one point of view. Many pictures are needed to present it in its manifoldness before the mental eye; and though the same features appear more or less in all, they are shown in different relations and in varying proportions. The remark applies not only to Christ's doctrine of righteousness, but to many other parts of His teaching. His great words baffle all attempts at exhaustive treatment by a single train of thought.

3. The righteousness of God, here imperfectly described, may seem high and difficult to fulfil. It is

---

[1] Matt. vi. 1. For δικαιοσύνην the T. R. has ἐλεημοσύνην, a reading due to the feeling that the term righteousness was not applicable to such matters as those afterwards referred to, or to almsgiving in particular. צדקה (righteousness) was a current name for alms among the scribes. *Vide* Weber, p. 276.

indeed high, like the great mountains,[1] whose snowy summits it is not easy to reach. But the commandments of Christ, though difficult, are not grievous. Laws are grievous which are merely positive or ritual in their character, having no apparent reason for their observance beyond the arbitrary will of the legislator. Such for the most part were the commandments of the scribes. Even moral laws, such as commend themselves to conscience, become grievous when they are enforced mainly by threatened penalties appealing to fear. Christ's commands are not grievous in either respect. They are essentially spiritual, and as such self-evidently reasonable. What more reasonable than the requirement to be God-like in charity, Christ-like in meekness and in fidelity to duty, or to be a true son of God in spirit? These precepts simply present, in the form of a task, that which our own spiritual intelligence recognises as the moral ideal. The ideal is high, but an ideal is never burdensome because it is high; on the contrary, it is the low moral ideal that is felt to be burdensome. How intolerable, for example, were the model prescribed not the loving Father in heaven, but the immoral divinities of paganism! If there be nothing grievous in the nature of the commandments, as little is there in the motives on which reliance is placed to ensure obedience. For these consist not in intimidations, like those brought into play at Sinai, but in aspirations and inspirations. The divine ideal is exhibited, and is left to draw us towards itself by its own unearthly beauty. A perfect example is set before us, and its power

[1] Ps. xxxvi. 6, "Thy righteousness is like the great mountains."

to awaken enthusiasm is confidently relied on. The righteousness of the kingdom acts on us as the mountain peaks on the strong-limbed climber, or the model picture of a great master on the young artist. In either case a hard task is set, but the very arduousness is a part of the charm. To catch the spirit of the old masters is the aspirant's own ambition. Scaling the high Alps is the tourist's holiday work. Even so is it the delight of the disciple to do the will of the Father, and to follow in the footsteps of Christ. Who would not rather ascend the high hills of God in the kingdom of heaven than walk the treadmill in the prison-house of Rabbinism!

CHAPTER X.

THE DEATH OF JESUS AND ITS SIGNIFICANCE.

According to the united testimony of the Synoptical Evangelists, Jesus for the first time spoke plainly to His disciples concerning the fact and the manner of His death, towards the close of the Galilean ministry, on the visit to the neighbourhood of Cæsarea Philippi. Then "He began to teach them that the Son of Man must suffer many things, and be rejected of the elders, and of the chief priests and scribes, and be killed."[1] Thereafter He repeated the startling intimation with added particulars, from time to time as His own mood or outward circumstances prompted.[2] Up till then He had alluded to the tragic issue of His life only in vague, mystic terms, as when He hinted that days would come when the Bridegroom should be taken away and the children of the bridechamber should have cause to mourn.[3]

In introducing the approaching passion as a subject of explicit prediction, in familiar intercourse with His disciples, Jesus deemed it expedient also to begin to instruct them as to its cause and meaning, that the unwelcome event might be rendered more tolerable by insight into its

---

[1] Mark viii. 31.   [2] Matt. xvii. 22, xx. 17.   [3] Matt. ix. 15.

rationale. From the view-point of an elaborate theology the instruction He communicated may appear very meagre, consisting at most of four lessons conveyed in very brief sayings. But instead of indulging in idle regrets that more was not spoken or recorded on so vitally important a topic, let us endeavour to penetrate into the meaning of the few precious words which embody our Lord's *doctrine of the cross.*

The *first* lesson Jesus taught His disciples in this abstruse doctrine was, that His death was the natural effect of fidelity to righteousness in an unrighteous world. Such is the import of the words He spoke to Peter in rebuke of his counsel of self-preservation: "Thou savourest not the things that be of God, but those that be of men."[1] It is implied that the divine interest and the individual human interest are to a certain extent incompatible, so that a choice must be made between them, and that the path of duty, in all cases of collision, is to sacrifice the personal interest to the divine. On this view the sufferings of Christ are not to be regarded as singular or exceptional, at least in kind, but rather as the highest instance of a general law, according to which all who are loyal to the divine claims must more or less suffer for righteousness' sake. This accordingly Jesus proceeded immediately to declare in these terms: "If any man will come after Me, let him deny himself, and take up his cross, and follow Me."[2] Thereby He intimated that cross-bearing was the normal law of every life regulated by supreme devotion to the divine kingdom; or, in other words, that the righteousness of the kingdom was so

[1] Matt. xvi. 23.   [2] Matt. xvi. 24.

utterly diverse from the way of the world, that reaction against it might be reckoned on as certain.

In the case of Jesus Himself the truth of this hard doctrine is apparent. Simply by being righteous in the true sense of the word, He exposed Himself to a deadly opposition which naturally culminated in His crucifixion. Three features of His public conduct, closely connected, inevitably provoked the bitter hostility of the religious world, above all things to be feared. These were His unflinching exposure of the righteousness of the scribes; His habit of fraternizing with the people of the land, *Am Haarcz*, who neither knew nor kept the laws manufactured by the scribes; and His personal disregard of many Rabbinical prescriptions, such as those connected with fasting, ritual ablutions, and Sabbath keeping. These characteristics, early manifested and early noticed, indicated a complete breach with Pharisaism, which to the lynx-eyed suspicious spirit of religious conservatism must have appeared a thing of evil omen, portending, in fact, nothing less than a revolution, a catastrophe by all means fair or foul to be averted. In all the three lines of action Jesus was but putting in practice the righteousness of the kingdom: in the first, witnessing for truth against current plausible falsehood; in the second, loving those whom cruel caste-pride abandoned to neglect and did its best to ruin; in the third, backing up a protest in words by a more powerful protest in deeds, and refusing to lend the sanction of His example to a moral system in which virtues and sins were alike artificial. Yet against such truth, love, and sincerity, genuine elements of the righteousness of God, there was a law: the law of established custom, which would not suffer itself to be broken with impunity. This law made its voice very soon heard, in censure of Christ's nonconforming ways; the tone of condemnation increasing in emphasis and truculence as time went on, till at last it became brutal and murderous. Jesus knew well what the voice meant, even in its first mutterings of discontent. Probably He did not need to wait for open manifestations of the spirit of antagonism in order to know what lay before Him. He could divine His fate from the treatment experienced by the prophets,[1] and through clear insight into the deep irreconcilable contrariety between the righteousness of the kingdom and that of the scribes. Hence apparently trivial occurrences were fraught with ominous import to His mind; in a small cloud like a man's hand He could discern the signs of a coming storm. The question, "Why do Thy disciples fast not?" which to any other person might seem very innocent and peaceable, led Him to speak of days when His bereaved disciples would have good cause to fast, the thought underlying the allusion obviously being: "at the end of this way of nonconformity stands a cross."[2] The demand for a sign from heaven made by the Pharisees at a later period, by a logic not apparent to the disciples, awakened in His mind the most gloomy forebodings.[3]

It was a mere question of time how long it would take Pharisaic hostility to ripen into a fixed purpose to get rid of the obnoxious man by violence. To that it must come sooner or later. At first it might content itself with expressions of simple disapprobation, or at worst with

[1] Matt. v. 12, xxiii. 29-31, 37.   [2] Matt. ix. 15.   [3] Matt. xvi. 1-4.

slanderous misrepresentations; but if these means failed it would not hesitate to have recourse to more effectual methods of neutralizing the offender's influence. That influence was too great to be treated with contempt. Jesus was formidable by His miracles, His wisdom, His goodness secretly acknowledged, though in word denied, by the claims to be some exceptionally great one which all these suggested, by His popularity which, though subject to fluctuation, ever broke out anew like an epidemic, so that no one could tell what might come out of it. Such indeed was the favour which His works of healing, His teaching, and His character had won for Him among the people, that had He chosen to use it as an instrument of self-defence He might have set Pharisees, priests, scribes, and unprincipled rulers at defiance. He had only to flatter popular prejudices and yield Himself up to patriotic enthusiasms. But He was not a man of the world who could play off one party against another, or make friends by even seeming acquiescence in prevalent delusions. And so He became completely isolated, a man without a party on whose support He could rely; and His enemies without much risk might do unto Him whatever they listed.

It thus appears that the sufferings of Jesus followed in the way of natural causality from the faithful discharge of the duties of His prophetic calling. On this view as a foundation all higher theological constructions of the passion must rest. Whatever more is to be said as to the significance of Christ's death, this at least is certain, that He died as a faithful martyr for truth and love. And in this aspect of His sufferings He is not isolated.

He has companions thus far, and is a Captain leading a host to battle. The antagonism between the divine kingdom and the world, though not always so acute as in the experience of the Saviour, is chronic, and there is always occasion in some form for the sacrifice pointed at in the striking paradox: "Whosoever will save his life shall lose it; and whosoever will lose his life for My sake shall find it."[1]

The *second* lesson in the doctrine of the cross was given in connection with the ambitious request of the two sons of Zebedee, on which occasion Jesus said: "The Son of Man came not to be ministered unto, but to minister, and to give His life a ransom for many."[2] The saying comes in with startling abruptness, without anything in the context to prepare us for the introduction of the one remarkable word it contains, the term λύτρον (ransom). On this account, and also because of the aspect of theological theorizing on the subject of Christ's death which the text wears, the authenticity of this *logion* has been called in question by Dr. Baur and others. The solitariness of the utterance has also been pressed into the service of a suspicious criticism, there being no other text in the Synoptical records the least like it, save that occurring in the account of the institution of the Supper, to be hereafter noticed. But the genuineness of this word can hardly be doubted in view of the fact that it is recorded by both Matthew and Mark, though the absence of a text so Pauline in character from Luke's narrative is certainly-surprising. And, if we leave out of account the one word λύτρον, the relevancy of the

[1] Matt. xvi. 25. [2] Matt. xx. 28; Mark x. 45.

saying to the connection of thought is indisputable. The ambition of the two disciples was to obtain places of distinction in the Messianic kingdom. Jesus gave them and their fellow-disciples to understand that in this kingdom power was not to be got by solicitation or by inheritance, but solely by service; he being the greatest who in love humbled himself to be the least. How natural and how convincing to follow up the statement of this general principle by a reference to the conduct of One whom the disciples regarded as the King of this kingdom, with the view of showing how He sought power. For that was the point to be emphasized. The reference made by Jesus to His own manner of acting was not meant to exemplify His humility, but to explain His method of gaining sovereignty. "The Son of Man," He says in effect, "seeks His place, that of sovereign, not by self-assertion, not by demanding His rights and enforcing them with a high hand, but by stooping to be a servant to His own future subjects, carrying service to the limit of possibility, even to the extent of laying down His life for the good of many."

Thus understood, this text, omitting the term $\lambda\acute{v}\tau\rho o\nu$, teaches as the second lesson in the doctrine of the cross, that Jesus died not merely for righteousness' sake, but for the benefit of men whom by this act of self-humbling love He sought to make His devoted subjects. But the omitted term must now be taken into account, and we must inquire what is to be understood by this very peculiar form in which the fact of the passion is framed?

A priori it was to be expected that Jesus would frame the fact in some remarkable thought forms. After He had begun to think much, and with deep emotion, on the fact that He must die on the cross, it was inevitable that His mind should set itself to invest the harsh prosaic fact with poetic, mystic, spiritual meanings. He could not be content to regard His death as a mere fate: He must see in it an event ordained of God for beneficent ends, destined to prove eventually in an eminent degree serviceable to the kingdom, instead of being, as might well appear to be the case, a fatal blow to its prospects. This much we should expect, even if we regarded Jesus only as a man of wonderful religious genius. From such an one, as even Keim admits, some deep pregnant utterances concerning the meaning of this anticipated death by violence were to be looked for, comparing it to redemption money, or to the seal of a new covenant, or to a corn of wheat dying that it may become fruitful—words worthy of one whose genius, not to speak of anything higher, was able to cope with death, and rob it of its sting and its repulsiveness, and invest it with beauty, clothing the unsightly skeleton of rude reality with the flesh and blood of spiritual significance.

This thought concerning the ransom, which comes in so abruptly and stands so isolated, like a detached rock which has resisted successfully the disintegrating force of the elements, had doubtless a secret history in the mind of Jesus, which, if known, would help us to understand its meaning. In absence of any explanatory statements by the speaker, it is natural to seek light in the Old Testament, and to regard the saying as the result of a combination of texts drawn from the ancient Scriptures. Thus Ritschl finds the roots of the idea in these two texts: "None of them can by any means redeem his brother, nor give to God a ransom for him;"[1] and, "If there be a messenger with him, an interpreter, one among a thousand, to show unto man his uprightness: then he is gracious unto him, and saith, Deliver him from going down to the pit; I have found a ransom."[2] From the former he draws the two inferences, that the "ransom" is a gift to God, not to the devil, and that Jesus represents Himself as able to render a service in the place of the many which no one of them could render either for himself or for another. From the latter he gathers a third inference, viz. that Jesus distinguishes Himself from the mass of men liable to death as being exempted from the natural doom of death, and conceives of His death as a voluntary act by which He surrenders His life to God. Assuming that these thoughts were all present to the speaker's mind when he uttered the saying now under consideration, it teaches that the Son of Man gave His life to God a ransom for the lives of men doomed to die, which He was able to do, because His life was that of an exceptional being, one among a thousand, not a brother mortal, but an angel who assumed flesh, and became a son of man that He might freely die.[3]

This construction, while exegetically legitimate, is open to the objection that it makes the saying the outcome of a process of reasoning much more in keeping with the habits of thought characteristic of the professional theologian than with the genial poetic way of Jesus. It would be more satisfactory if we could connect the saying with some occurrence in the recent history of the speaker

---

[1] Ps. xlix. 7.   [2] Job xxxiii. 23, 24.
[3] Ritschl, *Lehre von der Rechtfertigung und Versöhnung*, ii. 80.

which might naturally suggest the thought it embodies, and partly account for its utterance at the present time. May we not find such a point of contact in the *temple-tax* incident, which happened at Capernaum just before the final departure from Galilee?[1] On that occasion the collectors of the temple revenue demanded of Peter the *didrachmon* or half-shekel paid annually by every adult Jew, in accordance with the law laid down in Ex. xxx. 12. In that law the half-shekel is represented as a "ransom ($\lambda \acute{v} \tau \rho a$) for the soul," insuring the life of each man paying it against the risk of any plague breaking out in connection with the numbering of the people. When the customary tribute was called for, Jesus consented to pay it, under protest that as the King's Son He ought to be free; His purpose being not seriously to object to payment, but to direct the attention of His disciples to the conciliatory spirit by which His conduct was guided, in tacit rebuke of the ambitious passions which had led them to dispute by the way which of them should be the greatest in the kingdom. There are obvious points of resemblance between the two situations. In both there was an outburst of ambition within the disciple-circle to be dealt with; in both the Master, conscious of being a great one—a King's Son or a King—holds Himself up to His disciples as an example, as one who does not stand upon His rights and dignities, but assumes a servile position in a spirit of humility. There is not now, as then, a half-shekel to be paid in the form of a temple-tax; but there is a life to be demanded within the next few days, a tax also imposed in the name of religion, to

[1] Matt. xvii. 24.

be as cheerfully paid, and with greater ease; for the owner of this life was so poor that an exaction not exceeding in value half-a-crown was beyond His means. How natural that the mind of Jesus should revert to the incident which occurred in Capernaum three months ago, and, connecting the tribute then paid with its original purpose, as stated in the book of Exodus, should conceive of the new act of self-humbling service about to be performed as the paying of a ransom for the people, who in ignorance were on the point of throwing His life away as a thing of no value! It is as if He had said: "Then they asked of Me a small coin for their temple, which I had not to give; now they ask of Me my life, which it is in My power freely to lay down. This life, though they know it not, is, like the half-shekel, their ransom money, and I gladly yield it up to save their souls from death."

The foregoing account of the genesis of this saying I offer with diffidence, but not without a feeling that on various grounds it merits serious consideration. In the first place, it removes from the saying the aspect of isolation, by bringing it into natural association with known experiences and utterances of Jesus. It also divests it of that abstract theological aspect which has given rise to suspicion of its genuineness, and makes it appear, like all the words of Jesus, full of pathos and poetic spirit. It has this further recommendation, that it brings the saying in question into surprisingly close contact with a statement concerning the significance of Christ's death made by that apostle, who, as a disciple, played a principal part in the Capernaum incident. "Ye were not redeemed," writes Peter, "with corruptible things, as silver and gold, from your vain conversation received by tradition from your fathers; but with the precious blood of Christ."[1] One can hardly help thinking that he had the two evangelic incidents in his mind when he wrote that sentence, so that for himself it meant: your fathers paid half-a-shekel for the temple service as a ransom for their lives; it took something more and very different, even the life-blood of Jesus, to redeem you from the bondage of a vain religious tradition, and to make you Christians. The mention of silver connects the text with the earlier incident, the expression ἐλυτρώθητε (ye were redeemed) connects it with the memorable word in which Jesus spoke of His life given up to death as a λύτρον.

Thus far of what may be called the psychological history of this saying; what now is to be said as to its didactic significance? What precisely does it teach us? This much at least, that the death of Jesus, voluntarily endured, is somehow the means of delivering from death the souls of the many: He died that they might live; He died willingly, because He believed that thereby He could render this service. This much, and perhaps not much more. How the death of the Son of Man brings life to others, and whether the life thus procured could not be obtained in any other way, does not appear. We may have recourse to the sacrificial system in search of the needful supplementary explanations. In classic usage the term λύτρον was applied to expiatory sacrifices;[2] and it is also so used in the New Testament, as

[1] 1 Pet. i. 18.
[2] *Vide* on this Cremer's *Wörterbuch*, under the word λύτρον.

in the text quoted above from the First Epistle of Peter.[1] But to import exact theological determinations from other quarters into a text is not the function of strict exposition. In this profound saying our Lord has bequeathed to His Church a theological problem, rather than supplied her with a full solution.

As a sufferer for righteousness, Jesus, we saw, is not without companions. Is there companionship between Him and His disciples in this second aspect of suffering also? May Christians as well as their Lord lay down their lives as a ransom for others? It depends on the sense in which we understand the term. Companionship with Jesus in suffering for the spiritual good of others is possible. Jesus recognised this when He said to James and John, "Ye shall indeed drink of the cup that I drink of; and with the baptism that I am baptized withal shall ye be baptized."[2] Strictly interpreted, indeed, this was merely a prediction of suffering for the Christian faith, identical with the cross-bearing of the first lesson. But it is permissible to borrow light on this mystery of suffering from the beneficent function ascribed by Jesus to His own suffering, and to say that in all cases where suffering is endured for righteousness, there is reaction in the way of benefit, even to those who were the unrighteous cause of suffering. Saul's conversion was in part caused by Stephen's martyrdom, and the hand which

---

[1] Peter possibly combined the present saying of Jesus with that spoken at the institution of the Supper, to be considered farther on, and so got the idea of redemption by the sacrifice of Christ as a Lamb.

[2] Mark x. 39. In the corresponding passage in Matthew's narrative the second clause is not genuine.

he had in it. Thus good was returned for evil. The moral order of the divine kingdom provides for this happening on the great scale. Its citizens suffer through the world's sin, and their sufferings convince the world of sin, and make many conquests for the kingdom. The blood of the martyrs is the seed of the Church, and the knowledge of the fact helps them to die. Thus far there is companionship with Jesus. But when the benefit rendered by death is conceived of as an atonement for sin, He must be alone, for He alone is sinless. Righteousness, viewed impersonally, suffers for the unrighteous in all the citizens of the kingdom,[1] but only One can suffer as the Just for the unjust.

The *third* lesson in the doctrine of the cross was given in the house of Simon of Bethany, in connection with the anointing of Jesus by Mary. This lesson has not been recognised as one at all, or at least as available for theological purposes. I venture to include it, however, among the few precious hints communicated by Jesus to His disciples concerning the significance of His death, being convinced that in doing so I am acting in accordance with His own wish as expressed in the remarkable words recorded by the first two evangelists: "Verily I say unto you, Wheresoever the gospel shall be preached throughout the whole world, this also that she hath done shall be spoken of for a memorial of her."[2] As I understand this declaration, so solemnly introduced, it amounts

---

[1] This truth we are taught by Isa. liii., where the sufferer is in the first place the ideal Israel, the faithful portion of the nation bearing the sins of the unfaithful.

[2] Matt. xxvi. 13 ; Mark xiv. 9.

to an intimation by Jesus that His own deed in dying was in spirit similar to the deed performed by Mary on Himself, when, regardless of expense, she broke the alabaster vase, and poured its precious contents on His head. However much He might desire that compensation might be made to Mary for the wrong done to her by churlish critics, through her praises being sung in after ages, He would hardly have deemed her act worthy of perpetual eulogy, unless He had regarded it as possessing moral affinity to His own act in shedding His life-blood, and therefore as fit to be used in illustration of its meaning. He thinks of that tragic act for the moment as the great theme of the preacher. "The gospel" He speaks of is not merely the general gospel of the kingdom, but more specifically the gospel in His death. A not unimportant part of the third lesson consists just in this application of the term "gospel" to an impending catastrophe, which to the uninstructed eye can appear only as a horrible, disastrous fate. It teaches that ultimate great good to many will come out of this evil. But the most valuable contribution to the doctrine of the cross consists in the light thrown on the ethical character of Christ's action in submitting to crucifixion, by the suggested comparison between His deed in dying and Mary's deed in anointing Him. A gospel already, inasmuch as out of a temporary calamity comes permanent good, that death is revealed to be doubly a gospel when it is made to appear as a deed done out of pure, generous, uncalculating love to men. The gospel in Christ's death thus becomes "this gospel," as it is called in Matthew's narrative,—the gospel in a death of which Mary's act of love is an apt emblem. As such it is a gospel of that generous, magnificent character which to the eye of the churl is apt to appear wastefulness. There can be little doubt that Jesus had in view to point out the affinity between His deed and Mary's in this respect in speaking of His gospel as one to be preached in the whole world,—a very remarkable statement, containing, as has been observed, the most reliable word of the last period of Christ's life concerning the universal destination of Christianity.[1] Thereby He set the large aim of His redeeming love side by side with the munificence which had exposed Mary to censure. He would defend her by pleading guilty to the same charge of waste in the broadest possible terms. Waste is relative to the critic's point of view. From Peter's point of view at Cæsarea, it was waste in Jesus to die at all. From a Judaist's point of view, it was waste to die for more than the chosen race. From the Calvinist's point of view, it may appear waste in the Saviour to die for more than the elect. As against all these possible charges of waste, Jesus in effect replies: I die because I love My countrymen, and would fain ransom their souls from bondage; I die for pagans as well as for Jews, because I love them also; I die for every human creature, because all men are My brethren and God's prodigal children. The mind of Jesus in this matter has not been understood and appreciated by all His followers. Many have even denied the wastefulness which He virtually acknowledges; but in vain, for this grand, large-hearted way, which to the narrow-hearted

[1] Keim, *Jesu von Nazara*.

wears the aspect of waste, is characteristic of all the noble. It is the way of God Himself, and of all who are worthy to be called His sons. Here also Jesus has companions. Prophets, apostles, martyrs throw their lives away for the world's good, and the world calls them fools for their pains, and is benefited by those of whom it is not worthy.

The *fourth* lesson in the doctrine of the cross is contained in the words spoken by Jesus when He put into the hands of His disciples the sacramental cup at the institution of the Holy Supper. Negative criticism has been very active here, cutting down the genuine utterance of our Lord to very small dimensions, by treating as later additions the words εἰς ἄφεσιν ἁμαρτιῶν ("for the remission of sins") found only in Matthew; the expressions περὶ πολλῶν, ὑπὲρ ὑμῶν (shed "for *many*," "for *you*"), which give to the death of Jesus a sacrificial character; and the very remarkable phrase ἡ καινὴ διαθήκη occurring in Luke's account of the institution, and also in Paul's, and supposed to owe its origin to the apostle's influence, being as it were a summary embodiment of his universalistic view of Christianity. In connection with this last phrase stress is laid on the fact that in both Matthew and Mark the best attested reading is not τῆς καινῆς διαθήκης, but simply τῆς διαθήκης. Baur admits that the sense remains substantially the same though the epithet "new" be omitted, seeing that if the blood of Jesus be the blood of a covenant, the covenant formed through His blood can only be a new one; but just on that account he doubts the genuineness even of the shorter reading, and thinks that the reference to a covenant giving to the death of Jesus a sacrificial character found its way into the Gospels through the influence of Paul's doctrinal construction of the evangelic tradition concerning the Supper. But this is criticism carried to an extreme in the interest of a theory. The reference to a covenant, occurring in all the four accounts of the institution, must be accepted as genuine; and its acceptance carries along with it, if not the genuineness, at least the substantial accuracy of the other phrases, viewed as interpretive glosses added to the original utterance. The covenant referred to, from the nature of the case, must be new. Being a covenant in Christ's blood it is a covenant founded on sacrifice, and the expressions shed "for many" and "for you" are justified; which, however, may be accepted as genuine in their own right as occurring with insignificant variations as to form in all the narratives. And according to all the analogies of the Old Testament sacrificial system, what can "blood shed for many" mean, but blood shed for the remission of sins? Instead therefore of following the example of the Tübingen critics, and reducing the words of Jesus to the bald formula: This bread broken is (represents) My body, this wine poured out is My blood, we shall come nearer the truth, at least as to meaning, if, with Keim and Reuss, we accept the account obtained by combination of all the narratives as a correct version of the words of institution. On Baur's view of what Jesus said all that was intended by the breaking of the bread and the pouring out of the wine was to make a pathetic symbolic announcement of the approaching passion. It is morally certain that Jesus uttered words which gave His disciples a most important hint as to the significance of His passion, affording clearer insight into the mystery than any previously spoken. Virtually, if not in so many words, He said: This cup denotes My blood, the blood of a new covenant shed for many for the remission of sins.[1]

It is natural to assume that in uttering these words, or words of similar import, Jesus had present to His mind the paschal lamb, slain at the feast then being celebrated, which commemorated the deliverance of the children of Israel out of Egypt; the solemn rites connected with the ratification of the covenant at Sinai;[2] and the prophetic oracle of the prophet Jeremiah concerning a new covenant of grace, having for its leading blessings the law written on the heart, the knowledge of God brought within the reach of all, and the full forgiveness of all sin.[3] He might thus be regarded as offering Himself to the faith of His followers at once as a paschal lamb whose blood shields from the destroying angel; as a peace-offering whose blood sprinkled on the members of the holy commonwealth consecrates them to the Lord; as a sin-offering on the ground of which God bestows on men the forgiveness of their sins. The last of these three views is the one chiefly to be emphasized, as the gist or kernel of the final lesson taught by Jesus concerning the significance of His death. In this lesson advantage is taken of the ancient sacrificial system as an aid to the comprehension of the mystery. It does help

---

[1] For Baur's views, *vide Neutestamentliche Theologie*, SS. 101-5.
[2] Ex. xxiv. 5-8.   [3] Jer. xxxi. 31.

us so far, but after we have made the most of it we are still much in the dark as to the connection between the death of the sacrificial victim and the pardon of sin. The Levitical sacrifices did not deal effectually with the problem. They were merely putative atonements for artificial sins; for the ignorances or ritual errors of the people, not for their great moral transgressions. More light comes to us by reflection on the nature of the sacrifice by which the new covenant is inaugurated than from the whole Levitical system. Here for the first time we have priest and victim united in one. Christ's sacrifice is Himself. Here the virtue lies not in the blood, though that is formally mentioned, but in the offering of a perfect will through the eternal spirit of holy love. In this offering God can take pleasure, not because of the pain and the blood-shedding, but in spite of these. By the virtue of this offering God is reconciled to the world, and can regard with a benignant eye a guilty race. We are accepted in the Beloved, the Messianic King and His subjects being an organic unity in God's sight.

By this sacrifice of nobler name Jesus not only procured for us the forgiveness of sin, but inaugurated a new era. His death was the signal for the passing away of the old world of Judaism, and for the incoming of the new world of Christianity. This truth He proclaimed when He called His blood the blood of a new covenant. In the Sermon on the Mount He said, "I came not to destroy;" on the eve of His passion He virtually declares the contrary. The contrast has been adduced to prove that on the later occasion He cannot have spoken as the evangelists represent.[1] But the argument is without force. There is a time for everything; a time to be silent and a time to speak. That Jesus anticipated extensive innovation as the ultimate result of His work, is admitted by the objector. If so, now was the time for Him to speak out, when He was about to endure His last sufferings, brought upon Him not by any unseasonable utterances against the existing order of things, but simply by faithful witness-bearing for truth and righteousness.

The characteristics of the new era are such as flow naturally from the sacrifice on Calvary.

1. Levitical sacrifices, never of real value, pass away, henceforth utterly meaningless, and are replaced by the spiritual sacrifices of a thankful mind and a Christ-like life. With these antiquated sacrifices passes away also the institution of an official priesthood. In one sense Christ is the only Priest; in another sense all are priests who live in Christ's spirit, devoted to the kingdom, obeying the law of love.

2. The law is written on the heart, not on stone slabs as of old. Duty is made easy by assuming the form of personal attachment to the Crucified. In treating of the righteousness of the kingdom, I said that its commands though difficult were not grievous, because the motives consist not in intimidations, but in inspirations and aspirations. Among these I named imitation of Christ. In presence of the cross we come in view of a still more inspiring motive, grateful devotion to One whom faith apprehends as a Redeemer. Hereby the love of righteousness is transformed into a passionate desire to live

[1] So Baur.

lives worthy of the price by which redemption is achieved.

2. A new brotherhood comes into being based on faith in Jesus as the common Lord, and on mutual love. Israel was made a nation by the consciousness of common deliverance out of Egypt commemorated in the Passover. Even so Christendom takes its rise, a well-compacted kingdom of God, out of the consciousness of redemption from sin through Jesus Christ shared by every one who bears His name. In this community love comes to its rights. It not only becomes the royal law of the kingdom, but it is honoured with a divine throne. The cross is the symbol of dominion, and the Crucified is worshipped as God. The moral order of the universe is believed to be carried on in the interest of holy love, giving love scope to bear the burdens of others, letting it feel their full weight, and assigning to it a full reward in power to bless those whose sin and misery it has borne.

These characteristics find recognition and expression in the Holy Supper. Therein we remember the one sacrifice which effectually dealt with the problem of sin; declare our obligation to Him who redeemed us, and our devotion to His service; acknowledge that we are a brotherhood bound to walk in love; and honour love crucified as the most worshipful thing in the universe. We cannot doubt that a rite capable of giving symbolic utterance to so much meaning was intended to be repeated. Jesus said in effect, if not in so many words, "Do this in remembrance of Me." To perform so pathetic an act once was to make it a standing institution.

evangelis‘
force.
si¹

CHAPTER XI.

THE KINGDOM AND THE CHURCH.

The kingdom of God, in one view of it, is an ideal hovering in heavenly purity above all earthly realities, and not to be sought or found in any existing society, civil or ecclesiastical. It is an inspiration rather than an institution. It possesses the quality of inwardness. It comes not with observation, but has its seat in the heart. Wherever there is a human soul believing in the Fatherhood of God, and cherishing towards God the spirit of sonship and towards man the spirit of brotherhood, there is the kingdom manifesting its presence in righteousness, peace, and spiritual joy, and in philanthropic deeds.

But all ideals crave embodiment. Every great thought which takes a powerful hold of the human mind tends to assume visibility as a historical movement, and to become the organizing principle of a new society. Man is a social being, and his social instinct comes into play in connection with everything that deeply stirs him; therefore very specially in religion, which, when sincere, is the most powerful of all factors in human conduct. In connection with such a religious ideal as that set forth in the teaching of Jesus, association was inevitable. The very term " kingdom " is suggestive of society, and when it is considered that among the elements entering into the idea expressed by the term are the great truths of the Fatherhood of God, and the brotherhood of men as the children of God, it becomes apparent that reception of the idea, independently of any originative action on the part of Christ, must lead spontaneously to the creation of a society having for its aim to give expression to the fellowship of its members in faith and life.

It cannot therefore surprise us to learn from the Gospel records that Jesus contemplated, not only as a probable occurrence, but as a thing to be desired, the formation of such a society. The first distinct intimation of His wish or purpose was given on the occasion of the visit to Cæsarea Philippi, in other respects so memorable. There can, however, be little doubt that He had the momentous step in view at a much earlier period, at least as early as the choice of the twelve. It has indeed been maintained that at that time Jesus aimed at converting to righteousness the whole Jewish people, and so setting up the theocratic kingdom, and that He called together the twelve merely that they might act as His assistants in carrying on that work.[1] The choice certainly had a close connection, both in time and in purpose, with the evangelistic mission in Galilee; but that it had an ulterior object in view may be inferred from the terms in which the second evangelist describes the transaction: "He ordained twelve *that they should be with Him*, and that He might send them forth to preach," etc.[2] The chief end of the choice, according to this account, evidently was companionship and discipleship

[1] Weiss, *Leben Jesu*, ii. SS. 38, 79. [2] Mark iii. 14.

in order to training for a future vocation known to the Master, though not at first fully explained to the men whom He associated with Himself. The composition of the disciple-circle supplies a significant hint as to the nature of that vocation. The admission to the society of such a man as Matthew or Levi, belonging to a class obnoxious to all Jews who cherished the sentiment of national independence, was most impolitic and therefore most improbable, if the one aim of Jesus was the erection of a theocratic kingdom confined to Israel, and embracing, if possible, the whole nation. It was, on the other hand, not only unobjectionable but felicitously emblematic, if the end contemplated were the gathering together from all parts of the world of an eclectic society in which distinctions of class and nation were to be ignored.

Of this society, foreshadowed by the constitution of the apostolic band, Jesus at length, when His end drew near, began to speak as an institution about to come into existence. "I will build My *Church*."[1] The name, ἐκκλησία is appropriate, as denoting a new institution of an eclectic character, distinct both from the Jewish nation and from the synagogue, though familiar to all readers of the Septuagint as a title applied to the people of Israel in its religious aspect as a chosen race in covenant with God.[2] The manner of the announcement, "I will build *My* Church"—not *a* church, is significant, specially as showing that the idea, though new probably to the disciples, is familiar to the speaker. The time selected for making the announcement is seasonable. Jesus is now within measurable distance of His end, and

[1] Matt. xvi. 18.   [2] *Vide* Cremer's *Wörterbuch*.

it is fitting that, in referring for the first time in explicit terms to that unwelcome fact, He should say: "I am about to die, but I will leave behind Me an enduring society bearing My name." At the moment He is a fugitive from the scenes of His public ministry, rejected by His countrymen, and finds Himself in the proximity of the pagan world; how natural that He should seek consolation in the thought of a brotherhood of faith which will make Him independent of unbelieving Israel for disciples, and give Him in compensation the heathen for an inheritance. Of the universal outlook indeed nothing is said, but the situation makes it almost certain that it is a subject of thought. It may be taken for granted that when Christ began to speak of a Church, His prospect, narrowed in regard to Israel, widened out in another direction. Whatever may have been His early hopes respecting His own people, He expects now only the few to whom the things of the kingdom are revealed to accept Him as the Christ; but His comfort is that He has all the world to choose from.

While elective in character, the new society is not vindictively conceived by the Founder. He does not mean it to be a menace against unbelief, nor will its constitution be a definitive sentence of exclusion against all not immediately embraced in the *ecclesia*. The reference to the gates of Hades in the address to Peter does indeed wear an aspect of threatening or defiance natural in the circumstances. At this point the tone of Christ's utterances on this occasion resembles that audible in the saying, "Neither knoweth any man the Father save the Son, and he to whomsoever the Son is pleased to reveal Him." But the deepest wish of His heart now, as on the earlier occasion, is not exclusion, but the widest possible inclusiveness. He does not intend His Church to be a mere fortress with drawn bridge and closed gates, its occupants prepared for defence, and thinking of nothing beyond. His purpose is that the host which bears His name, though necessarily defensive at first, should ultimately march forth to conquer the world. Election is but the method by which He uses the few to bless the many. This truth He taught in the familiar sayings uttered to and concerning disciples: "Ye are the salt of the earth;" "Ye are the light of the world;"[1] as also in the parable which likens the kingdom of heaven to leaven put into a measure of meal, that it may leaven the whole lump.[2] That disciple to whom such prominence was given when the Church was first spoken of, showed how well he understood the mind of the Master on this subject when he characterized the *ecclesia*, now actually in existence, as a chosen generation called out of darkness to show forth the virtues of Him to whom they owed their high privileges.[3] Only when so conceived is election either scriptural or wholesome. When it is thought of as involving monopoly of divine favour and reprobation of all without, as it was by the Jews in our Lord's day, then the salt loses its savour, and the light is extinguished by being placed under a bushel. The salt exists that it may preserve the mass liable to corruption; the light is meant to shine that God the Father may be glorified, and the darkened souls of men spiritually illumined. The

[1] Matt. v. 13, 14. [2] Matt. xiii. 33. [3] 1 Pet. ii. 9.

principle, "natural law in the spiritual world," is emphatically false here. In nature the few are chosen, and the many are ruthlessly cast away; the fit survive, the unfit perish, and the unconscious cosmos sheds no tear. In the kingdom of God it is far otherwise. The chosen few seek the good of the many; the fit strive to preserve the unfit. This is their very vocation, and when they cease to pursue it they themselves become unfit, useless, reprobate.

An important step towards the founding of the Church was taken when the new society was furnished with symbolic rites serving as bonds of union and means of fellowship. Of one of these, baptism, no mention is made in the evangelic records till after the resurrection of Jesus. To those who interpret the Gospel narratives on the basis of naturalism, by whom therefore all that belongs to the post-resurrection period must be pronounced unhistorical, this fact may appear to prove that Christian baptism has no sanction in the teaching of our Lord. This, however, is not a necessary conclusion even on naturalistic principles. It is conceivable that a direction given by Jesus to His disciples concerning the rite, before His death, say on the eve of the passion, at the same time that the Holy Supper was instituted, might have been transferred by the evangelist to what was deemed a specially suitable place in the history—the final leave-taking, there to assume the character of a last instruction by the Master just before His ascension, to the future apostles. This were only to suppose that Matthew took a liberty with words relating to baptism similar to that taken by Luke in placing the account of

R

Christ's preaching in the synagogue of Nazareth near the beginning of his Gospel. This view, accordingly, is regarded favourably by Keim, who thinks it highly improbable that baptism would have obtained universal recognition in the apostolic Church unless it had been known to have on its side the authority of Jesus.[1]

Not only the time at which, but also the precise terms in which, Jesus is reported to have given directions concerning the initiatory rite, have been the subject of doubting criticism. The assailable points are the explicit universalism: "Go ye therefore and make disciples of all the nations," and the Trinitarian baptismal formula, "baptizing them into the name of the Father, and of the Son, and of the Holy Ghost."[2] As to the former, it is sufficient to remark that the universalism of the final directory is little more pronounced than that of the well-authenticated words spoken on the occasion of the anointing in Bethany: "Wheresoever this gospel shall be preached in the whole world." Then with reference to the Trinity of the baptismal formula, it is to be observed that it simply sums up in brief compass the teaching of Jesus. He taught His own disciples to regard God as their Father, and to accept Himself as God's Son, the revealer of the Father and the prototype of sonship. Of the Holy Spirit He seldom spoke, so far as appears from the synoptical records, wherein functions which, following Pauline usage, we should ascribe to the Spirit, are assigned to the Father and the Son. The Father reveals the things of the kingdom to the "babes;"[3]

---

[1] Keim, *Jesu von Nazara*, iii. 286.   [2] Matt. xxviii. 19.
[3] Matt. xi. 25.

Peter's insight into the doctrine of the Christ comes from the same source;[1] the Son who alone knows the Father reveals Him to such as He deems worthy.[2] But the few texts referring to the Spirit ascribe to Him the same function of spiritual illumination, and represent Him as the source of spiritual energy and sanctity. When disciples are called on to answer for their faith, it is the Spirit of their Father who speaketh in them,[3] and it is but a corollary from this that it is the same Spirit who reveals to them the faith which by His aid they are enabled to defend. That the Spirit is the sanctifier is implied in the closing words of the great lesson on prayer: "How much more shall your heavenly Father give the Holy Spirit to them that ask Him."[4] That He is also the source of all spiritual might, Jesus emphatically taught when He represented His own miraculous deeds as done through His inspiration.[5] All these positions are implicitly contained in the representation of the Holy Ghost as the object of that form of blasphemy which is unpardonable. Blasphemy against the Spirit can be unpardonable only because He is the fountain of light, and purity, and goodness, and power. It is thus in no wise improbable that in summarizing His teaching for baptismal purposes, Jesus added to the names of the Father and the Son that of the Holy Spirit. Neither is it any more improbable that He furnished such a summary in connection with instructions concerning baptism, than that He explained the mystic significance of the bread and the wine in instituting the Holy Supper.

[1] Matt. xvi. 17. [2] Matt. xi. 27. [3] Matt. x. 20.
[4] Luke xi. 13. [5] Matt. xii. 28.

It might seem so if we identified the rudimentary, moral, and religious Trinity of the Gospel with the developed, metaphysical, and speculative Trinity of theology, which, however, as Reuss has remarked, it is not necessary to do.[1] It is certainly true that in the history of the apostolic Church we find no trace of the use of the Trinitarian formula in connection with baptism. The confession of faith made by converts consisted simply in the acknowledgment of Jesus as the Christ. It does not follow from this that the apostles knew nothing of such a formula, but only that they did not consider themselves under bondage to a form of words, but felt free to use an equivalent form which expressed exactly what was necessarily implied in becoming a Christian. There can be no doubt that Jesus taught His disciples a form of prayer, though there is no evidence that the apostles were in the habit of using it; why then should non-use of the baptismal formula be accepted as conclusive proof of its non-authenticity?

The nature of the Church and its relation to the kingdom of God are explained in the remarkable words addressed by Jesus to Peter after his bold profession of faith in the Messiahship of his Master.[2] In these words, which are highly animated and dramatic, Peter appears as a most important man. He is the rock on which the Church is to be built; into his hands are committed the

---

[1] *Théologie Chrétienne*, i. 243.

[2] Matt. xvi. 18, 19. In the commentary of Ephrem Syrus on Tatian's *Diatessaron* this passage is reduced to these words: "Tu es Petra, et portæ inferi te non vincent." Some critics take this to be the original form of the saying, whence it would follow that Christ on this occasion said nothing about the Church. (So Wendt,

keys of the kingdom; his acts in binding and loosing, forbidding and permitting, are valid in heaven. All this belongs to the form rather than to the essence of the thought. It says in a highly emotional and Hebrew manner what can be expressed in abstract didactic language which eliminates Peter's personality as of no fundamental moment. The imagination that the fact is otherwise is one of the gigantic tragic mistakes through which the Church has become to a large extent a deplorable failure. In connection with this it is important to note that the famous utterance of our Lord to His disciples is found only in the first Gospel. This fact is no just ground for suspecting the genuineness of the saying; for it is far too remarkable to have proceeded from any one but Jesus: the very vehemence and absoluteness of its assertions which make it so liable to misunderstanding are guarantees of its originality. But the absence of the words from the other synoptical records provokes reflection as to the reasons for omission. In the case of the third evangelist the motive may have been a consciousness that the words were being used already for party purposes, in which case their exclusion from his pages is a silent protest against a prelatic or hierarchical spirit manifesting itself in the bud. The omission in Mark, on the other hand, may be due to the influence of Peter himself. We can imagine the apostle,

Die Lehre Jesu, S. 181.) But, as Zahn (*Forschungen zur Geschichte des neutestamentlichen Kanons*, Erster Thiel, S. 163) contends, Christ's words here, as often elsewhere, are probably abbreviated by Ephrem. The passage concerning the Church is in Cureton's Syriac version, which, according to Zahn, was that used by Tatian.

no longer the forward, self-asserting man that he was as a disciple, passing over in silence the strong language addressed to himself by the Master at Cæsarea Philippi from a feeling of modesty, and doing so the more readily because he was conscious that he did not thereby sacrifice any important truth, or seriously mutilate his testimony.

In treating the personality of Peter as of subordinate importance, I do not mean to affirm that the address to him was a matter of idle form. It was natural in the circumstances, and characteristic, that Jesus should put the truth concerning the Church to be founded in that concrete dramatic way. Here He was a fugitive from an unbelieving people, in presence of the first man who had said with clear intelligence and firm conviction, " Thou art the Christ, the Son of the living God." How natural that He should speak of this man as the first stone of the new edifice; and that, as if in gratitude to him, He should ascribe to him supreme power and privilege in the society about to be instituted! Nevertheless, all that is said admits of being translated into impersonal language; nor is the sense clear till this has been done. Jesus then gave utterance to three great truths: first, that the Church to be founded was to be *Christian,* or to put it otherwise, that the person of the Founder was of fundamental importance; second, that as such it should be practically identical with the kingdom of God He had hitherto preached; third, that in this Church the righteousness of the kingdom should find its home. The first truth He taught when He said to Peter: " Thou art Peter, and on this rock I will build My Church." The sample showed the quality of the edifice. Peter, the first stone, was a man who believed Jesus to be the Christ, the revealer of the Father, the prototype of Sonship, and who had received this faith as a revelation from heaven. To say that he was to be laid as the foundation of a new spiritual building, was to say in effect that that building should consist of men receiving from the same source, and holding firmly, the same faith. In other words, the new society was to be *Christian*, confessing Christ's name, animated by His Spirit, receiving Him at once as revealed by the Father and as revealer of the Father; the Son of Man who was pre-eminently the Son of God, and who thoroughly knew God and could declare Him. To say of the Church that it is Christian, is to utter a truism now; but it was not so then. The sacred historian of the apostolic Church, while passing over many events of importance, took care to note when the disciples of Jesus were first called Christians.[1] In like manner we ought to regard it as an eventful moment in the life of Jesus when He said: I mean to found a new society, and it shall be in character Christian; its *raison d'être* will be to confess me as Christ, the object of its faith and love, and the satisfier of all its religious wants. This He said when He spoke the words: "On this rock will I build My Church." And this commonplace truth is the truth above all to be laid to heart. The question of questions for the Church is not who is primate, or any question of the like kind, but how far is it Christian in faith and life? Lacking Christianity, an ecclesiastical society, whether acknowledging Peter's primacy or repudiating

[1] Acts xi. 26.

it, is a community against which the gates of hell shall prevail, nay, have already prevailed.

The second truth, that the new Christian society should be practically identical with the kingdom of heaven, Jesus declared when He said: "I will give unto thee the keys of the kingdom of heaven." These keys and what they are, and the power to use them and what it imports, and who may wield it, have been the subject of endless controversy, a horror to think of, with which I have no inclination to intermeddle. Nor have I any call to do so, for in my humble opinion the "power of the keys," in the ecclesiastical sense of the expression, was not in all Christ's thoughts. His purpose was not to determine with whom lay the power authoritatively to admit into or exclude from the Church assumed to be identical with the kingdom of God, but rather to indicate the connection between the Church and the kingdom, and the conditions under which the one might be identified with the other. In promising to Peter the keys of the kingdom, He meant to say that a society of men cordially joining in his confession, calling Jesus Lord by the Holy Ghost, was the ideal of the kingdom realized. Such a declaration was to be expected from Him. He had been speaking all along of a kingdom of God to be sought as the chief good; He had taught many truths relating to the kingdom; He had indicated very distinctly where it was not to be found, viz. in the religious world of Pharisaism. But He had not hitherto assigned to it a positive locality. He had left the heavenly commonwealth in the clouds or in the air, and had not brought it down to the earth and given to it there a local habitation and a name. Now at length He acknowledges the lack, and supplies what was needed to complete His doctrine of the kingdom; saying in effect: I am the Kingdom; in Me Fatherhood and Sonship meet; those who confess Me form a brotherhood in which all the blessings of the kingdom are enjoyed.

In subordination to this general truth, Jesus, by the words now under consideration, recognised the importance of Peter, and (of course) of his brother disciples, as sources of knowledge concerning Himself. In this connection the first apostles of the faith performed a function in which they can have no successors. They were the companions of the Church's Head and Lord, were intimately acquainted with His doctrine, had been deeply imbued with His spirit, and were thus qualified to convey to the world at least an approximately true reflection of His image. In a very real and important sense the key of knowledge was committed to them, whereby they opened the kingdom of heaven to the faith of men.

The identity of Church and kingdom is not absolute but relative only. The two categories do not entirely coincide, even when the Church as a visible society is all it ought to be; its members all truly Christian in faith and life. The kingdom is the larger category. It embraces all who by the key of a true knowledge of the historical Christ are admitted within its portals; but also many more, the children of the Father in every land who have unconsciously loved the Christ in the person of His representatives, the poor, the suffering, the sorrowful. For such no apostle or church-officer opens the door; the Son of Man Himself admits them into the kingdom prepared for them from the foundation of the world.[1]

The third truth—that in the new society the righteousness of the kingdom should be realized—Jesus taught when He said: "Whatsoever thou shalt bind on earth shall be bound in heaven; and whatsoever thou shalt loose on earth shall be loosed in heaven." Translated into abstract language, this amounts to a declaration that the moral judgment of the Church about to be founded shall be sound, wholesome, in all its actings in accordance with eternal truth. Such a spirit of wisdom and understanding shall pervade its membership that they shall know instinctively what to do and what to avoid. The representative men at the head will give right directions as to conduct, and the enlightened conscience of the community will accept and enforce their counsels. That will be declared to be right which is right in God's sight and in the divine kingdom, nothing will be declared to be wrong which is lawful and commendable. In other words, the state of matters in the new society will be exactly the reverse of that which prevailed in Rabbindom. The Rabbis to a very large extent bound what should be loosed, and loosed what should be bound. They permitted what was sinful, they forbade what might be done without sin, and they enjoined many things which might very reasonably be disregarded. Speaking generally, their laws and penalties were directed against the wrong men and the wrong practices. Under their *régime* bad men, hypocrites, were likely to prosper, and

---

[1] Matt. xxv. 34. *Vide* chap. xiv.

good men were in danger of judgment. The godless, wearing a cloak of religion, were admitted within the pale, and the saints were thrust out. There can be little doubt that Jesus had the scribe-ruled religious world of Israel in His view when He uttered the words I now comment on, and meant to hint at a radical contrast. Of the righteousness of the scribes He had said that it stood in no relation to the kingdom of heaven, bore no correspondence to its righteousness, formed no preparation for citizenship therein. Of the holy commonwealth which is to bear His name He affirms the reverse. Rabbinism, He says in effect, has utterly failed to realize the moral ideal; nascent Christendom will be a more successful attempt.

The prediction, however, is not unconditional. It goes on the assumption that the faith of the Church will continue to be of the same character as Peter's, not in the letter merely or chiefly, but in spirit, a revelation to the soul from heaven, not a tradition of flesh and blood. If ever the traditional principle should enter the Church there would be no guarantee against Rabbinism, in new forms, reinvading with all its blindness and perversity. Was there any risk in that direction? Great risk. The spirit of tradition can manifest itself in connection with every conceivable creed or religion; and the usual course of religions is to begin in the spirit and end in the flesh, to originate in inspiration and terminate in custom. Peter did not, and could not, receive his faith in Jesus as Christ from tradition or custom, for all the voices of that kind cried out: This cannot be the Christ; He is an unholy man, a law-breaker, a blasphemer, a glutton, a drunkard, a "friend of publicans and sinners;" or at best a good man fatally disqualified for being the Messiah by indifference to legitimate patriotic aspirations. But *we* can call Jesus Lord and Christ otherwise than through the Holy Ghost; when Christendom grew to be a great fact many did. When this happens much that at first was avowedly and manifestly antagonistic to Christ may be associated with His name; Rabbinism may enter into the Church and Christianity may be driven out.

Christ was not unaware of the risk to which the new experiment at realizing the ideal of a divine kingdom was exposed. He revealed His anxiety when He said to His disciples: "Ye are the salt of the earth; but if the salt have lost its savour, wherewith shall it be salted?" He had before His eyes the tragic result of a past experiment, and He feared lest a similar fate should befall the one with which His own name was to be associated. "The old election," He meant to say, "has become a savourless salt through lack of genuine righteousness; see that the new one go not the same way." He did His utmost to prevent the result by subjecting to a wholesome discipline the men on whom so much was to depend, at least in the initial stage of the Church's history. There are traces in the Gospel records of special pains taken with this view after the time when the subject of the Church was first mentioned. Perhaps the warning against savourless salt, though occurring in the Sermon on the Mount as reported by the first evangelist, belongs to this period. Mark introduces it very appropriately as a part of the admonitions addressed to the twelve in connection with their first dispute concerning places of distinction.[1] It is certain, at all events, that from the time the spirit of ambition began to manifest itself in the disciple-circle, Jesus strove to make sure that the future apostles should have salt in themselves. By the manner in which He met the demand for the temple-tax He gave them a lesson in meekness;[2] through a little child He taught them humility;[3] from the anecdote of the exorcist, related by John, He drew the moral of tolerance;[4] by directions as to the mode of dealing with an offending brother He urged the importance of taking all possible pains to prevent total and final alienation;[5] by a promise of His presence He sought to foster the spirit of fellowship in prayer;[6] by the parable of *The Unmerciful Servant* He enforced the duty of forgiveness.[7] On another occasion, by the parable of *The Hours*, He chastised the spirit of self-complacency, and by reference to His own example initiated ambitious aspirants to greatness into the mystery of honour gained by lowly service.[8] At a still later time He warned the multitude and the twelve at once against servile subjection to, and against arrogant assumption of, authority, saying: "Call no man your father upon the earth; neither be ye called masters;"[9] so guarding against the return of that Rabbinical dominion over faith and conduct which He was in the act of denouncing.

[1] Mark ix. 50.
[2] Matt. xvii. 24.
[3] Matt. xviii. 21.
[4] Mark ix. 38–40; Luke ix. 50.
[5] Matt. xviii. 15–17.
[6] Matt. xviii. 19, 20.
[7] Matt. xviii. 21–35.
[8] Matt. xx. 1–28.
[9] Matt. xxiii. 9, 10.

Such was the contribution of Jesus towards the shaping of the future character of His Church. He provided for it no ecclesiastical constitution, issued no authoritative instructions concerning forms of church government, clerical offices and orders, or even worship. These He left to be determined by the self-organizing life of the society. He concerned Himself with the spirit, believing that if that was right all would be right. He taught the apostles humility, brotherly equality, charity, patience, concord; and for the rest left them to their discretion. Neither of the three forms which ecclesiastical organization has assumed is either justified or condemned by His instructions. Prelacy is possible under Presbytery, humility is compatible with Episcopal dignity, and catholicity is not irreconcilable with Congregationalism.

Notwithstanding all His care, the evils dreaded by the Founder of the Church made their appearance. Rabbinism reinvaded, priestcraft crept in, legalism resumed its malign dominion in the shape of salvation by sacraments or by dogmatic othodoxy, endless divisions, alienations, and contentions ensued, making the history of the Church a tragic, humiliating, disenchanting tale. As in view of the evils that are in the world we are tempted to ask, Why did God create man? so in presence of the evils that have come into existence in the course of ecclesiastical history we are tempted to ask, Why did Christ create the Church? We certainly cannot say that He acted in ignorance of what was to happen. He knew that there was not only a risk, but a certainty of evil developing itself within the Church; He even predicted in outline, as we shall see, its chequered history. The promise that the gates of Hades should not prevail against it, is neither an indication that He laboured under a delusion nor a guarantee against failure. The promise or prophecy, as already hinted, is conditional. The Church will stand if the faith of its members continue to be of the right quality. But why then enter on the enterprise? Why lay the foundation of this building? In the first place, because the thing had to be. A powerful religious impulse once communicated will run its course; it cannot be prevented from taking its place in history as an institution. In the second place, because it was good on the whole. The Christian Church gave to the spirit of Christ a body; to the light of Christ, an atmosphere. It brought down to this earth the city of God, whose presence has surely conferred many benefits on mankind. Since its descent from heaven the celestial city has lost much of its beauty, could not help losing, for all historical realizations of divine ideals (save one— the perfect Man!) are necessarily imperfect. At times the spiritual Salem has resembled certain terrestrial cities known to us as they appear in the time of frost, enveloped in a grimy fog which shuts out the sun and blue sky visible in the surrounding country. At such unhappy periods the question suggests itself, Is the Church of any use; were it not well that it perished, that Christianity might the better thrive? Then, instead of claiming for the Church that within it alone is salvation to be found, earnest men are more inclined to ask whether salvation is to be found in it at all, and does not rather consist in escaping from its influence. A good many are asking such revolutionary questions even now, and it is foolish for Churchmen simply to be shocked, and to characterize them as profane. The Church is only a means to an end. It is good only in so far as it is Christian. There is no merit or profit in mere ecclesiasticism. Whatever reveals the true Christ is of value and will live. Whatever hides Christ, be it pope, priest, or presbyter, sacraments or ecclesiastical misrule, is pernicious, and must pass away. But we may hope that there will always be enough of Christ's spirit in the society which bears His name to keep it from becoming utterly savourless, and to bring about such reforms as may be necessary to make it serve the end for which it was instituted. Should this hope be disappointed, then the visible Church, as we know it, must and will pass away, leaving the spirit of Christ free room to make a new experiment, under happier auspices, at self-realization. To be enthusiastic about the Church in its present condition is impossible, to hope for its future is not impossible; but if it were, there is no cause for despair. Christ will ever remain, the same yesterday, to-day, and for ever; and the kingdom of God will remain, a kingdom that cannot be moved.

CHAPTER XII.

THE PAROUSIA AND THE CHRISTIAN ERA.

THERE is no subject on which it is more difficult to ascertain the teaching of Christ than that which relates to the future of the kingdom. The difficulty arises in part from the fact that there are two classes of texts bearing on the topic, one of which by obvious implication, if not by direct statement, seems to assign to the kingdom, as an earthly institution, a lengthened history, in the course of which it is to pass through a gradual process of development; while the other seems not less plainly to predict the speedy approach of the grand consummation, involving the advent of Messiah, the setting up of His kingdom in splendour, the separation of the good and evil, and the allotment to each of their respective destinies. Various methods have been resorted to for solving the problem presented in these apparently conflicting oracles. Some, admitting the equal authenticity of the two sets of statements, and denying their reconcilability, maintain that Jesus had not a uniform manner of speaking on the subject, but either vacillated in opinion, or at one time spoke His own sentiments, and at another accommodated His utterances to existing ideas and hopes. Others, also regarding the two classes of texts as irreconcilable, but not believing either in self-contradiction or in illegitimate accommodation on the part of Jesus, have recourse to the expedient of treating the texts which foretell a speedy consummation as a corrupt, unauthentic element in the evangelic tradition, and accepting as genuine those only which are most remote from the apocalyptic ideas then current among the Jews. If the choice lay between these two views I should certainly adopt in preference the latter alternative; for it is *à priori* more credible that the reporters of Christ's words concerning the future coloured them with their own opinions, than that the outlook of the Master was as limited as we know theirs to have been. In that case we should have to regard those sayings of Jesus which give to the kingdom a lengthened career as the most authentic and reliable words preserved pure by the evangelists, involuntarily and in spite of their bias. In these sayings we should, as it were, see the morning sun of the Christian era struggling into sight through the mist of contemporary Jewish eschatology. I trust, however, that we are not shut up to either of the foregoing alternatives. In that hope, though without foregone conclusions, I proceed to look at the two classes of texts, and to consider how far they are capable of being reconciled. I begin by remarking that the mere fact of Christ's resolving to institute a Church raises a presumption in favour of the view that He anticipated for the kingdom, not consummation by an early catastrophe, but a lengthened history. Why set about building an edifice on rock foundations, and with walls strong enough to defy time, if the end was to come before the work of construction had been well begun?

Among the texts which point in the same direction a foremost place is due to those in which we find the kingdom associated with the idea of *growth*, with which the idea of early catastophe is irreconcilable. Now there is a whole group of parables in which the kingdom is represented as subject to the law of growth; those, viz., in which it is compared to seed — the parables of *The Sower, The Wheat and Tares, The Mustard Seed,* and *The Seed growing gradually.* The last of the four is the most important; because while growth is clearly implied in all the rest, the express design of this one is to teach that the kingdom of God is subject to the law of gradual growth in accordance with the analogy of nature. The parable has an important application to the divine life in the individual, but its applicability to the kingdom as an institution will not be disputed. From it we learn, therefore, that the kingdom of God, as a historical movement, has to pass through stages at a rate of progress so slow that the servants of the kingdom will cease to expect the consummation forthwith, and that there will be a striking contrast between the tedious process of growth and the sudden oncoming of the harvest when the grain is ripe for the sickle. Catastrophe is recognised in connection with the latter: "immediately he putteth in the sickle;" but it is catastrophe coming at the end of a lengthened development. The significant point in the parable is the description of the farmer's habit after the seed is sown. He sleeps and rises night and day. He knows that his part is done, and that the rest must be left to the soil; therefore he resigns himself to easy-minded passivity, leaving the earth to bring forth of itself. He knows also that growth cannot be hastened by bustling activity, therefore he is patient. He knows further that the harvest season will come eventually; he has faith in the soil and the seasons; therefore he is free from feverish anxiety. By the parable Jesus taught His disciples that they must strive to resemble the farmer in these respects, and that they should have need and opportunity to do so in connection with the work of the kingdom, need and opportunity for passivity, patience, and faith. The mood recommended is not indifference, but that which is natural to one interested in a process demanding time for its completion. It is the opposite of the mood described by Paul as prevalent in the Thessalonian Church, that, viz., of men shaken in mind and disturbed to distraction.[1] The cause of that disorder was the notion that the day of the Lord was just at hand. The radical cure for it is Christ's doctrine of growth. But that doctrine the apostolic generation failed to grasp, and even Paul himself but imperfectly understood.

A second important group of texts consists of those which suggest the thought of a *delayed parousia*. These texts do not, of course, like those containing the idea of growth, imply a lengthened period of development. Their significance lies in this, that they open up the question as to a plurality of senses to be attached to the coming of the Son of Man; for if there be a coming which may be delayed, there is also a coming, as we shall see, which will certainly take place within a generation. To this second group of texts belong the

[1] 2 Thess. ii. 1, 2.

two parables which inculcate perseverance in prayer, viz., *The Selfish Neighbour* and *The Unjust Judge*. Apart from the connection in which, in Luke's narrative, the former stands with the Lord's Prayer, it may be taken for granted that in exhorting the future apostles to be on their guard against fainting in prayer, Jesus had very specially in view the kingdom which He ever taught them to regard as the supreme object of desire. He spoke to men whom He assumed to be ever saying in their hearts, "Thy kingdom come." It is thus implied in the parable that the kingdom may come so slowly, so much later than was anticipated, that men interested in its advancement will be tempted to despondency. This truth comes out still more clearly in the parable of the Unjust Judge, in which the source of temptation is the delay of Providence in espousing the cause of those who devote their lives to the kingdom. The delay is so long that the faithful are in danger of losing heart. "Nevertheless, when the Son of Man cometh shall He find faith in the earth." When the Son of Man comes the divine interest in the cause of His kingdom will be manifest, and the prayers of the saints at length heard; but so long will His coming be deferred that faith in it will almost have died out, even among the most devoted. Hope deferred will have made their hearts sick, and when deliverance comes they will be like the Israelites in Babylon when recalled from captivity—like men that dream, unable to believe welcome tidings, because to heavy hearts they seem too good to be true. Some critics see in the last two verses an unauthentic addition to the words of Jesus, made at a later time when it had become evident that the coming of the Lord was not to take place so soon as had been anticipated. Such doubt, however gratuitous, has this value, that it betrays a feeling that delay beyond expectation is plainly implied in the passage.

A deferred *parousia* is implied in all texts, and they are not few, containing exhortations to *watch*. These exhortations imply two things: the uncertainty of the *parousia*,—it may come on you unawares, therefore be ever ready,—and a risk of being off guard arising out of delay. That such delay was in the view of Jesus, in some cases at least, is beyond question. As an instance may be cited the counsel to watch, at the close of the parable of *The Ten Virgins*, in which the situation is thus described: "While the bridegroom tarried, they all nodded and slept."[1] All, the wise not less than the foolish; those virgins young and eager, and in full sympathy with the occasion. Long delay was necessary to cast an eagerly expectant Church into such a state of somnolency.

The parable concerning *The Upper Servant playing the tyrant over the Inferior Servants in the absence of the Master* emphatically points the same moral.[2] Luke introduces it in a very appropriate connection. Interrogated in reference to another parable enforcing the duty of watching, whether it was meant for the twelve or for the multitude, Jesus spoke this second parable to indicate the temptations to which men occupying higher places in the kingdom would be exposed by the Master delaying His coming. While the inferior servant is represented as simply liable to fall asleep instead of watching, the

[1] Matt. xxv. 5. [2] Luke xii. 42-46.

steward of the house is conceived as in danger of beginning to play the tyrant and the reveller. Obviously a process of demoralization culminating in such scandalous misbehaviour demands a considerable lapse of time. The head men of a religious community cannot be thought of as falling from a high moral level of fidelity to the low condition supposed suddenly; we are rather led to think of a slow secular process of declension extending over generations or even centuries. There was, indeed, a certain risk of demoralization setting in at the close of the apostolic age as soon as it began to be suspected that the day of the Lord was not to come, as had been generally anticipated, in the first Christian generation. Strained expectation of a speedy coming might then give place to scepticism as to its ever coming, leading on to utter unbelief and moral licence. Some traces of such a reaction occur in the Second Epistle of Peter,[1] in view of which one might be disposed to regard the parable now under consideration as the invention of a later time, embodying cautions suggested by observation of the evil consequences of disappointed hope. But the hypothesis is refuted by the simple consideration that such evil consequences in the apostolic age were confined to the obscurer members of the Church, and did not appear among those of whom the steward in the parable is the natural representative. There were no facts to suggest or justify so dark a picture of misbehaviour among the office-bearers of the Church. The authenticity of the parable is therefore above all doubt, and it is to be regarded as one of the most convincing proofs that Christ contemplated, as

[1] 2 Pet. ii. 4.

at least a probability, a parousia delayed not merely a little beyond expectation, but even indefinitely.

A third group of texts favouring the hypothesis of a Christian era, as against that of a speedy end of the world, embraces those which contain or suggest the idea of a *Gentile day of grace*. To this class belongs the word spoken in the house of Simon the leper, in which it is indirectly declared that the gospel is to be preached in the whole world.[1] Another utterance of the same kind, still more explicit in its terms, occurs in the great eschatological discourse as recorded by the same two evangelists who have preserved the former. Matthew makes Christ say, "This Gospel of the kingdom shall be preached in all the world for a witness unto all nations;"[2] Mark, "The gospel must first be published among all nations."[3] The authenticity of this saying has been questioned. There may be room for reasonable doubt whether it has its proper historical place in the discourse in which it is embedded; but there is really no ground for disputing its genuineness. On the contrary, the very variations with which it is given by the two evangelists is an argument in favour of genuineness, as either pointing to two independent sources of information, or, as has recently been suggested by Dr. Abbott, to independent use of one elliptical document whose laconic phrases might easily be differently construed by readers.[4] Weiss, in his work on the life of Jesus, while admitting

---

[1] Matt. xxvi. 13; Mark xiv. 9.
[2] Matt. xxiv. 14.   [3] Mark xiii. 10.
[4] *The Common Tradition of the Synoptic Gospels*, Introduction, p. xxxiii.

the genuineness, does his utmost to evacuate the saying of significance, and to reconcile it with the hypothesis that Jesus believed and thought that the final catastrophe would happen within a generation. His argument is to this effect : In our modern sense Jesus never thought of His work as for the world in general, because He could only think of it in the form which the Scripture gave to His hand. No doubt the Gentiles were concerned in the Messianic salvation, and a single generation may seem a most inadequate time to allow for their conversion. But, in the first place, Jesus was ignorant of the extent of the world, just as Paul was, who actually thought and said that the gospel had already been preached in the whole world. Then, and above all, it must be borne in mind that though Jesus expected to get some converts from heathendom, yet His experience of disappointment even among a prepared people left little room for hope of extensive conversions among unprepared pagans.[1] This train of thought provokes the reflection often suggested by this author's treatment of the great biography, that while Jesus in his hands is officially a very important person—the Messiah, He is a very commonplace man, morally and intellectually. The comparison between Jews and Gentiles as to the reception of the gospel is in direct contradiction to the whole spirit of Christ's teaching, which was to the effect that the last might be first, that publicans and sinners were more likely to receive the good tidings than the Pharisees, the babes than the wise men ; and that a faith might be forthcoming among pagans, the like of which was not to be

[1] *Das Leben Jesu*, ii. 483-4.

found even in prepared, privileged Israel. The remark concerning Christ's ignorance as to the extent of the world, even if true, is irrelevant. Supposing the Gentile world to consist of the nations bordering on the Mediterranean Sea, the question is, was not a generation, say forty years, an utterly inadequate period for the effective evangelization of even so limited a world? Was it not mocking the Gentiles to offer them a single generation, when Israel had had many centuries? Could the gospel be preached to them in that short time for a witness, that is, as a basis of judgment, that all men might know of the mercy of God before the end came— assuming that the words "for a witness" are to be connected with the preaching to the Gentiles, which is doubtful, Mark connecting them rather with the appearing of the apostles before rulers and kings testifying for Christ and against their oppressors. There is something unsympathetic in the tone of Christ's words as reported by Matthew, which inclines one to prefer Mark's version as the more accurate. Christ would have His gospel preached to the pagans not merely for a witness, as if to justify their condemnation, unbelief being taken for granted; but rather for their salvation, and in the hope that many would gladly accept the boon offered. It is a mere unfounded assertion to say that Christ did not and could not seriously entertain the thought of a thoroughgoing evangelization of the Gentiles, but at most only contemplated the throwing of a few crumbs to the pagan dogs after the children of the house of Israel had been filled. Why not He as well as Paul? It is probably nearer the truth to say that the mind of the Master, in this respect as in others, was wider in its range of ideas than the apostle's, and that He had in view a leavening of the whole lump of humanity by the gospel of the kingdom to a degree of completeness whereof Paul, as he made his hasty missionary excursions hither and thither in Asia and Europe, had no conception. It is not clearly indicated in the parable of the leaven that the lump is the world at large, but the method on which the kingdom works, wherever it goes, is explained. If the kingdom is to go into the Gentile world it will work there as a leaven as well as in Palestine. And the method demands time, its manner of working is slow but sure; its process needs not a generation, but an era for its accomplishment. The Pauline evangelist Luke, in his version of the eschatological discourse, uses a significant phrase which indicates a remarkable appreciation of the requirements as to time of the work of Gentile evangelization. It is "the times of the Gentiles" ($\kappa\alpha\iota\rho o\grave{\iota}\ \dot{\epsilon}\theta\nu\hat{\omega}\nu$).[1] It is the equivalent, in his account, of the preaching of the gospel to Gentiles spoken of by Matthew and Mark. It points to a Gentile day of grace analogous to Israel's time of gracious visitation, to which Jesus alluded in His lament over Jerusalem.[2] As soon as the two things are brought together we feel the absurdity of the notion that Gentile opportunity was to be limited to a generation. The Jewish *kairos* lasted for many centuries—from the conquest of Canaan to the destruction of Jerusalem now impending. And the *kairos* of the great Gentile world, how long is it to last? For forty or fifty years? Verily a crumb for pagan dogs! It is not necessary to

[1] Luke xxi. 24. [2] Luke xix. 44.

assume that the expression I comment on was coined by Jesus. If Luke invented it he thereby simply put into felicitous words the inevitable inference from Gentile evangelization, viz. that Gentile opportunities must be commensurate with the magnitude of the work, and in analogy with God's way of dealing with men in grace as revealed in the past history of Israel.

In passing now to the other class of texts which seem to teach that the final consummation was to come very soon, I may cite as a first sample a saying of Jesus preserved by Matthew in his account of the instructions given to the disciples in connection with the Galilean mission: " When they persecute you in this city flee ye to the next; for verily I say unto you, Ye shall not have gone through the cities of Israel till the Son of Man be come." [1] Assuming that the coming of the Son of Man and the end of the world coincide, the plain meaning of this statement is, that the wind-up of the world's history was to take place in the lifetime of the apostles, and while they were engaged in their evangelistic enterprise among their countrymen. But is the assumption correct? There is room for reasonable doubt on the point. Looking into the connection of thought to which the text belongs, we observe that Jesus has in view something which specially concerns the Jewish nation. The parousia is referred to as a reason why the disciples being persecuted in one city should flee to another; and the thought intended seems to be: You need not hesitate to flee from any city which does not give you welcome, for it is desirable that all the cities of Israel should hear the

[1] Matt. x. 23.

gospel of the kingdom, and however diligent you may be, you will not have time to go over them all before Israel's crisis comes. The coming of the Son of Man thus appears, at least in this instance, to signify the coming of Israel's judgment-day, involving destruction to the impenitent portion of the nation. This inference is wholly independent of the question whether Matthew has given this saying in its proper historical position. Some portions of Matthew's mission discourse appear in the eschatological discourse as reported by the other evangelists,[1] and even Matthew himself repeats certain sayings already given in the earlier discourse in his version of the later;[2] and it is not improbable that the saying now under consideration really belongs to the closing period of Christ's life. All that is necessary for our purpose is that the saying, at whatever time uttered, had reference to the preaching of the gospel in Israel by the apostles. This, indeed, has been denied, and the text thus construed: Ye shall not have finished *fleeing* from city to city till the Son of Man be come;[3] the motive for the interpretation being a desire to eliminate all reference to Israel's judgment-day. But this seems a very forced construction. It is intrinsically probable that Christ referred to His coming as a reason for diligence in the work of preaching the gospel to Israel; and it could be that only on the supposition that His coming meant the judgment-day of Israel.

---

[1] Compare Matt. x. 16–22 with Mark xiii. 9–13, Luke xxi. 12–19.
[2] Matt. x. 22; cf. Matt. xxiii. 9, 13.
[3] So Pünjer, "Die Wiederkunftsreden Jesu," in Hilgenfeld's *Zeitschrift*, 1878.

The same reference to the judgment of Israel seems to have been in Christ's mind when He uttered the words: "There be some standing here that shall not taste of death till they see the Son of Man coming in His kingdom."[1] The section of the history to which the text belongs begins with the account of a request made by certain Pharisees for a sign which led Jesus to return an answer tinged with the melancholy characteristic of all His replies to requests of that sort. He saw in the spirit which prompted these demands a sure proof that the Jewish people were approaching their doom, and also an ominous indication of the fate which awaited Himself. Therefore He told the sign-seekers that no sign should be given them but that of the prophet Jonah, meaning probably to set the reception given by Nineveh to Jonah's preaching in contrast to the reception given by Israel to Himself, and to hint that the doom Nineveh had escaped by repentance would come on her. The encounter with unbelief troubled His spirit and coloured all His thoughts for a while. It cast Him into a brooding mood as they rowed Him across the lake, and prompted the abrupt word of warning: "Take heed and beware of the leaven of the Pharisees and of the Sadducees."[2] It led Him to think of His approaching death, and to feel that it was now time to inform His followers of what was coming. It led Him, finally, to speak of His coming in His kingdom still with conscious reference to the wicked and adulterous generation, and with this thought in His mind: then parties will change places; the Son of

---

[1] Matt. xvi. 28.   [2] Matt. xvi. 6.

Man, soon to be crucified, will then be Judge; and this people, at whose hands He is about to suffer, will receive its doom.

These texts, thus explained, suggest the thought that there may be more than one kind of coming of the Son of Man referred to in the words of Jesus. Students of the Gospels not specially biassed in favour of orthodoxy, such as Holtzmann, have recognised three distinct comings: an *apocalyptic* coming at the end of the world, a *historical* coming at any great crisis, as in the destruction of the Jewish state, and a *dynamical* coming in the hearts of believers.[1] The parousia assumes this third aspect chiefly in the fourth Gospel, but traces of it are not wanting in the Synoptics, as in the saying: "The kingdom of God cometh not with observation, the kingdom of God is within you;" and in the promise: "Where two or three are gathered together in My name, there am I in the midst of them."[2] The three senses are all intelligible and important, and it is *à priori* perfectly credible that they were all present to the mind of Jesus. Such a free plastic manner of conceiving the parousia is quite in accordance with His ideal poetic habit of thought. We have another instance of His free treatment of prophetic ideas in the identification of John the Baptist with Elijah. "If ye are willing to receive it," He said, "this is Elijah which is to come."[3] Why should He not also say in like manner, in reference to the judgment of Israel, preparing the way for Gentile Christianity, or to His spiritual presence in believers, If

---

[1] *Die Synoptischen Evangelien*, S. 409.
[2] Luke xvii. 20, 21; Matt. xviii. 20.   [3] Matt. xi. 14.

ye will receive it, this is the promised coming of the Son of Man? Critics are not willing to receive it; but neither were the people of Israel willing to receive the Baptist as Elijah. Elijah came, and they "knew him not, but did unto him whatsoever they listed."[1]

The most important and difficult text remains to be considered, that at the close of the great eschatological discourse containing this solemn declaration: "Verily I say unto you, This generation shall not pass away till all these things be accomplished."[2] This text, as it stands in Matthew's narrative, seems conclusively to prove that Jesus really did expect the final consummation to happen within the lifetime of His contemporaries. For the discourse on the Mount of Olives, as reported by the first evangelist, takes the form of a reply to three questions apparently assumed by the questioners to be equivalent in import, of which the first referred to the destruction of the temple which had just been predicted, the second to the sign of Christ's coming, and the third to the end of the age or world.[3] The apocalypse vouchsafed consists of three parts: the first containing a description of the birth-pangs, the things which are to precede the crisis of Israel;[4] the second being occupied with the "affliction" or $\theta\lambda\hat{\imath}\psi\iota\varsigma$, the dread visitation of judgment on that doomed people;[5] while the third describes the end, the coming of the Son of Man, which is represented as taking place immediately after the $\theta\lambda\hat{\imath}\psi\iota\varsigma$. The coming is something distinct from the

---

[1] Matt. xvii. 12.
[2] Matt xxiv. 34; Mark xiii. 30; Luke xxi. 32.
[3] Matt. xxiv. 3.   [4] Matt. xxiv. 4-14.   [5] Vers. 15-22.

θλίψις, yet it follows closely on the back of it. It is the great final coming, to be accompanied by the judgment of the unbelieving world, and the gathering together of the elect from the four winds of heaven for a happy meeting with the Lord; and it is among the things whereof it is declared: This generation shall not pass till all these things be fulfilled.[1]

Such seems to be the plain meaning of Matthew's report of the apocalyptic discourse. Yet there are certain things which suggest the thought that, after his usual manner, he has gathered together in one place words spoken on different occasions, and connected future events more closely in time than the actual utterances of Jesus justified. In the first place, the main subject of the discourse was undoubtedly the judgment of Israel. This is manifest even from Matthew's record, and on turning to Mark and Luke we find that the one subject of inquiry on the part of the disciples was when the predicted destruction of the temple should take place.[2] Then the εὐθέως, "forthwith," connecting that event with the coming of the Son of Man, strictly interpreted, does not seem compatible with a remarkable saying embedded in the discourse, to which I have not yet alluded, that, viz., in which Jesus declares that "of that day and hour knoweth no one, not even the angels of heaven, neither the Son, but the Father only."[3] Such a declaration

---

[1] Matt. xxiv. 29–31.   [2] Mark xiii. 4; Luke xxi. 7.

[3] Matt. xxiv. 36. The clause οὐδὲ ὁ υἱός is not in the T. R.; but the best ancient authorities have it, and it is restored in critical editions.

could not be made, either with regard to an event concerning which it was known that it would happen within the living generation, or with reference to another event concerning which it was known that it would happen immediately after the other. The two declarations: "All will happen in this generation," "No one knows the time," are irreconcilable, taken as referring to the same event. It may, indeed, be attempted to harmonize them by taking the one as referring to the general epoch, and the other to the precise time, say the particular year. But this interpretation is hardly compatible with the peculiar solemnity with which the Speaker proclaims His ignorance. The declaration evidently refers to something concerning which He knows less than He knows about Israel's impending calamities. Some, indeed, take it as referring to those calamities, and regard it as the direct reply of Jesus to the question of the disciples, viewing all that lies between as an apocalyptic writing of Judeo-Christian authorship interpolated into the narrative, the incompatibility between the two texts being cited in proof of the hypothesis.[1] There is, however, no reason to doubt that Jesus did on several occasions speak of Israel's judgment-day as very near. The prophetic insight of the Son of Man enabled Him to read the signs of the times, and to predict that the fateful day would fall within the existing generation. The profession of ignorance, therefore, must be taken to refer to another day, separated from the former by an unknown, indefinite interval.

[1] So Colani, *Jesus Christ et les Croyances Messianiques de son Temps*, p. 209.

The narratives of Mark and Luke present variations which are very significant in view of the declaration of nescience. Mark connects the coming of the Son of Man with the affliction of Israel more loosely than Matthew. His phrase is: "In those days, after that tribulation;"[1] which leaves room for the lapse of time, and makes it conceivable how Jesus might declare Himself ignorant of the day and hour[2] (of His final coming), while so positively affirming that Israel's judgment-day would fall within the existing generation. Luke, on the other hand, altogether avoids using words expressive of sequence, introducing the paragraph concerning the coming of the Son of Man with the words: "*And there shall be signs in the sun*," etc.[3] He does not mean to represent what follows in his narrative as taking place after the times of the Gentiles mentioned in the verse immediately preceding. He rather thinks of the coming of the Son of Man as contemporaneous with the destruction of Jerusalem. That is to say, it is no longer the final, apocalyptic coming that is spoken of, but the historical coming at the Jewish crisis; a coming not following, but going before the times of the Gentiles, in the description of which some apocalyptic features are still retained, but very much toned down as compared with Matthew's version. And what of the declaration of ignorance? It is omitted altogether. In explanation of this it has been suggested that, when Luke's Gospel was written, the feeling of the Church could no longer bear to have such ignorance ascribed to Jesus. A more likely explanation is that the evangelist, having made his

[1] Mark xiii. 24.   [2] Ver. 25.   [3] Luke xxi. 25.

version of the discourse have reference solely to things connected with the judgment of Israel, felt that the profession of nescience could not suitably be introduced into it alongside of the announcement that all should happen within " this generation." The omission confirms the view that the two declarations could not be made with reference to the same events.

CHAPTER XIII.

THE HISTORY OF THE KINGDOM IN OUTLINE.

Jesus knew and taught not only that the kingdom of God should have a history on the earth, but what the general course and character of that history should be. The synoptical records supply us with materials for sketching in outline the fortunes of the kingdom from its cradle to its consummation, presenting a picture full of moral if not of political interest. In reference to the initial stage, the relative utterances are in one view simple statements of facts based on personal observation of what was actually taking place; only such as refer to the more advanced stages can be considered prophetical. Yet even in the statements of fact there is, as we shall see, a prophetic element, in virtue of which, while telling what now is, they at the same time foreshadow what shall be.

The general impression made by these sayings of Jesus concerning the future is, that the history of the kingdom is to be of a chequered character. They teach that there will be much in its course throughout tending to disappoint and disenchant, and that the ideal will be far enough from being satisfactorily realized. A few utterances, taken by themselves, might lead us to form an opposite expectation. The most outstanding of these are the two parables of *The Mustard Seed* and *The Leaven*,[1] which seem to predict for the kingdom a career of unimpeded progress, through which it will spread itself on all sides till it cover the earth, and work with an all-pervading intensive force till it has made its influence felt in every department of human life. Had these parables stood alone, we should have formed from them the most sanguine and optimistic idea of the prospects of Christianity, which would have stood in strange saddening contrast with the facts as they lie before us in the pages of church history. But they do not stand alone; for, though full of the spirit of hope, Jesus was no shallow optimist or unthinking enthusiast. He took a very sober and even sombre view of the course the kingdom of heaven was to run on earth, as will be apparent from the texts about to come under review. The drift of these texts is this: the kingdom will not be as universal in fact as it is in design, or as pure in reality as it is in its own nature. Its development will be hindered in various ways. By some it will be rejected altogether; by others it will be received only in an abortive manner or in corrupt form.

This part of our Lord's teaching to a large extent assumed the parabolic form; very naturally, as the parable suits the mood of despondency and the mystic style of prophecy. Among the most important parabolic contributions to the doctrine of the future is the familiar parable of *The Sower*,[2] which appears to have been the

---

[1] Matt. xiii. 31-33; Luke xiii. 18-21.
[2] Matt. xiii. 3-9, *et parall.*

first formal instance of the use by Jesus of that method of setting forth thought. It teaches that among those who are invited to receive the truths of the kingdom will ever be found many in whose case the good seed will come to nothing, and whose spiritual experiences will turn out abortive. The parable is, in the first place, a record of observation. The Speaker has found among His own hearers the classes of men typified by the *beaten path*, the *rocky soil*, the *soil foul with thorn roots or seeds*, and the *good soil, soft, deep, and clean:* some curious about Himself, His doctrine, and His kingdom, yet with minds so hard-trodden by the current thoughts of the world that no distinct ideas could be communicated to them—all they heard being forthwith forgotten; others, lively and impressionable, easily touched on the emotional, imaginative side of their nature, catching up with enthusiasm the new doctrine of the kingdom, but only to be forthwith disenchanted and scared by the sober realities of discipleship; a third class, more deliberate and thoughtful, and likely to persevere with anything they take in hand, but men of divided heart, interested in the kingdom sufficiently to persevere in discipleship beyond the blade into the green ear, but still more interested in themselves, and therefore unable to bring forth fruit unto perfection; a few choice rare ones, such as Peter and John, of noble generous spirit, receiving the doctrine into mind, heart, and conscience, and giving the kingdom the first place in their regards, and therefore destined to bring forth in due season an abundant harvest of spiritual character. The parable, while a history, is at the same time a prophecy. Jesus offers His experience as a sample of what the preachers of the kingdom may expect, proceeding on the assumption that human nature will remain constant, and that the types of character depicted will reproduce themselves in every generation. The assumption, which made prediction possible, has been amply justified by the event. There have always been examples of the diverse classes of hearers. Of the best class, the men of noble and generous heart, there have sometimes been too few—heroic virtue is, indeed, always rare; but of the baser sorts there is always an abundant supply. The disproportion between the noble and the ignoble is one of the things which make the earthly realization of the kingdom of heaven so disappointing to all the Christ-like.

But another feature still more disappointing is brought before us in two other parables. The diverse types of unsatisfactory hearers in the parable of *The Sower* may be regarded merely as varieties of human infirmity manifesting itself in well-meaning men. In the parables of *The Tares* and *The Drag Net*,[1] especially in the former, we are warned that in the future history of the kingdom there will appear a revolting and unnatural mixture of good and bad men, Christians and anti-Christians, children of the heavenly Father and children of Satan. The evil are to resemble the good as "tares" (ζιζάνια, bearded darnel) resemble wheat, the resemblance being so close that till the plants reach the ear they cannot easily be distinguished. They are in the kingdom and bear the Christian name. But they are not the better on

[1] Matt. xiii. 24-29, 47-50.

account of this external similitude, but rather the worse; counterfeit citizens of the kingdom, children of darkness wearing the guise of children of the light, wolves in sheep's clothing, Christians in name, only to be all the more thoroughly anti-Christian in spirit. The feelings likely to be awakened by the appearance of these ungenial and unwelcome characters in the Church were just such as are described in the parable—surprise and impatience. "Sir, didst not thou sow good seed in thy field, from whence then hath it tares?" It is the question of honest men to whom the strange mixture is at once an astonishment and a vexation. Of course the impulse of faithful servants is at once to get rid of the intruders. "Wilt thou then that we go and gather them up?" Fully appreciating the naturalness of the proposal, and the praiseworthiness of the zeal out of which it springs, Jesus nevertheless negatives it, making the master say in reply to his servants: "No, lest while ye gather up the tares, ye root up also the wheat with them. Let them both grow together until the harvest." That the Founder of the kingdom should recommend this policy of patience has probably been little less of a surprise to His followers than the appearance of the evils to be tolerated. It seems so right and reasonable that plants known to be noxious weeds, which is the case supposed, should at once be removed. Yet Christ deliberately recommends patience as the least of two evils, the other being the uprooting of wheat along with tares in headlong zeal to get rid of the noxious crop; which implies a close interrelationship between the two kinds of growths that may well seem an additional calamity. Practically, the Church has not been able to work out this policy of patience. To wait calmly for the final separation, when the scandals and the workers of iniquity shall be gathered together and thrown into the fire, and the righteous shall at length shine forth as the sun in the kingdom of their Father, seems a task too severe for frail human tempers. God alone can so wait. All through the history of the Church the servants of truth and righteousness have been busily occupied in getting rid of the scandalous, especially in connection with matters of faith. "Out with the heretics" has been the watchword of nearly all faithful men; and the result is that instead of one Church in the world an approximate realization of the divine kingdom, there are hundreds of Churches, each, in theory at least, justifying its own separate existence by accusing all the rest of being tares. A futile quest after purity, which has too often ended by propagating within the most exclusive societies tares of the worst description, viz. spiritual pride and self-righteousness, and all the vices of a self-satisfied Pharisaism. Yet we cannot greatly wonder that men have not been able to wait for the last judgment. The moral order of the world itself does not wait, but is incessantly judging and sifting, and at critical times in human history makes great collections of scandals and kindles judicial bonfires.

It was an act of mercy in Jesus to utter that parable of *The Tares*. He spoke it not merely to teach His followers patience, but to keep them from despair. For nothing can tempt more fiercely to despair concerning the realization of all ideals, and to treat them as idle dreams, than to see that pure heavenly thing which Jesus conceived, the kingdom of God, defiled and bemired by the presence of evil unworthy elements: the divine amalgamated with the Satanic, heaven with hell, the best with the worst. We are prone to ask in bitterness what mischiefs hath not religion wrought, had we not better do without it? If only we could! But the Christian religion is the best, as its counterfeit may be the worst of all things. We cannot do without our religious ideals, and if along with these come hideous caricatures, our Master has taught us to find in the one a sedative and place of refuge from the other.

Jesus taught that the kingdom would meet with a variable reception depending not merely on psychological differences between individuals (as in the parable of the Sower), but on social distinctions. This truth He hinted at when He spoke of the things of the kingdom as being hid from the wise and understanding, and revealed to babes. The word was in the first place a statement of fact and personal experience, but it was, moreover, the suggestion of a principle, and the prediction of a recurrent experience. He meant to say that men of the type represented by the scribes, learned in the law, were not likely to receive the doctrine of the kingdom, and that disciples were more likely to be found among illiterate laics. The unreceptivity of the former class He partly explained in the parable of *The Children in the Marketplace*,[1] in which He virtually represented the generation of the scribes and their disciples as whimsical, unreasonable triflers, who could not be pleased with any form of true moral earnestness simply because they themselves, with

[1] Matt. xi. 16-19.

all their zeal for the law, were not in earnest, but were only playing at being religious and righteous. But the parable should not be taken as a complete description of the class, or as intended to negative their claim to some estimable qualities; all the more that the very qualities denoted by the attributes "wise and understanding" ascribed to them by Jesus acted as hindrances to faith. Pride and self-righteousness apart, the scribes, just because they were in a way wise, were all but doomed to an attitude of unbelief. Their snare was mental preoccupation, the power of which in producing indifference or aversion to the doctrine of the kingdom Jesus illustrated in a popular manner in the parable of *The Great Supper*.[1] The forms of preoccupation therein mentioned are such as are most suited to parabolic narration, such, namely, as arise from the business and pleasures of ordinary life. They are not the only forms, or even the most important, or such as chiefly beset the class of men represented at the dinner-table when the parable was spoken. The preoccupations of the wise and learned were of a more dignified and respectable character, and just on that account the source of a subtler temptation. They consisted in a system of fixed opinions on all the matters on which Christ in His teaching touched: on God, man, the kingdom, the Messiah. There was nothing on which it was possible for a religious and ethical teacher to speak on which they had not already formed their theories and drawn their sapient conclusions. Their minds were full and satisfied, and there was no room or taste for new ideas. Therefore Christ's chief chance of a hearing was

[1] Luke xiv. 16-24.

among the ἀγράμματοι καὶ ἰδιῶται,[1] the unlearned laity, who were comparatively empty, unbiassed, open-minded. He offered to teach them, and they received Him gladly, and eagerly drank in the good tidings. So it came to pass that the empty and the hungry were filled with the good things of the kingdom, while the rich in reputation for wisdom went away empty. And the experience of that age was prophetic: the same phenomenon recurs from age to age, at every new era when the kingdom comes in fresh power, under new aspects. The "wise" espouse no cause when it is new. When the new thing has become an established institution, they will patronize it. Their interest then is not in the thing itself, but in its secular adjuncts. They love the kingdom, not as a kingdom of heaven, but only in so far as it is become a kingdom of this world.

The experience of Jesus repeated itself in the apostolic Church. Paul alludes to and describes the fact in these terms: "Ye see your calling, brethren, how that there are not many wise men after the flesh, not many mighty, not many noble; but the foolish things of the world hath God chosen, that He might confound the wise," etc.[2] He makes it a matter of sovereign divine election. So also did Christ when He said: "Thou hast hid these things from the wise, and revealed them unto babes." This is the religious view of the phenomenon, most important in its own place; but it does not exclude natural causes or interdict inquiry into these. The diversities in question are not confined to the religious sphere. They repeat themselves in connection with

[1] Acts iv. 13.   [2] 1 Cor. i. 26, 27.

every new movement of thought, and they are perfectly intelligible. Possession, wealth in every form, is conservative, cautious, slow in sympathy, and languid in support; whether it be the intellectual wealth of knowledge, or the moral wealth of character, or the material wealth of outward property. The *rôle* of the rich in wisdom, worth, or gold is not that of the ardent pioneer, but of the tardy patron; so they miss the glory of martyrdom and also its pains. Their place in the history of the kingdom is a very mean one—in the more heroic phases of that history they are mainly conspicuous by their absence.

Jesus proclaimed another most important truth concerning the future history of the kingdom when He taught that it was destined to find a welcome, not among the people who might be regarded as its natural heirs, the Jews, but rather among the pagan nations that had hitherto been aliens from the commonwealth of Israel, and strangers to the covenants of promise. This is the burden of a whole series of parables, such as *The Barren Fig-Tree*,[1] *The Great Supper, The Royal Wedding*,[2] *The Two Sons*,[3] *The Wicked Vine-Dressers*,[4] every one of which points more or less clearly to the rejection of the Jews and the calling of the Gentiles. The fig-tree is threatened with ejection because it cumbers the ground, that is, occupies a space that might be more profitably filled with another tree. The very selection of a fig-tree instead of a vine to represent Israel is significant, as a virtual denial of her supposed prescriptive rights as the chosen

---

[1] Luke xiii. 6–12.
[2] Matt xxii. 1–13.
[3] Matt. xxi. 28–32.
[4] Matt. xxi. 33–40.

people. In the parables of *The Great Supper* and *The Royal Wedding*, the guests, brought in from the highways and hedges and lanes, may in the first intention represent the spiritually-neglected Jewish populace as opposed to the self-satisfied scribes and Pharisees; but the principle involved is: the kingdom and its blessings for the hungry anywhere and everywhere, there is plenty of room, and I will have my house full; and the probable application is: privileged Israel, self-excluded by her indifference, unprivileged heathendom rendered eligible by destitution. In the last parable of the group the moral is more plainly pointed. The wicked husbandmen,—the leaders of Israel,—representative of the nation in its corporative capacity, are to be destroyed, and the vineyard given to others who will render its fruits. The whole drift of Christ's teaching is in harmony with this view. While faithfully labouring for her salvation He never seems to have had any hope of Israel escaping the doom of unbelief and impenitence. To His prophetic eye that people seemed abandoned to ruin, and the kingdom He preached appeared in the panorama of the future shaking the dust off its feet as it forsook the Holy Land and marched forth full of faith and hope into the Gentile world. His clear vision of the future migration was the result of perfect insight into the moral conditions of faith and unbelief. The unbelief of the Jews and the faith of the Gentiles were but illustrations of the great ethical principles enunciated in His teaching: the things of the kingdom hid from the wise, revealed unto babes; the hungry filled, the rich sent empty away; grace given to the lowly, the proud regarded afar off; the first in their own esteem last in the esteem of God, the last in their own esteem first in the esteem of God. These principles received illustration on a small scale and within the boundaries of Israel in Christ's own lifetime. The subsequent transition of Christianity from the soil of Judæa to the wide world of the Gentiles was but an illustration of the same principles on a wider scale. And as these principles are of perpetual validity, new exemplifications of them may be expected while the Christian era lasts.

Among the words of Jesus which show the bright side of the prophetic picture, must be reckoned those in which He declared that His death would be followed by resurrection. To each one of the three preannouncements of His passion such a declaration is appended.[1] The doleful tidings of coming suffering ever wind up with the cheerful words, "And be raised again." It is easy to understand the motive for this constant transition from the minor to the major key. The reference to the resurrection was meant to make the announcement of the passion bearable. "I am about to die," Jesus would say, "but grieve not, I shall return to you very soon." All the evangelists agree in ascribing to Jesus such explicit predictions of His rising again, and they must be regarded as an authentic part of the evangelic tradition. The only question that can legitimately be raised is, what do these announcements mean? Do they point to a literal rising from the grave of the crucified One, or are they to be taken in a pregnant sense as intimating that the cause of Jesus would not perish with His life; that, on the contrary, it would live on in spite of that apparently

[1] Matt. xvi. 21, xvii. 23, xx. 19.

crushing blow, and even thrive by means of it? There is no reason to oppose these two interpretations; they are probably both covered by the words. Jesus, I apprehend, meant to say at once: I, the crucified, will rise again, and the cause I have at heart will rise again: the kingdom will come, and will receive a mighty forward impulse through my death. Viewed in the latter sense, the prophecy of resurrection was but a special application and instance of the general law of progress through antagonism, life saved by losing it, peace the conquest of the sword.[1] Faith in that law enabled Jesus to predict with unwavering confidence the survival and rapid spread of His religion after His death, and to go forward, in consequence, with firm step to meet His own fate. In that sense He might have said, "I will rise again," though He had meant nothing more. But that He did mean something more, even His own personal resurrection, we can have no doubt, when we remember how much the future of the kingdom depended on the apostles. The cause of Jesus could only revive and thrive through them. If they lost heart, then, humanly speaking, it was all over with the Christian faith; the kingdom was dead irretrievably, henceforth to remain in men's memories a generous but fond dream. But how were the apostles to be inspired with heart and hope? By faith in the resurrection of their Master. That this faith was indispensable is universally acknowledged. Naturalism admits the need of the apostolic faith in the resurrection of the Lord; it only denies that the fact of the resurrection was the cause of the faith. For those to whom the miraculous is

[1] Matt. x. 34.

impossible such denial is inevitable; the only course left for them is to invent theories to account for the faith while denying the fact. But from the point of view of Jesus the faith and the fact went together. If He regarded it as necessary for the future success of His cause that His disciples should believe in His resurrection, He must also have regarded it as necessary that He should actually rise from the dead. Therefore, to His mind, the thought, "My cause shall rise again," involved the other, "I shall rise again," and in predicting the one event He also predicted the other.

The resurrection of Jesus being in itself a welcome event, there was not the same urgent necessity as in the case of His death for bringing into play the religious imagination to invest it with mystic meanings. The doctrine of a crucified Christ could become tolerable only in the light of its rationale. Jesus risen would be hailed by His mourning disciples whatever the theological import of His rising again might be, or even though it had none. We are not surprised therefore to miss in the synoptic records sayings concerning the resurrection analogous to those in which the spiritual significance of the passion is unfolded. The solitary exception, if it be one, is that which refers to destroying the temple and raising it again in three days. Of the authenticity of this remarkable saying there can be no doubt, seeing it is preserved, not only in the fourth Gospel,[1] but also, in a slightly altered form, by two of the Synoptics, Matthew and Mark.[2] There is less certainty as to when and in what precise terms it was uttered, and there is also much difference

[1] John ii. 19.   [2] Matt. xxvi. 61; Mark xiv. 58.

of opinion among interpreters as to its meaning. The author of the fourth Gospel places it at the beginning of the history, and in connection with the cleansing of the temple, which in his narrative appears as an initial act of zeal on the part of Jesus protesting against the profanation of the sanctuary. Asked by what authority He acted, He replied: Destroy this temple, and in three days I will raise it up. The evangelist adds the explanatory comment: "He spake of the temple of His body," so making the words bear a hidden allusion to the resurrection. The synoptical evangelists introduce the saying into their account of Christ's trial, putting it into the mouth of certain witnesses as a word they professed to have heard Him utter. They give no indication of the occasion on which it was originally spoken; they do not even so much as state distinctly whether Jesus ever spoke it at all. From the fact that they characterize the witnesses as false, one might infer that they meant to hint that the story was a pure fabrication. The probability, however, is that the falsehood consisted in reporting Christ's words in a perverted form, fitted to create a prejudice against Him, the witnesses making Him say, "I will destroy this temple," instead of "destroy this temple," as reported in the fourth Gospel. The historical connection assigned to the saying in the same Gospel seems very suitable. No more appropriate occasion for such an utterance can be thought of than the solemn moment when, overtaken by an irresistible impulse of zeal, Jesus drove the crowd of profane traffickers out of the sacred precincts. At such an hour He might very seasonably speak of the destruction of the temple as the sure ultimate result of the encouragement or tolerance of such unholy traffic on the part of irreverent officials. Asked for a sign of His right to act as He did, He might very well reply, Destroy ye this temple, for that is the work ye are busily engaged in; my part will be to build it again. Truly interpreted such words would not necessarily mean more than that in the view of Jesus what was going on in the religious world of Judæa tended surely to the ruin of existing religious institutions, and that it was His hope to replace these by a new and purer worship, even by the setting up of the kingdom of God. It would not occur to us, apart from the hint of the evangelist, to find in the saying any reference to the resurrection. The specification of "three days" as the time within which the re-edification of the ruined sanctuary is to take place does not necessarily involve any such reference, for it may be nothing more than a proverbial phrase for a short time. If the cleansing of the temple took place at the beginning of His public ministry, as the fourth Gospel represents, it is difficult to believe that at so early a period Jesus had His resurrection distinctly in view. Accordingly some writers, such as Weiss, who accept John's narrative as otherwise correct, hold that he is mistaken in thinking that the words had a reference to that event. I sympathize with this view so far as to admit that, while the cleansing of the temple seems most appropriately placed at the beginning of the history, the saying concerning destroying the temple, if it contained any *immediate* and *conscious* allusion to the resurrection, appears suitable only to a more advanced period. But it is not necessary to assume any allusion of that description in order to vindicate the substantial accuracy of John's representation. The true state of the case I conceive to have been somewhat as follows. The words in question were spoken in connection with the cleansing of the temple at the opening of Christ's public career, and their meaning was: I will show my right to do what I have done by setting up the kingdom of God in place of this sanctuary which ye are doing your best to destroy. But as time went on the saying proved to be one of those mystic pregnant words which imply more than they explicitly state, or than any one thought of when they were first uttered. It became apparent that the destroying of the temple had a close connection with destroying Jesus, and the raising of it again with His resurrection. A dim presentiment of this was probably present to Christ's thoughts from the first, but it grew clearer with the progress of events. Before the end came it had grown evident to Him that His own death and the ruin of the Jewish sanctuary and state were connected together as inevitable common effects of the same causes, and on the other, bright, side of the picture His prophetic eye saw His personal resurrection and the resurrection of true religion in the apostolic Church linked together as means and end. When the witnesses at the trial reminded Him of the word He had spoken three years before He silently reaffirmed it charged with all that new meaning. He said nothing— how could He make Himself intelligible to such an audience?—but He thought much. A whole apocalypse of the future flashed through His mind, in the vivid light of which He saw at the same moment: Himself a victim on the cross, Jerusalem in ruins, the crucified One risen, the new Christian world ushered into being, the whole vision capable of being summed up in the pregnant oracle: Destroy this temple, and in three days I will raise it again.

Thus viewed, the saying under consideration had a real connection in our Lord's mind both with His resurrection as a means and with the inbringing of the true religion as an end. At first the end was mainly thought of, but gradually the means came distinctly into consciousness. The second and fourth evangelists by their explanatory glosses give, between them, the full significance of the saying, Mark making the last part of it point to the building of another temple made without hands (putting, doubtless, his own thought into the mouth of the witnesses), while John finds in it a reference to the temple of Christ's risen body. The two glosses represent different ways of interpreting the oracle current in the Church, easily reconcilable with each other. The gloss of the second Gospel comes nearest to what may be supposed to have been in Christ's mind when He uttered the words; that of the fourth to the reflections of Jesus on hearing them repeated three years later, when He stood a prisoner at the bar of the Sanhedrim. From the two combined we learn to regard the resurrection of our Lord as at once a cause and a symbol of the new spiritual life embodied in Christendom. As with His death the old world passed away, so with His resurrection a new world sprang into being.

CHAPTER XIV.

THE END.

FROM the texts cited in the foregoing chapter it plainly appears that Jesus did not expect the kingdom of God during the period of its earthly development to be other than an imperfect disappointing thing. But He did not on that account despair as to the final fortunes of the kingdom. He believed that the ideal would eventually be realized, that the kingdom would at length come in all its perfection and purity.

This consummation might be reached in either of two ways: either by all men being transformed into genuine sons of the kingdom, or by a judicial separation between genuine and counterfeit, between friends and foes. In the recorded sayings of Christ relative to this subject purity is represented as being reached by separation. So in the parable of *The Tares*: *Let both grow together until the harvest: and in the time of harvest I will say to the reapers, Gather ye together first the tares, and bind them in bundles to burn them: but gather the wheat into my barn;*[1] and in its interpretation: *As therefore the tares are gathered and burned in the fire; so shall it be in the end of this world. The Son of Man shall send forth His angels, and*

[1] Matt. xiii. 30.

they shall gather out of His kingdom all things that offend (τὰ σκάνδαλα), *and them that do iniquity, and shall cast them into a furnace of fire: there shall be wailing and gnashing of teeth. Then shall the righteous shine forth as the sun in the kingdom of their Father.*[1]

These words point to a process of judgment within the kingdom. When we collect together all Christ's sayings concerning the end, we find that they may be grouped into what may be called three judgment programmes. There is the judgment of citizens or of Christendom, the judgment of opponents or of antichristendom, and the judgment of those who stand in no conscious relation to the kingdom, or of heathendom.

Many of Christ's sternest sayings relate to the first of these judicial processes, and contain severe sentences on the various sins of false discipleship and unfaithful disloyal citizenship. *Not every one that saith unto me, Lord, Lord,*[2] pronounces a sentence of exclusion on lip-homage, and zeal in technical service combined with godless conduct, in which we have to note the keen insight and moral discrimination of Jesus shown in conceiving of such a combination as possible. It is a common enough occurrence, yet how many have ever refused to recognise the fact, and have accepted religious talk and religious zeal as conclusive evidence of goodness! *Whosoever shall deny me before men, him will I also deny before my Father which is in heaven,*[3] pronounces a doom of repudiation on faithless disciples who, through cowardly, selfish fear, prove disloyal to the divine interest in critical, perilous

---

[1] Matt. xiii. 40-43.   [2] Matt. vii. 21-23.
[3] Matt. x. 33; Luke ix. 26.

times. Ambition and mercilessness are proclaimed to be utterly alien to the kingdom in the sayings: *Except ye be converted, and become as little children, ye shall not enter into the kingdom of heaven;*[1] and, *So likewise shall my heavenly Father do also unto you, if ye from your hearts forgive not every one his brother their trespasses.*[2] Tyranny gets its appropriate penalty in the word which declares that the lord of the upper servant who maltreats his humbler fellow-servant *will cut him in sunder, and will appoint him his portion with the unbelievers.*[3] Mere negligence is relentlessly judged: *Cast ye the unprofitable servant into the outer darkness; there shall be the weeping and gnashing of teeth.*[4]

The materials relating to the second judgment programme are less abundant. In one sense, indeed, they are exceptionally copious, for the whole of Christ's criticism on Pharisaism may be said to belong to this category. His judgment on contemporary Pharisaism anticipates the final judgment on that phase of human character, and reveals the principles on which it will be based. That judgment in effect was this, that the righteousness in vogue in Judæa was in spirit, tendency, and result wholly alien and hostile to the kingdom of God.[5] That was not the judgment of those who practised it on themselves. They claimed to be the rightful heirs of the kingdom and its honours. This claim Jesus recognised as a fact, but refused to homologate when He said: *Many shall come from the east and west, and shall sit down with Abraham and Isaac and Jacob in the kingdom of heaven.*

[1] Matt. xviii. 3.   [2] Matt. xviii. 35.   [3] Luke xii. 46.
[4] Matt. xxv. 30.   [5] Matt. v. 20.

But the children of the kingdom shall be cast out into the outer darkness.[1] The very essence of Pharisaism was that it combined exclusive pretensions to the rights of citizenship in the divine kingdom with bitter hostility to all its true interests. The "children of the kingdom" in their own esteem, the Pharisees were the implacable enemies of the kingdom in Christ's esteem. Their type of character is not to be confounded with that of the men who say, "Lord, Lord," and do not the will of the Father in heaven. The vice of the latter is inconsistency, duality of character, two-souledness, the combination of religiosity with a low moral tone, after the manner of Balaam and Judas. There is weakness as well as wickedness in men of this class, and withal a consciousness of weakness, a tendency, doubtless, to self-deception, and to make pious phrases and technically "good" works an atonement and cloak for moral faults, yet not without an insuppressible sense of wrong which causes trouble to a conscience not altogether corrupted. The sin and wickedness of Pharisaism are far in advance of this. Its spirit is opposed to God, truth, and goodness, allied to falsehood, selfishness, inhumanity, pride, and every evil passion; yet it has a good conscience, is thoroughly self-satisfied, believes itself to be on God's side, and in possession of the divine favour, and knows nothing of the weakness of self-distrust and self-division. The individual Pharisee may not have attained to this pitch of iniquity, but this is the goal to which the system tends. Christ's phrase for the bad ideal was *blasphemy against the Holy Ghost*, and how intensely wicked He deemed it He showed when

[1] Matt. viii. 10, 12.

He said: *Whosoever speaketh against the Holy Ghost it shall not be forgiven him, neither in this world, neither in the world to come.*[1] From this unpardonable sin He distinguished, as easily pardonable, blasphemy against the Son of Man, which is a sin of misunderstanding, an unfavourable judgment on one whose true character is unknown, in the interest of that which the misjudged one really loves and is. This sin is often committed by truly good men; who, indeed, has not been guilty of it, and had occasion afterwards for bitter repentance? There is even a blasphemy against God which is of the same pardonable character, a passionate protest against a conventional deity not worthy of trust or reverence, worshipped by men whose conduct brings into discredit their creed; an atheistic reaction against a base theism in the interest of a God unknown but worth knowing. The *Holy Ghost* in the saying of Jesus signifies God as He is in truth, God in His very spirit of righteousness, wisdom, and love, and the blasphemers of Him are men who invest with every sacred attribute an idol of their own creation, and charge with impiety all who worship not at its shrine.

The judgment of heathendom is pictorially represented in Matt. xxv. 31–46. The Gentile peoples ($\tau\grave{a}$ ἔθνη) are conceived of as gathered together to be judged by the Son of Man, and they are judged by the manner in which they have treated Him. The difficulty at once presents itself, how can they be judged by their behaviour towards one whom they know not? The difficulty is met by the Judge treating what is done to His brethren as done to Himself. The question next arises, who are the

[1] Matt. xii. 32, 33.

"brethren"? Some answer: disciples, Christians. All pagans are accounted righteous who show kindness to those bearing Christ's name, giving them a cup of cold water in the name of a disciple, or in any way ministering to their necessities.[1] The answer is true so far as it goes, but it does not adequately meet the case. There are many pagans who have never even seen a Christian, not to speak of seeing Christ. The "brethren" must receive as comprehensive a definition as is given to "neighbour" in the parable of the Good Samaritan, and be made coextensive with all in every land who need the offices of love. The brethren of the Son of Man in this judgment programme are all the poor, suffering, sorrow-laden sons of men, and the principle on which judgment proceeds is that as men treat these they would have treated the Judge had they had the opportunity.

It is noticeable that in none of these judgment programmes, or indeed in any sayings having a judicial reference, is mention made of the classes whom the Pharisees shunned and Jesus pitied. The one word that might seem to wear an aspect of judicial severity is "lost;" but that term, as we have seen, does not describe

---

[1] So Weizsäcker, *Untersuchungen*, S. 199, and Pfleiderer, *Urchristenthum*, S. 532. The latter regards the judgment scene as a composition of the evangelist, and compliments him on the ethical human style of his thought, as shown in replacing the lacking Christian faith in the case of the heathen by Christ-like love, and so placing by the side of Paul's dogmatic universalism his ethically grounded universalism and humanism. Weiss and Wendt regard the passage as a genuine logion of Jesus, with exception of the last verse, "These shall go away into everlasting punishment, but the righteous into life eternal," which they both regard as a gloss (*vide Das Matthäus-Evangelium* and *Die Lehre Jesu*).

a state of perdition, but merely of ignorance, error, and foolishness.[1] It is a word of compassion rather than of doom. Jesus launched His stern sentences at "the unwedgeable and gnarled oak," not at the "lowly myrtle." He may have had the classes above mentioned in view when He said: "He that knew not, and did commit things worthy of stripes, shall be beaten with few stripes."[2]

The final separation takes place in the interest of an ideal purity, for which all earnest ones constantly strive, and the grounds of separation are such as commend themselves to every unsophisticated conscience. In connection with the faults of unfaithful citizens of the kingdom one may have a doubt whether the characters in which they appear are purely and irredeemably bad; but one cannot doubt that doublemindedness, cowardice, ambition, implacability, tyranny, and sloth are very evil qualities. With reference to the moral perversity of counterfeit holiness, and the inhumanity of a Dives who can let a Lazarus lie at his gate without a thought of mitigating his misery, our assent to the sentence of exclusion is more intense and unreserved. To every healthy moral nature hatred of true goodness, and pitiless selfishness, must needs appear altogether damnable. Christ's doctrine approves itself as of the highest moral quality in fixing on these as the unpardonable sins. Nothing can be conceived more ethically dignified and wholesome than that judgment programme in Matt. xxv. The judgment of the pagans proceeds on a purely ethical basis. Pagans are not condemned because they are ignorant of Christ, or because they worship idols, or

[1] *Vide* p. 136.   [2] Luke xii. 48.

because they are in an unregenerate state of natural depravity, or on any disputable or indisputable theological ground, but simply and solely because they have lacked the love which in the view of the Judge is the essence of goodness. All who live in the spirit of love the Son of Man recognises as Christians unawares, and therefore as heirs of the kingdom. All who live a loveless life of selfishness He relegates to the congenial society of the devil and his angels.

From these judgments we cannot withhold our assent. Even when we think of them as final, eternal, we cannot help saying, Amen. On the vexed question of "the eternity" of future punishments I do not mean here to enter. It is a subject to which I have ever felt a decided aversion, on which I have little light for myself, and therefore little to offer to others. I may simply say that so far as I can see finality is involved in Christ's whole way of viewing the consummation of the kingdom. The "end," whensoever it may come, means for Him the time when the process of historical development is complete, when characters have become fixed, and men are what they will be. Whether the end for the individual be the hour of death, or whether development of character may go on beyond that crisis, is a question for the determination of which few materials are to be found in the Gospels. The parable of Dives and Lazarus, when it speaks of the great gulf fixed that cannot be passed from either side, seems rather discouraging to those who cherish "the larger hope." In any case, when the "end" has come finality seems a matter of course. Some of Christ's words regarding the future expressly point at finality, *e.g.* that regarding the unpardonable sin. "It shall not be forgiven, neither in this world, neither in that to come." The form in which this saying occurs in Mark, according to the best accredited reading, suggests the rationale of this eternal unpardonableness. The blasphemer of the Holy Ghost is there pronounced guilty of an "eternal sin" (αἰωνίου ἁμαρτήματος).[1] He has reached the final stage of complete moral perversity, in which no change for the better is to be looked for, and therefore must remain for ever excluded from the bliss of forgiveness and reconciliation accessible to all the penitent.

The significant expression "an eternal sin," suggests the thought that eternal damnation is the doom only of the utterly and hopelessly bad. The same inference may be drawn from the expression "prepared for the devil and his angels," occurring in Matthew's judgment programme. The words obviously imply that "the everlasting fire" was not originally kindled with reference to mankind; that God created man for a better destiny, and that if any man be consigned to it for his misdeeds, it is an accident in his history. But they imply more, this, viz., that no man will find his home in the everlasting fire till he has become a fit companion for devils, till, in fact, he has himself become diabolic. Putting the two texts together the doctrine of Christ appears to be that final, eternal damnation awaits those, and those only, who have become diabolized through moral perversity and inhuman selfishness. To this doctrine one can say, Amen, though with subdued voice. What does

[1] Mark iii. 29.

it amount to but the expression in terms of duration of the universal sense of the absolute badness of the character described? The robust conscience habitually damns such characters in unqualified terms and with passionate earnestness. Even the man who accepts the modern theory of the universe, according to which there is no future world, and the eternal is immanent in the temporal, in his own way pronounces a sentence of eternal damnation on all that is diabolic in human conduct. And I suspect that there are only two ways of it: either to acquiesce in the old Jewish mode of expressing absolute reprobation of iniquity by attaching to it a penalty of unending future retribution,[1] or to find satisfaction to our moral resentment in the conception of a moral order of the universe acting incessantly throughout all the ages as a gnawing worm consuming rotting carcases, and as a glowing fire burning up the waste matter of the spiritual world.

"Who shall dwell with the devouring fire?" It may be hoped few. It is permissible to hope that few will become so utterly depraved and dehumanized as to be fit companions for devils. Certain it is that Christ had no pleasure in contemplating that as the ultimate state

[1] The everlasting fire does not necessarily imply perpetual existence of the individual. The furnace in the parable of the Tares consumes the tares as waste. From the point of view of that parable the wicked are the waste of the moral world, and they are cast into the consuming fire, not so much to punish them, as to get rid of them. How far the category of waste can be properly applied to human souls is a question of the same sort as that which asks, Can a being endowed with freewill fitly be compared to clay in the hands of a potter? These analogies, like most others, can easily be carried to an undue length.

of any man, and that He regarded damnation of human beings as abnormal, and contrary to the divine order. This, as I have above indicated, is a fair inference from the phrase, "prepared for the devil and his angels." For whomsoever the everlasting fire was prepared, it was not, in the view of Jesus, prepared for *man*. It is important to note how studiously He avoids using any words which might suggest such a thought. The sentence put into the mouth of the Judge with reference to those on the left hand runs thus: "Go from me, cursed, into the everlasting fire, that prepared for the devil and his angels." There are several points of contrast between this sentence and that pronounced on those on the right hand. The article is wanting before κατηραμένοι. They are not "the cursed ones," as the others are "the blessed ones," but simply those who are in a cursed moral state, and therefore must receive an appropriate doom. Neither are they cursed of the Father, as those on the right hand are blessed of the Father. Jesus will not make His Father the source of man's cursed condition, but will rather teach that men, by the abuse of their freedom, bring that condition on themselves. The fire is not prepared for these self-cursed ones, as the kingdom is prepared for the righteous; not for them, but for the spirit of evil and his servants. Finally, the fire is not prepared even for the devil and his angels *from the foundation of the world*, as in the case of the kingdom, but only when it is called for by their lapse into rebellion against the Creator and Lord of all.[1]

[1] These points are noticed by Weiss, *vide Das Matthäus-Evangelium*, S. 539.

God's original purpose was to bless all His creatures, angels and men alike.

How far Jesus was from regarding men, all or any of them, as predestined to damnation, appears from His doctrine of election. He did not think of the elect as chosen to an exclusive salvation, or as enjoying a monopoly of divine favour. He regarded them rather as chosen to the noble vocation and function of saviours to their fellow-men. "Ye are the salt of the earth," "Ye are the light of the world;" such was the language He employed to indicate the purpose of their election. The aim is universal human salvation, and the elect of any age are God's agents in the execution of the beneficent plan. If any are unsaved it is a miscarriage for which God is not responsible, and which wrings from the Redeemer's heart tears of bitter regret. "I would, ye would not."[1] It is true, indeed, that from some texts we might gather that even Christ cared only for the elect, and without a pang left all the rest of mankind outside the chosen few to their fate. Thus in the discourse on the last things we read, "He shall send His angels with a great sound of a trumpet, and they shall gather His elect from the four winds, from one end of heaven to the other."[2] Again, in the same discourse it is stated that the days of tribulation preceding the second advent shall be shortened, "for the elect's sake."[3] I do not envy the man who can extract from these texts in an obscure apocalyptic discourse the meaning: what does it matter what happens to the rest of mankind, either in this world or in the next, if only the dear elect are safe?

[1] Matt. xxiii. 37 [2] Matt. xxiv. 31. [3] Matt. xxiv. 22.

in defiance of the general scope of Christ's teaching, and the broad human sympathies that are the very essence of His gospel. Such men, if they exist, belong to an elect that has lost its savour, and is fit only to be trampled under foot. There are crises, doubtless, when all that can be done is to gather out of a corrupt mass that has become utterly degenerate and ripe for judgment the few elect ones. Such was the case of Sodom at the time of its overthrow. Then Providence looked after the safety of Lot and his family before proceeding to the work of destruction. But how far the true elect are from thinking that their safety alone is of importance appears from the noble intercession of Abraham, who prayed that the few righteous men in the city might shield the many from a too well-deserved doom; a prayer which would not have been in vain had there been a sufficient number of righteous men in Sodom to serve the purpose of a preservative salt.

Within or without—such are the two alternatives involved in the judgment. The faithful are admitted within the kingdom, the unfaithful and unworthy are shut out. The alternatives are presented, especially in parabolic narratives, as rewards and punishments. In such parables as *The Labourers in the Vineyard*,[1] *The Talents*,[2] and *The Pounds*,[3] we find a doctrine of Work and Wages in the kingdom. The work is done by the servants (δοῦλοι) of the King on a contract, and the wages are paid at the end of the day—that is, at the consummation of all things. The representation seems contrary to the nature of the kingdom as a kingdom of

[1] Matt. xx. 1-20. [2] Matt. xxv. 14-30. [3] Luke xix. 12-28.

grace. Its adoption is due in part to the parabolic form in which our Lord clothed His thoughts on this subject, and also in part to the fact that it is in a certain respect in accordance with truth. The absolute magnitude of the reward, which is out of all proportion to the service, guarantees and guards its graciousness. Eternal life, admission into the everlasting kingdom, entrance into the joy of the Lord, recovery an hundredfold of the things renounced for the sake of the kingdom, who can think of such blessedness as wages that have been strictly earned? With reference to so great a recompense all must say, " We are unprofitable servants." It is in connection with the graduated apportionment of reward in accordance with the amount and the quality of work done that we see the relative truth of the legal point of view. For the rewards and punishments of the great hereafter, while in one sense all alike, do also, according to the teaching of Christ, vary on certain definite principles. The law of the case, as gathered from the three above named parables, is that the reward varies according to the quantity of work done, the ability of the worker, and the motive. Ability being equal, quantity determines relative value: such is the lesson of the parable of *The Pounds;* ability varying, then, not the quantity viewed absolutely, but its relation to ability determines value: such is the truth taught in the parable of *The Talents.* The supreme importance of *motive* is the special contribution of the parable of *The Labourers in the Vineyard.* In the first of these parables all receive one pound, but use it with unequal diligence, one making ten pounds, another only five, and the rewards are proportioned to the diligence. In the second, two servants make equally diligent use of a different number of talents, one getting five and making other five, the other getting two and making other two; and both are rewarded alike. In the third, while all get the "penny," the men who entered the vineyard first are paid last, and those who entered last are paid first, and much more than their legal due: a day's wages for an hour's work; the reason of the diverse treatment lying in the diverse dispositions of the workers, the first mercenary, the last devoted and uncalculating.[1]

Admission into or exclusion from the kingdom, while represented as depending on the decision of the Judge, may be said to come about by natural law. These are admitted within the kingdom, because the kingdom is within them; those are excluded, because no trace of the spirit of the kingdom can be discovered in them. The Judge judges according to fact, recognises and publicly proclaims the fact. It is only necessary to consider for a moment the grounds of admission or exclusion to see the truth of this statement. The loving—how can they be shut out? They are in the kingdom, the spirit of the kingdom is in them; where they are the kingdom is. The unloving—how can they be admitted? They have nothing in common with the kingdom; where they are is the outer darkness. Christ said, the ambitious cannot enter the kingdom. Is the sentence surprising? Ambitious men often do much work ostensibly for the kingdom, which may seem to constitute a claim not only to a

---

[1] For a full discussion of these parables, *vide The Training of the Twelve*, chap. xvi., and *The Parabolic Teaching of Christ*.

place, but to a high place therein. But all they do is done really for themselves, to gain popularity and power. They are self-seekers, and of such is *not* the kingdom of God. So with all the other conditions, for it is needless to prove what to spiritual discernment is self-evident.

The rewards and punishments of the end are thus to continue to be, and to be in perfection, what you have been. "He that is righteous, let him be righteous still," and "he that is unjust, let him be unjust still." When the great separation takes place the righteous shall simply "shine forth as the sun in the kingdom of their Father,"[1] be clearly seen to be what they really are, instead of having their character obscured by mixture with the unrighteous, and even being in danger of being confounded with their moral opposites.

Of these rewards and punishments the words of Christ give a variety of figurative representations. The righteous sit on thrones,[2] rule over cities,[3] share the joy of their Lord,[4] a joy like that of a wedding-feast.[5] The unrighteous go into the everlasting fire,[6] are in prison for debt,[7] receive stripes as slaves guilty of misconduct,[8] pass into the outer darkness, where is the weeping and gnashing of teeth.[9] These are all alike figures, symbols of spiritual truths, valuable as such, but misleading when taken as literal descriptions of eternal destinies. The everlasting fire is, not less than the other figures, only a

---

[1] Matt. xiii. 43.
[2] Matt. xix. 28.
[3] Luke xix. 17, 18.
[4] Matt. xxv. 21, 23.
[5] Matt. xxv. 1–11.
[6] Matt. xxv. 41; Luke xvi. 23.
[7] Matt. xviii. 34.
[8] Luke xii. 47.
[9] Matt. viii. 12, xxv. 30.

symbol, as appears from the fact that, taken literally, it excludes from the region of possibility the "outer darkness." All these figures are the products of the religious imagination, and express in sensuous terms the intense conviction of the enlightened conscience as to the blessedness of being good and the misery of being evil. To be bad is to be as one dwelling in an everlasting fire; to be negligent of duty is to be as one left out in the cold dark night, while the faithful merrily feast in the brilliantly lighted hall. What the good dread is the badness, not the fire which is its symbol. What the bad fear is the fire, not the evil that is within them. If one came from the dead and assured them that the hell of which they had heard had no existence, and that the only torment known in the other world was that of an evil conscience, it would comfort them, and encourage them to sin with a high hand. It may seem, therefore, as if the symbolical character of Scripture representations of future states should be treated as an esoteric doctrine, to be carefully kept for the ears of the initiated and hid from the profane multitude. The policy has been pursued, but whether with much success for the real interests of the kingdom of God may be doubted. Dives wished one sent from the dead to give a glowing description of the place of torment to his brethren, that they might not come into it. But our Lord represents Abraham as replying, "If they hear not Moses and the prophets, neither will they be persuaded though one rose from the dead."[1] Moses and the prophets had little to say about hell, or indeed about a life to come

[1] Luke xvi. 31.

in any form. The theme of their preaching was righteousness here and now. Christ meant to teach that he who has no ear for their doctrine cannot be made a citizen of the divine kingdom by the terrors of hell, however vividly depicted.

CHAPTER XV.

THE CHRISTIANITY OF CHRIST.

THE recent revival of the conception of the kingdom of God, which is so prominent in Christ's teaching as reported in the synoptical Gospels, and which throughout the greater part of the Church's history, from the apostolic age downwards, has been eclipsed by other notions, is justly regarded as a wholesome movement for various reasons, and specially as supplying a needed antidote to religious individualism. This return to Christ's way of regarding salvation as a social thing is but a single phase of a much wider movement going on all around us, which may be described as a return to the *Christianity of Christ*. On all sides the cry is "back to Christ." "To reconceive the Christ is the special task of our age," says one, in whose mouth it means the disentanglement of the real historical elements in the life of Jesus from all miraculous accretions assumed to be unreal and mythological. It is possible heartily to sympathize with the sentiment, without sharing the naturalistic bias against the miraculous. Beyond doubt, to reconceive the Christ in a spirit of historic fidelity is an urgent task of vital consequence to the life and prosperity of the Church. The ecclesiastical Christ is to a large extent not the Christ of the Gospels, but a creation of scholastic theology. Notwithstanding all our preaching, Jesus Christ is not well known. That He is not well known, is partly the fault of our preaching. Men are not permitted to see Jesus with open face, but only through the thick veil of a dogmatic system. The religious spirit of Jesus, His attitude towards the religion in vogue in Judæa in His time, and its grounds, His humane sympathies, His thoughts of God, His ethical ideal, have been allowed to fall into the background. Hence types of piety have sprung up within the Church which, whatever virtues they may possess, are not characteristically Christian. It has become possible to be very religious and yet to be very unchristian, not only largely ignorant of Christ, but antagonistic to Him in spirit; to be, in short, a modern reproduction of the Pharisee, imagining oneself to be one of the most faithful friends of Jesus, while hostile to all the true Christian interests of the time. This is apparent to many without the Churches, and constitutes one of their reasons for keeping aloof from them as institutions having little real goodness in them. It is also apparent to an increasing number within the Churches, whose highest aim is to know Christ, and their constant endeavour to unearth the Christianity of Christ and exhibit it to their fellowmen.

The growth of this tendency is greatly to be desired. There is nothing more likely to regenerate the Church, to give it a new lease of life, and to make it a fresh source of moral power. Nominal Christianity will become real Christianity endowed with something of its pristine energy and beauty. My hope is that this is what is before us: Christianity renewing its youth by remounting to the fountain of inspiration, instead of tarrying longer by cisterns in which the waters of life have become putrid and unwholesome. I propose to conclude this study of the teaching of Jesus according to the synoptical presentation by indicating some directions the new Christian revival may take, and some of the good fruits it may yield.

If the desired rejuvenescence is to become a great fact, the restored intuition will make its appearance through a sufficient number of representative men in the pulpit. For we must be careful not to undervalue this institution as an instrument of religious regeneration. The pulpit is the place of the *prophet*, to whose utterances men never have been and never will be indifferent; to speech, that is to say, about God and the great questions of religion at first hand, by men who see with their own eyes, and feel deeply and truly, and speak as they see and feel; not in hackneyed phraseology, but in their own natural tongue. The pulpit is a perennial institution, an invaluable means for diffusing among the people the elevating influence of healthy religious thought, requiring in order to its full usefulness to be carefully guarded against enslavement, whether by traditional creeds or by current opinion, but when able to assert its liberty sure to command general respect and wield great spiritual power. Therefore the desiderated revival, if it is to acquire momentum, must show itself here.

It will show itself in the form of a race of *Gospellers:* men to whom return to the evangelic fountains has been a necessity of their own spiritual life, possessing the power of historical imagination to place themselves side by side with Jesus as if they had belonged to the circle of His personal companions and disciples, so gaining a clear vivid vision of His spirit, character, and life, and becoming thoroughly imbued with His enthusiasms, His sympathies, and His antipathies; and with this experience behind them, the fruit of much thought and careful study, coming forth and saying to their fellow-men in effect: "That which was from the beginning, which we have heard, which we have seen with our eyes — declare we unto you." It would be the apostolic age returned, the companions of Jesus come to life again, showing the Son of Man as He was in word and deed and way. For it is the Son of Man we need to know; not as denying His divinity, but as knowing whom we affirm to be divine. What avails it to confess that an unknown Man is God? The vital matter is to confess that God is this well-known Man.

The public would not be indifferent to such preaching. To some sorts of preaching thoughtful earnest people, not less than the thoughtless, listen very languidly, or with ill-concealed impatience, *e.g.* to the platitudes of a merely traditional "evangelicalism," and to the cold unsympathetic negations of an anti-evangelic reaction not far removed from pure unmitigated naturalism. The great public cares neither for second-hand threadbare dogmatism nor for barren denial; it desiderates religious utterances at once positive and fresh, such as would be forthcoming from the gospellers I speak of.

A general return to the Christianity of Christ would

have a most important effect on the religious training of the young. At present, it is to be feared, this department of the Church's work suffers greatly from our being in a transition time. All know what an important place the Shorter Catechism occupied in the religious education of the youth of Scotland. Whether it was ever a good instrument for the purpose, is a question that need not be here discussed. What is certain is, that the most was made of it in bygone times by all concerned, parents, teachers, ministers; whose faithfulness in the discharge of duty is worthy of all praise. Now this thoroughness lingers only in odd corners of the land. Large numbers of people have become doubtful as to the value of a dogmatic catechism as an instrument of religious training, and in consequence the Westminster Assembly's Catechism has extensively fallen into desuetude. And as yet there is nothing to take its place, nothing fitted and intended to insure that the young shall have impressed upon their minds indelibly the things most important to be known, and most worthy to be believed concerning the Lord Jesus Christ and the religion called by His name. The result is that many children are growing up to maturity very slightly informed as to these things; not the children of the non-church-going alone, but those of Church members not less. Is this state of matters to continue indefinitely? Is the Church, in a spirit of conservatism, or timidity, or listlessness, to say: The Westminster Catechism or nothing? Or is she to content herself with producing commentaries on the Catechism of a purely scholastic type, as a means of reviving interest in it? It seems to me that a bolder policy is called for. What is wanted is not a dogmatic catechism, or commentaries on it written in a Rabbinical spirit, but a *Christian* Catechism or Primer, framed on a historical method: a little book intended to do for the young of our time what Luke did for his friend Theophilus; telling them the story of Jesus of Nazareth in a way suited to their years, and fitted to captivate their imaginations and their hearts, including the chief of His golden sayings, some representative acts and experiences, and telling briefly the story of His death and resurrection. Recall the eight questions in the Shorter Catechism relating to Christ, making mention in technical terms of His double nature, offices, humiliation and exaltation, and think what an abstract Christ is thus presented to view compared with the Christ of the evangelists, and the Christ that might be reproduced on a smaller scale—a photograph as it were from a large painting—in our new Christian Primer!

Who is to prepare the Primer? Not, I think, any Church, or Assembly, or Assembly's committee. Ecclesiastical bodies are too conservative, too slow, too much given to drift, too prone to make fetishes and Nehushtans of past means of grace. The work must be done, in the first place, by some individual Christian man, who has seen with open face the beauty of Jesus, and on whose heart it lies as a burden to show to others what he has himself seen, and to whom has been given the rare power to present spiritual truth in the poetic, naive, simple, yet not shallow way that wins children. And this man will not come from among those who make a saviour of Church, or creed, or sacrament. Completely emancipated from ecclesiasticism, and dogmatism, and sacramentarianism, he will have but one absorbing care and passion—to make the young know and love Jesus Christ. The advent of such a man, with such a mission, will be one of the sure signs and best fruits of the new Christian revival; and in proportion to its prevalence will be his welcome.

The Christward movement will make itself felt in connection with *creed* not less than with *catechism*. What to do with our creeds has become for all the Churches a burning question. That these creeds, centuries old, no longer express perfectly or even approximately the living faith of the Church, is being frankly acknowledged on every side. The free expression of the faith and spiritual life of former generations, they have become a bondage to the spirit and a snare to the conscience. Some Churches are even now occupied in considering what readjustments are necessary to make the situation bearable. Various solutions are proposed, two methods of meeting the difficulty finding special favour: altering the Confession directly or indirectly so as to bring it into line with present beliefs, and defining anew the attitude of the Church to the Confession.

Neither of these operations possesses much dignity, or rises much above the moral level of an artifice. The tinkering method of altering some details is a very partial cure, making the articles left untinkered press harder on the conscience because others have been altered to suit present exigencies as judged of by majorities. The other method of altering the formula of subscription amounts to touching your hat to a document venerable for its antiquity, and highly respectable on the score of theological acumen. The one thing to be said for it is, that it gets rid of the ecclesiastical scandal of making solemn pretence of receiving *ex animo* what is only submitted to reluctantly as a condition of office.

It will not be disputed that a written creed, to serve any high purpose, ought to be the faithful reflection of the living earnest faith of the Church. How far it is possible on the system of written creeds to satisfy this requirement is a question which may fairly be raised. Evidently a creed which is to continue approximately true to the faith of successive generations must be subjected to periodic revision. In making this remark I have in view not so much the theological opinions of individual subscribers, as the changes which come over the minds of whole communities. I do not think the purpose of a creed requires it to be at any time in exact accordance with the views of all the office-bearers of a Church. Individual subscription is an ecclesiastical device for securing external uniformity of opinion, for which, as essentially unspiritual, I entertain very little respect. The Holy Ghost is the only true guardian of genuine orthodoxy. It is enough if a creed be an honest, straightforward statement of the faith of a Church collectively as represented by its supreme court. But that it must be, if it is to have any weight as a testimony to what the Church regards as important truth.

If the existing Confession of Faith cannot claim for itself this character, why, it may be asked, not at once make a new one? A very natural, yet somewhat inconsiderate question. Creeds cannot be manufactured to order, nor is creed-making the business of every age.

Creed-tinkering is possible at any time, but making a new creed is a different affair. A new creed, fresh in conception and expression, is the work of a creative, not of a critical age, and the outcome of a new religious life. A fresh intuition of Christ and a new Christian enthusiasm such as I have been desiderating, would have for one of its results a fresh formulation of Christian belief bearing an entirely different stamp from that of the historical Protestant Confessions. Till the new life come we had better let the making of a new creed alone, and be content with acknowledging in one way or another that things as they are are far from satisfactory. For this is emphatically one of those matters to which the wise observation of the late William Denny applies: "There are problems in the spiritual and social world which are like some of our metals, altogether refractory to low temperatures. They will only melt with great heat, and there is no other possibility of melting them."[1] Whence is the needful heat to come? Not certainly from the friction of theological controversy, which has rent the Church asunder into innumerable fragments, but from the central Sun of the spiritual world, dispelling with His beams the mists of ages, and shining forth once more in full effulgence.

The reference just made to the divided state of the Church leads me to remark that ecclesiastical reunion or reconstruction is another of the problems to which Mr. Denny's observation applies. Reunion is possible only through refusion, and refusion is possible only through new religious intuitions and enthusiasms. There must

[1] *Vide* the *Life of William Denny*, p. 338.

come a change in the nature of our interest. At present the supreme interest of the majority is in their Church. For them, as for the woman of Samaria, the great question is—Gerizzim or Jerusalem, which of them is the place where men ought to worship? Union will come when men have learned that the vital question is not where, but how? "The hour cometh, and now is, when the true worshippers shall worship the Father in spirit and in truth." The "hour" Jesus spake of was the Christian era, which abolished old enmities, antiquated old institutions, upset partition walls, traversed party lines, and established a new society in which old distinctions were ignored, and once alienated men were formed into a close brotherhood. Can such an hour come again; or can a religion, can even Christianity, have such an hour only once in its history? If, as both faith and philosophy attest, Christianity be the absolute religion, perennial because perfect, not destined to be superseded by anything better, because better is impossible, it must possess the power of rejuvenescence. It must be able to shake itself clear of whatever hampers the free expression of its eternal vitality. It is the worship of the Spirit, and the Spirit must and will rid itself of all bonds. The need of a new hour of emancipation is a prophecy of its coming. One of the things that show the need is the divided state of the Church. Division is an infallible sign that the spirit of Christ immanent in the Church is in bondage. If Christ's spirit were among us in power, our divisions would appear ridiculous and intolerable. Hence we learn what is the hope of deliverance. It lies in the increase of men to whom Christ and Christianity are first, and everything else secondary. Every man to whom is given a fresh intuition of Christ will become an apostle of union, if not in the sense of ecclesiastical reconstruction, which may or may not be a great boon according to circumstances, at least in the sense of a real spiritual fellowship that will either make existing Churches serve its purpose, or create for itself new media of self-manifestation.

The new Christward movement must exercise an important influence on the methods of apologetic. No great movement of Christian thought can leave that department of theology untouched. It is easy to see in what way the methods of apologetic must be modified in order to be in sympathy with the movement I have sketched. The new apologetic will make it its first and fundamental task to ascertain and state what Christianity really is, and will rely largely on the result of this inquiry as its best armour of defence against antichristian prejudices whencesoever arising. It will not begin, as of old, with proofs of the being of a God, but will inquire what was Christ's idea of God, and what its speculative presuppositions, and show that these are more worthy of acceptation than any other thoughts of God, and theories of the universe that have ever been propounded. On such a method there is some hope of apologetic achieving its purpose. The task of an apologist is desperate if he is supposed to be the advocate of the *status quo* in theology. It is otherwise if he appear as the expositor or advocate of the Christianity of Christ. In performing this *rôle* he may fail to convince confirmed sceptics, or to give satisfaction to dogmatists who regard an apologist as a sort of prize-fighter for all the details of a traditional creed, but he is likely to commend Christianity to men of open mind and ingenuous spirit, like those who gathered about Jesus by the banks of the Jordan, drawn by a charm uncomprehended but irresistible. Christianity will never, probably, be the uncontradicted religion of all men. But there will be cause for satisfaction if it win to its side the noble, the truth-loving, the men who have a passion for righteousness. I should not despair of that if such men only saw Christ truly. The apologetic of the future must make it its business to communicate the vision to the few, that they in turn may communicate it to the many.

It may be doubted, indeed, whether a real knowledge of the historical Christ be now possible. Strauss writes: "We know very little about Jesus. The evangelists have daubed His life-image so thick with supernatural colours that the natural colours can no longer be restored. The Jesus of history is simply a problem, and a problem cannot be the object of faith or the exemplar of life. It is the penalty He pays for having been a God."[1] Of course the apologist cannot begin by assuming a doctrine of inspiration which is internal to faith, or postulating the infallibility of the evangelists. He must use the Gospels as sources of information concerning Christ under the ordinary critical conditions. But much that is of vital significance can be ascertained even under these conditions: that Jesus habitually spoke of God as Father; that He called Himself Son of Man, and asserted with new emphasis the worth of human nature;

[1] *Der Alte und der Neue Glaube*, S. 76.

that He preached His gospel of the kingdom to the poor; that He was the friend of publicans and sinners, and the enemy of Pharisaism; that He regarded it as His vocation to save the " lost," to be the healer of moral disease; that He accepted the Messianic idea, and even regarded Himself as the Messiah; that while thus associating Himself closely with the faith and hopes of His countrymen He taught a religion which was in spirit, tendency, and inevitable result universal; and that by sympathies wide and deep, but totally contrary to the prevailing habits of thought and feeling in His age and nation, He brought on Himself the temporary disgrace and eternal honour of crucifixion. These things at least are true; how much they imply!

INDEX

OF THE MORE IMPORTANT DISCOURSES, PARABLES, AND INCIDENTS IN CONNECTION WITH WHICH SAYINGS WERE SPOKEN, WITH THE RELATIVE GOSPEL TEXTS, AND REFERENCES TO PAGES IN THIS WORK.

SUBJECT.	GOSPEL TEXTS.	PAGE.
I. DISCOURSES.		
The Sermon on the Mount,	Matt. v.–vii.; Luke vi. 20–49,	5-8, 10, 11, 12, 22, 28, 63, 68, 88, 111, 187, 189, 204, 211, 212, 214, 217, 227, 233, 249, 268, 312.
Discourse on the mission of the Twelve,	Matt. x.; Mark vi. 7-13; Luke ix. 1–6,	117, 138, 284, 285, 312.
Discourse on Blasphemy,	Matt. xii. 22-37; Mark iii. 21-30; Luke xi. 14-26,	17, 172, 259, 314, 319.
,, Humility,	Matt. xviii.; Mark ix. 33-50; Luke ix. 46-50,	19, 90, 269, 287, 313.
,, Pharisaism,	Matt. xxiii., . . .	22, 189, 191, 193, 194, 195-205, 233, 269.
,, Last Things,	Matt. xxiv.; Mark xiii.; Luke xxi.,	185, 280, 285, 288-292, 322.
II. PARABLES.		
The Sower, . . .	Matt. xiii. 3-9; Mark iv. 3-9; Luke viii. 5-8,	275, 294-296.
The Tares, . . .	Matt. xiii. 24-30, . .	275, 296, 297, 311.
Mustard Seed, . .	Matt. xiii. 31, 32; Mark iv. 30-32; Luke xiii. 18, 19,	275, 294.
The Leaven, . . .	Matt. xiii. 33; Luke xiii. 20, 21,	256, 283, 294.
The Treasure and the Pearl,	Matt. xiii. 44-46, . .	222.
The Drag Net. . .	Matt. xiii. 47-50, . .	296.
The Seed growing gradually,	Mark iv. 26-29, . .	124, 275.
The Two Debtors, . .	Luke vii. 36-50, . .	143.
The Good Samaritan, .	Luke x. 38-42, . .	38, 212, 316.

INDEX.

SUBJECT.	GOSPEL TEXTS.	PAGE.
II. PARABLES—*contd.*		
The Selfish Neighbour, and the Unjust Judge,	Luke xi. 5-8, xviii. 1-8,	120, 277.
The Unfaithful Upper Servant,	Luke xii. 42-46,	278, 313, 326.
The Barren Fig Tree,	Luke xiii. 6-12,	302.
The Great Supper,	Luke xiv. 16-24,	300.
The Finding of the Lost,	Luke xv.,	112, 133, 136, 190.
Dives and Lazarus,	Luke xvi. 19-31,	141, 317, 318, 327.
Extra Service,	Luke xvii. 7-10,	225.
Pharisee and Publican,	Luke xviii. 9-14,	190, 201.
Children in the Market Place,	Matt. xi. 16-19,	299.
The Unmerciful Servant,	Matt. xviii. 21-35,	269, 313, 326.
The Labourers in the Vineyard,	Matt. xxi. 1-16,	226, 269, 323, 324.
The Two Sons,	Matt. xxi. 28-32,	302.
The Wicked Vinedressers,	Matt. xxi. 33-41; Mark xii. 1-12; Luke xx. 9-16,	179, 303.
The Royal Wedding,	Matt. xxii. 1-14,	303.
✓ The Ten Virgins,	Matt. xxv. 1-13,	278, 326.
✓ The Talents,	Matt. xxv. 14-30,	313, 323, 324, 326.
The Pounds,	Luke xix. 12-28,	323, 324, 326.
III. INCIDENTS.		
The Temptation,	Matt. iv. 1-11; Luke iv. 1-13,	32, 162.
Scene in Nazareth Synagogue,	Luke iv. 16-30,	25, 33, 50, 160.
Healing of the Paralytic: Power to forgive sin,	Matt. ix. 6; Mark ii. 10; Luke v. 24,	173.
Call of Matthew: "I came not to call the righteous,"	Matt ix. 13; Luke v. 32,	8, 9, 53, 96, 190.
Neglect of Fasting,	Matt. ix. 14-17; Mark ii. 18-22; Luke v. 33-39,	45, 51, 52, 217, 230, 232, 233.
Rubbing ears of corn: Lord of the Sabbath,	Matt. xii. 8; Mark iii. 28; Luke vi. 5,	77, 173, 197.
The Sabbath made for man,	Mark ii. 27,	74.
Roman Centurion,	Matt. viii. 5-13; Luke vii. 1-10,	30, 100, 313.
John the Baptist's message to Christ and Christ's estimate of him,	Matt. xi. 1-19; Luke vii. 19-30,	51, 80, 153, 161, 188.
John's preaching of repentance,	Luke iii. 10-14,	86, 95.
The woman that was a sinner,	Luke vii. 36-50,	97, 143.
The mission of the seventy,	Luke x. 1-16,	27.
The gracious invitation,	Matt. xi. 27-30,	24, 35-38, 195, 202, 204, 218.

SUBJECT.	GOSPEL TEXTS.	PAGE.
III. INCIDENTS—*contd.*		
Martha and Mary,	Luke x. 38–42,	35.
The Lesson on Prayer,	Luke xi. 1–13,	17, 141.
The Lord's Prayer,	Matt. vi. 9–15; Luke xi. 1–4,	115.
"The harvest is great,"	Matt. ix. 37,	135, 140.
The filial consciousness of Jesus,	Matt. xi. 25–27; Luke x. 20–22,	180–184, 203, 301.
Jesus the Revealer of God,	Matt. xi. 27,	109, 156, 185.
"Behold my servant,"	Matt. xii. 18–21,	150.
Neglect of washing,	Matt. xv. 1–20; Mark vii. 1–23,	29, 69, 184, 199, 208.
Syro-Phœnician Woman,	Matt. xv. 21–28; Mark vii. 24–30.	8, 28, 30, 100, 103.
At Cæsarea Philippi: Peter's Confession,	Matt. xvi. 13–20; Mark viii. 27–30; Luke ix. 18–21,	16, 21, 24, 163, 167, 177, 178, 260, 265, 267.
The Founding of the Church,	Matt. xvi. 18–21,	254–272.
First lesson on the doctrine of the Cross,	Matt. xvi. 21–28; Mark viii. 31–33; Luke ix. 22 27,	230, 286.
The Three Aspirants,	Luke ix. 60–62,	222.
The Transfiguration,	Matt. xvii. 1–13; Mark ix. 2-13; Luke ix. 28–36,	162–164.
The Temple Tax,	Matt. xvii. 24–27.	239, 269.
"Forbid him not,".	Mark ix. 38–40; Luke ix. 50,	139, 269.
Question of Divorce,	Matt. xix. 1–12; Mark x. 2–12,	71.
Young man seeking eternal life,	Matt. xix. 16–22; Mark x. 17–27; Luke xviii. 27, 28,	78, 223.
Two Sons of Zebedee: Second lesson on doctrine of Cross,	Matt. xx. 20–28; Mark x. 35–45,	154, 220, 235.
Zacchæus,	Luke xix. 1–10,	137.
The Judgment Programme,	Matt. xxv. 31–46,	155, 175, 266, 315, 321.
Anointing in Bethany: Third lesson on doctrine of Cross,	Matt. xxvi. 6–13; Mark xiv. 3–9,	243, 280.
The Lord's Supper: Fourth lesson on doctrine of Cross,	Matt. xxvi. 26–29; Mark xiv. 22–25; Luke xxii. 19, 20,	246.
"Destroy this temple,"	Matt. xxvi. 61; Mark xiv. 58,	306–310.
Baptism: Trinitarian formula,	Matt. xxviii. 19,	258.

www.ingramcontent.com/pod-product-compliance
Lightning Source LLC
Chambersburg PA
CBHW020242240426
43672CB00006B/608